Reminiscences

of

Admiral James S. Russell

U. S. Navy (Retired)

## PREFACE

This volume contains the transcript of several taped interviews with Admiral James S. Russell, USN (Retired). They were obtained by John T. Mason, Jr. for the Oral History collection of the U. S. Naval Institute during a visit to Admiral Russell at his home on American Lake, Takoma, Washington in November, 1974.

The Admiral's career is a notable one. This account of it reflects in considerable measure the vigor and enthusiasm he invests in everything he does. Researchers will find of particular value the section dealing with Russell's experiences in Alaska during World War II. The account of these operations has an extra dimension in that Russell was able to talk with various Japanese participants and examine Japanese records of the campaign later when he served as a member of the Strategic Bombing Survey in Japan (1945-46). Of course there are other valuable portions of the narrative: Task Group 58.2 in the Pacific; Chief of the Bureau of Aeronautics; Vice Chief of Naval Operations under Admiral Burke; Cinc South, the NATO Command in the Mediterranean.....the researcher is urged to use the subject index (at end of the volume) in seeking these segments of the story.

An appendix precedes the Index. It contains the following:

1. A Profile of Admiral Russell - from the Armed Forces JOURNAL, September, 1974.

2. A short account of an interview with Secretary MacNamara - subject - TFX.

3. Copy of an Action Report covering March 14-27, 1945 - Task Group 58.2

John T. Mason, Jr.
Director of Oral History

September 1976.

ADMIRAL JAMES S. RUSSELL, UNITED STATES NAVY, RETIRED

James Sargent Russell was born in Tacoma, Washington, graduated from High School there, and first went to sea in 1918 as a seaman in the Merchant Marine when the Navy would not accept his enlistment for World War I because he was too young.

He entered the Naval Academy in 1922. Upon graduation in 1926 he reported aboard the battleship WEST VIRGINIA where he served until entering flight training at Pensacola. He was designated a Naval Aviator in 1929 and has been flying naval aircraft regularly ever since. There followed normal tours of aviation duty both aboard ship and ashore. The highlight during this period was his earning the degree of Master of Science in Aeronautical Engineering at the California Institute of Technology while in postgraduate training.

The beginning of World War II found Lieutenant Commander Russell in command of Patrol Squadron 42. During 1942 he led VP-42 in action against Japanese forces in the Aleutian Islands Campaign. He was awarded the Distinguished Flying Cross and the Air Medal for heroism and extraordinary achievement in aerial flights for leading his squadron against the enemy in the face of enemy opposition and extremely hazardous weather conditions. Later, in 1942, Commander Russell was awarded the Legion of Merit for exceptionally meritorious service in establishing advanced bases in the area and operating his squadron from them. His squadron was awarded the Navy Unit Commendation for its part in the Aleutian Campaign.

He returned to Washington for duty in the Office of the Chief of Naval Operations and the Bureau of Aeronautics. Captain Russell then returned to the Pacific area as Chief of Staff to Commander Carrier Division TWO, operating as a Task Group with the famed Task Forces 38 and 58. For his outstanding planning and coordination of the Striking Group in action against the Japanese he was awarded a Gold Star in lieu of a second Legion of Merit.

Captain Russell then commanded the attack carrier USS CORAL SEA which functioned as a unit of the powerful SIXTH Fleet in the Mediterranean. Following this duty he again served in the Office of the Chief of Naval Operations and was promoted to the rank of Rear Admiral in 1953. Next he commanded, in succession an Anti-Submarine Carrier Division and an Attack Carrier Division in the far Western Pacific. In 1955 he assumed the duties of Chief of the Bureau of Aeronautics. He was awarded the Collier Trophy for 1956, sharing that award with Mr. C. J. McCarthy of Chance Vought Aircraft, for the development of the supersonic CRUSADER Navy Fighter, the first ship based fighter aircraft to fly faster then 1000 miles per hour - the outstanding contribution to aviation in that year. He next served as Deputy Commander in Chief of the Atlantic Fleet With the rank of Vice Admiral. He reported as Vice

Adm. J. S. Russell, USN, Ret.

Chief of Naval Operations on July 21, 1958, with the four star rank of Admiral and for "exceptionally meritorious service...(in that capacity) from July 1958 to November 1961..." he was awarded the Distinguished Service Medal.

On January 2, 1962, he became Commander in Chief Allied Forces, Southern Europe and served as such until relieved of active duty pending his retirement, effective April 1, 1965. He was awarded a Gold Star in lieu of the Second Distinguished Service Medal for his "exceptionally meritorious service..." during the period January 1962 to January 1965.

Admiral Russell is employed by the Boeing Company as a part time consultant and his primary consultation is within the Aerospace Group in Seattle, Washington. He is also a consultant to the Boeing Company Commerical Airplane Division and VERTOL Division. He travels throughout the United States on these consultation tours. He is also very active in the Seattle and Tacoma Councils of the Navy League. He is a member of the Board of Directors of Alaska Airlines, Incorporated and a member of the Board of Directors of Airtronics, Incorporated.

Since his retirement he has served on the Puget Sound Oceanographic Study Committee and has been selected as Chairman of the Zoning Commission of Tacoma's Industrial Airport. During the periods August to October 19, 1967 and August to October 1968 he was on active duty as Senior Member of the Aircraft Carrier Combat Operations Safety Review Panal, Navy Department, and the second period as Head of a Special Study Group in the Office of the Secretary of Defense, Washington, D. C.

He is married to the former Miss Geraldine Haus, of Seattle, Washington. Admiral Russell has two sons, Donald Johnson Russell and Kenneth McDonald Russell. His home is on American Lake, just south of Tacoma in Washington State.

26 February 1969

ADMIRAL JAMES S. RUSSELL, UNITED STATES NAVY, RETIRED

PERSONAL DATA:

Born: 22 March 1903, Tacoma, Washington
Parents: Ambrose James and Loella Janet (Sargent) Russell, both now deceased
Wife's Maiden Name: Geraldine Haus of Seattle, Washington
Children: Donald Johnson and Kenneth McDonald Russell
Official Home Address: 7738 Walnut Avenue, S. W., Tacoma 99, Washington
Education: DeKoven Hall Boys School and Stadium High School, Tacoma, Wash.; U. S. Shipping Board Navigation School, University of Washington, Seattle; U. S. Naval Academy, Annapolis, Md.(BS, 1926); Naval Air Station, Pensacola, Fla. (flight training, 1928-1929); Postgraduate School, Annapolis, Md. (1932-1934); Postgraduate, California Institute of Technology, Pasadena (MS, 1935)

PROMOTIONS:

Appointed Midshipman, 20 June 1922
Commissioned Ensign, USN, 3 June 1926
Designated Naval Aviator #3495 in May 1929
Lieutenant (junior grade), USN, 3 June 1929
Lieutenant, USN, 12 June 1936
Lieutenant Commander, USN, 26 June 1940
Commander, USN, 17 September 1942
Captain, USN, 27 April 1944
Rear Admiral, USN, 1 July 1953
Vice Admiral, USN, 1 July 1957
Admiral, USN, 21 July 1958
Transferred to the Retired List of the U. S. Navy, 1 April 1965

MEDALS AND DECORATIONS:

Distinguished Service Medal
Gold Star in lieu of the Second Distinguished Service Medal
Legion of Merit with Combat "V"
Gold Star in lieu of Second Legion of Merit with Combat "V"
Gold Star in lieu of the Third Legion of Merit
Distinguished Flying Cross
Air Medal
Navy Unit Commendation Ribbon (Patrol Squadron 42)
American Defense Service Medal, Fleet Clasp
Asiatic-Pacific Campaign Medal with four stars
American Campaign Medal
World War II Victory Medal

Adm. J. S. Russell, USN, Ret.

Navy Occupation Service Medal, Asia and Europe Clasps
National Defense Service Medal with bronze star
Philippine Liberation Ribbon with two bronze stars
Korean Service Medal
United Nations Service Medal

FOREIGN DECORATIONS:

Order of Naval Merit (Grand Officer) by Brazil
Legion of Honor (Commander) by France
Peruvian Cross of Naval Merit (Great Cross) by Peru

CITATIONS:

Distinguished Service Medal: "For exceptionally meritorious service...as Vice Chief of Naval Operations from July 1958 to November 1961. Exercising administrative, planning, and operational ability of the highest caliber, Admiral Russell has been eminently successful in carrying out an extremely difficult and exacting assignment. As executive of the Chief of Naval Operations, he displayed sound judgment and keen foresight in resolving complex problems involving a Navy in transition to rocketry and nuclear power, politico-military actions resulting from the cold war, and world-wide commitments to our Allies. Through his progressive leadership, vision, and wide knowledge and background of naval operations and administration, coupled with his complete intellectual honesty in dealing with political and military officials, he was able to produce, through the very force of his personality, results of signal value to the United States..."

Gold Star in lieu of the Second Distinguished Service Medal: "For exceptionally meritorious service...as Commander in Chief, Allied Forces Southern Europe from January 1962 to January 1965. During this period of heightened world tensions, Admiral Russell made an outstanding contribution to the security of the United States and its North Atlantic Treaty Organization (NATO) Allies. His direction and coordination of the multinational forces allocated to his command contributed materially to their readiness. During the negotiations for an amicable settlement of the Cyprus crises, he exhibited unusual skill, clear-sightedness and objectivity in his relationships with officials of Allied Nations in the Southern Region and with commanders of contiguous national and NATO military commands. (He) initiated the preparation and negotiation of Civil-Military Cooperation agreements with the Governments of Greece, Italy and Turkey for the division of responsibilities in wartime between allied and national commanders. These agreements were the first of their nature to be completed within the Allied Command, Europe. Through his brilliant leadership, wise counsel, dedication and tireless efforts, (he) materially enhanced the military posture of his command, advanced the accomplishment of the NATO mission, and upheld the highest traditions of the United States Naval Service."

Adm. J. S. Russell, USN, Ret.

Legion of Merit: "For exceptionally meritorious conduct...in action against enemy Japanese forces during the Aleutian Islands Campaign from June 15 to October 14, 1942. Despite severe weather conditions and extremely limited facilities, Commander Russell established the Wing's first base at Cold Bay, maintaining and operating his squadron with efficiency and resourcefulness. Achieving a close cooperation and liaison between Naval and Army Air Corps units and ground troops at other bases which he built he contributed in great measure to their successful joint action and mutual understanding. After leading the first Naval air unit ever to base on and operate from Nome, he made many all night fog-enveloped patrols of the Upper Bering Sea, and during Task Force operations directed toward the bombardment of Kiska, he personally led units of his squadron at night in instrument weather..."

Gold Star in lieu of the Second Legion of Merit: "For exceptionally meritorious conduct...as Chief of Staff for the Commander of a Fast Carrier Task Group operating against enemy Japanese forces from August 1944 to March 25, 1945. Captain Russell organized the work of all the components of the Task Group into one coordinated striking force. By his excellent judgment in planning and executing extensive carrier operations in enemy controlled waters, in the face of repeated Japanese air attacks, he contributed in large measure to the efficient performance of the units of the command in inflicting a tremendous amount of damage on the enemy. His courage, inspiring leadership under aircraft bombing and suicide attack which on two occasions started fires on the flagship and the successful performance of duty reflects the highest credit upon Captain Russell and the United States Naval Service."

Gold Star in lieu of the Third Legion of Merit: "For exceptionally meritorious conduct...as Test Director and Commander, Task Group 7.1, Joint Task Force SEVEN, Operation SANDSTONE, from October 20, 1947 to May 27, 1948. Charged with the exacting task of meeting the requirements of many scientific groups and of agencies of the Army, Navy, and Air Force, Captain Russell conceived the basic plan and was responsible for conducting the test program. In a mission further complicated by the necessity of obtaining many scientific and technical measurements and data in tropical conditions far removed from normal support facilities, he was, in addition, personally responsible for the security and effective use of critical material...(He) contributed directly to the successful scientific completion of the Atomic tests at Eniwetok and thereby to the national security..."

Distinguished Flying Cross: "For heroism and extraordinary achievement...as Commander of Patrol Squadron FORTY-TWO in action against enemy Japanese forces throughout the Aleutian Islands Campaign beginning February 5, 1942...(He) contributed in large measure to the success of his squadron in carrying out numerous hazardous search, combat and patrol missions in this area under extremely adverse weather conditions and in the face of intense anti-aircraft fire and relentless enemy aerial opposition..."

Adm. J. S. Russell, USN, Ret.

Air Medal: "For meritorious achievement...during operations against enemy Japanese forces in the Aleutian Area from May 10 to October 14, 1942...(He) contributed materially to the success of his squadron despite hazardous weather conditions and active enemy opposition..."

Patrol Squadron FORTY TWO was awarded the Navy Unit Commendation for its part in the early Aleutian Campaign.

CHRONOLOGICAL TRANSCRIPT OF NAVAL SERVICE:

| | |
|---|---|
| Jul 1926 - Jul 1928 | USS WEST VIRGINIA |
| Aug 1928 - May 1929 | Naval Air Station, Pensacola, Fla (flight training) |
| Jul 1929 - Nov 1931 | USS WEST VIRGINIA (Air Unit) |
| Dec 1931 - Jun 1932 | Patrol Squadron ONE-B (Squadron Gunnery Officer) |
| Jun 1932 - Jun 1933 | Postgraduate School, Annapolis Md. (student, general line) |
| Jun 1933 - Jun 1934 | Postgraduate School, Annapolis, Md. (student, aeronautical engineering) |
| Jun 1934 - Jun 1935 | California Institute of Technology, Pasadena (student, aeronautical engineering) |
| Jun 1935 - Jun 1936 | Bombing Squadron FIVE-B (Squadron Eng. Officer) |
| Jun 1936 - Jun 1937 | Fitting out duty in USS YORKTOWN |
| Jun 1937 - Jun 1939 | USS YORKTOWN (W&D, Air Dept.) |
| Jun 1939 - Jun 1941 | Bureau of Aeronautics, Navy Dept. (Carriers) |
| Jul 1941 - Oct 1942 | Patrol Squadron 42 (Commanding Officer) |
| Nov 1942 - Dec 1942 | Office of the Chief of Naval Operations, Navy Dept. (Air Bases) |
| Jan 1943 - Jun 1944 | Bureau of Aeronautics, Navy Dept. (Director, Military Requirements Division) |
| Aug 1944 - Apr 1945 | Staff, Commander Carrier Division 2 (Chief of Staff) |
| May 1945 - Aug 1945 | Staff, Commander in Chief, U. S. Pacific Fleet |
| Sep 1945 - Mar 1946 | Air Technical Intelligence, Supreme Commander Allied Powers, Japan |
| | Naval Analysis Division, U. S. Strategic Bombing Survey (Pacific) (Member) |
| Apr 1946 - May 1947 | USS BAIROKO (Commanding Officer) |
| Jun 1947 - Jan 1948 | Atomic Energy Commission, Wash., D. C. (Head, Weapons Branch) |
| Feb 1948 - Jun 1948 | Commander Task Group 7.1 (USS ALBEMARLE) |
| Jul 1948 - Jan 1951 | Atomic Energy Commission, Wash., D. C. (Deputy Director Military Application Division) |
| Feb 1951 - Feb 1952 | USS CORAL SEA (Commanding Officer) |
| Mar 1952 - Jul 1953 | Office of the Chief of Naval Operations, Navy Dept. (Head, Military Requirements & New Developments Branch) |
| Jul 1953 - Apr 1954 | Office of the Chief of Naval Operations, Navy Dept. (Director, Air Warfare Division) |

Adm. J. S. Russell, USN, Ret.

| | |
|---|---|
| May 1954 - Oct 1954 | Commander Carrier Division 17 |
| Nov 1954 - Mar 1955 | Commander Carrier Division 5 |
| Mar 1955 - Jul 1957 | Chief, Bureau of Aeronautics, Navy Dept. |
| Aug 1957 - Jan 1958 | Deputy Commander in Chief, U. S. Atlantic Fleet & Chief of Staff & Aide, Commander in Chief, U. S. Atlantic Fleet |
| Aug 1958 - | Vice Chief of Naval Operations, Navy Dept. |
| Jan 1962 - | Commander in Chief Allied Forces, Southern Europe |
| 1 Apr 1965 | Retired |
| Aug 1967 - Oct 1967 | Active duty as Senior Member of the Aircraft Carrier Combat Operations Safety Review Panal, Navy Department |
| Aug 1968 - Oct 1968 | Active duty as Head of a Special Study Group, Office of the Secretary of Defense, Wash., D. C. |

NAVY - Office of Information
Internal Relations Division (OI-430)
26 February 1969

DECLARATION OF TRUST

The undersigned does hereby appoint and designate as his (her) Trustee herein, the Secretary-Treasurer and Publisher of the United States Naval Institute to perform and discharge the following duties, powers, and privileges in connection with the possession and use of a certain taped interview between the undersigned and the Oral History Department of the United States Naval Institute.

1. Classification of Transcript.

   (✓)a. If classified OPEN, the transcript(s) may be read or the recording(s) audited by the qualified personnel upon presentation of proper credentials, as determined by the Secretary-Treasurer of the U.S. Naval Institute.

   ( )b. If classified PERMISSION REQUIRED TO CITE OR QUOTE, the user will be required to obtain permission in writing from the interviewee prior to quoting or citing from either the transcript(s) or the recording(s).

   ( )c. If classified PERMISSION REQUIRED, permission must be obtained in writing from the interviewee before the transcribed interview(s) can be examined or the tape recording(s) audited.

   ( )d. If classified CLOSED, the transcribed interview(s) and the tape recording(s) will be sealed until a time specified by the interviewee. This may be until the death of the interviewee or for any specified number of years.

2. It is expressly understood that in giving this authorization, I am in no way precluded from placing such restrictions as I may desire upon use of the interview at any time during my lifetime, nor does this authorization in any way affect my rights to the copyright of my literary expressions that may be contained in the interview.

                    Witness my hand and seal this 29th day
                    of December 1975.

                              *James Sargent Russell*
                              Admiral, U.S. Navy (retired)

I hereby accept and consent to the foregoing Declaration of Trust and the powers therein conferred upon me as Trustee:

Interview #1 with Admiral James S. Russell

Date: Friday morning, 22 November 1974

Place: His residence in Tacoma, Washington

Subject: Biography

By: Dr. John T. Mason, Jr.


Q: Sir, it is great to be able to sit down with you and listen to this account of your remarkable naval career. Would you begin in the proper way with a biography by giving me the date and place of your birth, and tell me something about your family background - your father's activities, his business, that sort of thing?

ADM. R.: Jack Mason, that's a great pleasure. I was born in Tacoma, Washington, on the 22nd of March, 1903 - I was born at North Fifth and M Street - and my father was Ambrose James Russell who was born in Trivandrum, India, in the province of Kerala, the south of India, on the 28th of October, 1857.

Q: Did he come from a military family?

ADM. R.: He did not. My grandfather was a missionary,

Russell #1 - 2

a Scottish missionary, who married an Australian girl, Rhoda Foss of Sydney, and there were two children. Then my paternal grandmother, unfortunately, died. Trivandrum was rather an unwholesome place and she contracted a fever and died. The old missionary, grief-stricken, gathered up the two children, sailed in reverse around Cape Horn back to Scotland, their homeland.

Q: He obviously was a Presbyterian, was he?

ADM. R.: He was not; he was a Congregationalist. Father went to the schools in Scotland, and at the University of Glascow he won a scholorship in architecture to the Ecole des Beaux-Arts in Paris. His two roommates in Paris, Loredo Taft and Bernard Maybeck, were both Americans. So, after completing his course at the Beaux-Arts, he came to America seeking his fortune. The three of them started in Boston, all three of them married Kansas City girls, and Dad and Mother came to the Pacific Northwest in 1891.

Q: Loredo settled in Illinois, no?

ADM. R.: He went to Chicago. As a sculptor, he needed a large city in which to practice his art. Maybeck, an architect, went to San Francisco where he became quite

Russell #1 - 3

famous. He had classes in architecture - he did many of the buildings in that area and had classes at the University of California at Berkely.

Q: Did they maintain an intimate contact through the years?

ADM. R.: They did indeed. Father designed most of the nice residences in Tacoma. There are some rather famous ones. He did the Governor's mansion in Olympia. He did the Standard Bank Building in Vancouver. The mansion in Olympia, as you say, is now being restored. My boyhood was generally in the Tacoma neighborhood. We did a little traveling; we went once to eastern Washington to White Bluffs and Hanford, which is now the scene of the great atomic plants, - but remained largely in Tacoma. We camped on American Lake, where you find yourself today. This was originally my family's summer camp, beginning in the year 1907. It was a very pleasant place in those days - open prairie land - I had a pony, and we had a cow (we called her Violet) and I learned to milk a cow. We rented the cow. We were greatly favored by an old Norwegian ship's carpenter who got tired of the sea; his name was Mr. Nordeen. I remember him with a great deal of respect. He came here, he built a boat house, he lived in the boat house while he built a boat for my father and for my father's partner, Mr. Babcock. He built a tower - if you'll look over the lawn here you'll see there is a well. There used to be a wooden tank and windmill over that well, which Mr. Nordeen built. Now, importantly, he was a great sailor of course, and he made a sprit rig for the little boat he built for us, and he taught me how to sail. This really was sort of the genesis of my going to sea. I admired the old man very, very much. He was an expert carpenter, a real perfectionist, and really a great guy.

Well, I went to school - public school first and then to a private school. The private school was DeKoven Hall. I attended it largely because of a cousin who was taken on as a professor there. It was a very forward school, however the grades at that school didn't match the public grades. So, when it was decided that I would leave that school, there was some question as to where in the public school system I would be aligned - whether it would be in the seventh, eighth ninth or tenth grades, or just where. About this time my sister, who had spent a year going to the School on the Prairie here, was ready to go into Stadium High School at the normal age; she was then seventeen or eighteen, and she had to take exams to get into the public school, the high school. There were only two high schools in Tacoma at the time. They gave her trial examinations to study from, and I looked these over and I said to my mother, "I think I could pass those examinations."

Q: And you were then ten years old?

Russell #1 - 5

ADM. R.: I was ten years old, and mother said, "Oh, James, you're too young." Well, Father appeared on the scene at this time and being a hard-bitten old Scotsman he said, "Let him try it." So I took the examinations, I passed, and I got into high school at the age of ten. This put me out, a graduate of high school, in June of 1918, and if you'll remember we were in World War I in June of 1918.

Q: Wasn't this an inconvenience in one sense; you hadn't matured physically to the point where you were a high school graduate?

ADM. R.: You mean the girls didn't like me? You're quite right, Jack. But anyway, I was very much intent on getting into World War I. People were going off to the War, and we had befriended soldiers from the 91st Division which had sailed for France - they were then training here at Camp Lewis, now Fort Lewis - and so I tried to enlist in the Navy. I was downtown at the Recruiting Office, and I saw the Recruiting Officer. He said, "There, there, young man. Come back in a couple of years. We take them at seventeen, not fifteen." So I said, "But, sir, there's a war on." And he said, "We can't help that, son." So I was walking home very dejectedly along the street overlooking Puget Sound (we lived on North Fifth and M Street) and I saw there a camouflaged wooden merchant steamer, obviously with steam up. So I made my way down across the railroad tracks, out on the wharf, I got aboard the steamer and I found the first mate. I said to the first mate, "Sir, do you need a deck hand?" And he looked me over, smiled a bit, and he said, "You want to sign the shipping articles, son?" I said, "Yes, sir." He took me to his stateroom, where he broke out a very official looking paper, a contract between the seaman and the ship owner, I signed my name, I went home and got my gear, and went to sea in spite of the United States Navy. In World War I.

Q: And he didn't establish your age.

ADM. R.: He didn't give a damn how old I was. He thought I was big enough to steer the ship and do the other things required of seamen so he gave me the job.

Q: Did your father feel that you were old enough for this adventure?

ADM. R.: He thought it was wonderful. My mother didn't like it a bit.

Q: How many children were there in your family?

ADM. R.: I had one sister, Margaret, who's still alive and lives in our neighborhood here at American Lake, and a sister who died at the age of five before either of us was born. That was Janet. She died of acute appendicitis at the age of five, unfortunately.

Well, so off I went to sea and that was on the SS WISHKAH. Those steamers were Shipping Board steamers in World War I and they were named for rivers in the United States. WISHKAH went up to Nanaimo, British Columbia, and loaded coal. Coal, being a non-rigid cargo, is the worst thing you could put into a new wooden ship. We went to sea, and off Cape Flattery when we struck the heavy swells of the open Pacific, she started filling with water faster than the steam pumps could pump her out. The skipper turned and ran for the shelter of Cape Flattery. When we got back in the Straits and as the working of the ship got less, the steam pumps were able to take hold and we kept her afloat. We brought her in, discharged her coal, and put her in drydock. We found that (remember now, she was a wooden ship), we found that the timbers were green. That was the first deficiency. Secondly, the caulkers were green too, and they'd driven the caulking too far into her seams. You know, a wooden ship works in a seaway; down below you hear her squeak plank on plank. Well, the water was just pouring through the sides of the ship.

Q: This was because of the hurried construction - the War?

ADM. R.: Exactly, yes. So I left her, as we put her alongside to get repaired, and I found a job on the SS OSSINING, that was also named for a river, a steel steamer, and we took grain from the great inland empire of Washington State, filled her up with that and sailed for France. But my contract was only to the East Coast. We got to the East Coast (it was my first time on the East Coast) and was paid off. An East Coast crew took her on across, while I got a free ticket home, of course on the railroad, which was quite an exciting affair.

Q: You mean they didn't want you, as a minor, to go into a war zone?

ADM. R.: I was asked to go on. I was one of the few crew members who was asked to go on; apparently I had learned to steer well enough and behave like a seaman. The first mate really wanted me to go on but I told him that my contract was to the East Coast and I was rather intent on enjoying the train trip home. It was quite an adventure for me.

Q: You really didn't want to go into the War zone at that point then?

ADM. R.: Oh, it didn't matter. The war had just ended when we got to the East Coast - the eleventh of November.

Well I came home and I signed on the SS CITY OF SEATTLE which was my first experience on a passenger ship. Again, I was a seaman though I think by this time I qualified as an able-bodied seaman. We did the normal work of the crew, but in addition to that in Alaska we went only as far north as Skagway, because of the shortage of manpower in Alaska we worked the cargo. So we made quite a bit of money on that trip in overtime, getting up in the middle of the night and discharging cargo. I remember one of my experiences there was loading ingots of gold. These were carefully sewn into canvas so that they couldn't be seen as gold, but we took a hand truck up to where a safe was opened. We put these very heavy small objects on the hand truck and wheeled them down to the side of the ship, put them in a special sling - and there was a very heavy netting strung between the pier and the side of the ship so that if we dropped any of these gold ingots they wouldn't go in the water - and they were taken aboard and put in custody in a locked space in the steamer. That was the SS CITY OF SEATTLE.

Q: Was she a passenger steamer? The Alaskan route?

ADM. R.: Passenger and freight. Southeastern Alaska only. Our first port of call as I remember it was Ketchikan, and then Wrangell, Petersburg, Haines, Juneau and Skagway.

Russell #1 - 10

Skagway is as far north as we got. It was a beautiful trip, but it was winter and it was pretty cold and bitter. I remember going into Juneau and looking up and saying, "My heavens, what tall buildings they've built in Juneau." And when dawn came I discovered it was a gold mine, and what I was seeing was the sheds over the path of the gold as it was refined and brought down the hill.

Q: Obviously you took to this life?

ADM. R.: Then I tried my hand again on a wooden steamer. I tried to go to sea on a sailing ship, and about the only sailing ships we had in those days were cannery tenders. There were some square riggers that went up to Alaska, but I missed out on that. I got on another wooden steamer and this was the SS BOTTINEAU, named also for a river. She was loaded with Puget Sound lumber completely, including a deck load, and the deck load I remember was made up of things like smaller timbers that could be jettisoned if you got into a very bad storm. She was ballasted with gravel from Puget Sound. She was a very nice, smooth-riding ship but I discovered she was slightly unstable because if the wind was on the port side she'd list slightly to starboard. We got into quite a blow at the Gulf of Tehuantepec going down and I remember we hove to and she rode it out very nicely, with her nose into the sea and the wind. We went through the canal, we refueled (incidentally, she burned coal), we re-coaled in the Azores, and on up to Great Grimsby on the Humber River in England. There we discharged the lumber. We, again, helped the longshoremen in this case, and I was driving steam winches. I remember getting one great timber up, which was slung with just a single wire strap with a hook. I got it over the bulwark of the ship. As I slacked off on the stay side of the yard and stay tackle, it put just enough slack into the span to let the heel of that timber sit on the bulwark of the ship. That took the load off the wire strap that was holding the huge timber and it came unhooked. I watched this great timber slowly fall over the side. I knew there were men down below making the lumber into a raft. So I quickly turned the steam off the winch, went over to the side, and, thank God, I had hit nobody. But there was my great big timber lying across the raft down at the side of the ship.

Great Grimsby harbor was actually a dock because you went in and they closed a gate after you. There was quite a tide on that coast of England, and we were in stagnant water with real tidal gates behind us which kept the level of water up while the tide receded, and until it came back up again. So that was truly a dock; people confuse piers and docks, you know, and a dock really is that, I believe.

They tried to sell her over there, but there was no market for wooden ships. We celebrated the first anniversary of the signing of the Armistice on the eleventh of November, 1919, while I was over there. It was very impressive. Dad's sister was married to a Scottish professor at the University of Reading. I visited them and was very much impressed, going through London, with the respect they paid the Cenotaph, which was a memorial to the war dead. Well, we were unable to sell that ship so we brought her back, and all she had in her was the gravel ballast. My, what a great difference there was in the behavior of the ship at sea between going over with a complete load of lumber, and the gravel ballast with which we came back. It was just like having a cork with a lead weight on the bottom of it.

Q: There was no cargo available to bring back?

ADM. R.: No. Her roll was very short and snappy and it was almost destructive. The ship used to roll the lids off the galley stoves, and I remember in the wheelhouse I could put my two feet up against the side of the bulkhead as she snapped back, after rolling over to starboard as she started back again you could put your two feet up on the bulkhead and stand briefly on something that normally would be at 90 degrees to the deck. It was amazing. A very, very uncomfortable ride.

Q: They weren't able to get a cargo to come back?

AMD. R.: No cargo coming back. She had nothing but the gravel ballast in the bottom of her. She had a very high metacentric height in this case, you see, and her roll was very, very stiff. It was almost destructive. As I say, it rolled the lids off the galley stoves occasionally, if you had any sort of weather. Well, we left her, we were paid off in Newport News. We anchored her there, and a few days after I left her there was fog - she was rammed and sank. And I was on my way home by train.

The next trip was on the SS ROBIN GRAY. She was a beautiful 10,000 ton, flush deck, oil burning steamer. We had a completely Puget Sound crew, people from Seattle, Tacoma, Bellingham, Everett - people like that, and my roomate was a chap by the name of Ammundson. He'd been at the University of Washington where he was a boxer. And that's how I got my broken nose. We used to practice boxing out on the fantail of the ship; he was quite an expert. Ammundson is still alive; he lives in Portland presently. Well, that was a great trip. We took a variety of cargo; we took steel shapes, beams and such, bales of cotton, drums of chemicals, and from the Tacoma refinery that you saw yesterday, from the smelter, we took ingots of copper. We discharged that cargo in two ports in Japan; the first was Yokohama and the second was Kobe. Things in Japan were very different in those days.

Q: This was in 1920, or thereabouts?

ADM. R.: This was 1920 - yes, exactly. The Japanese among themselves were very honest. I remember a longshoring family, there used to be a papa-san and then a certain number of longshoremen who worked with him. One of these young men claimed more wages than was his due and they set upon him and he left that ship holding one eye open, they beat him so badly. So they were very honest among themselves, by anything which was on that ship they could steal. We were warned. They said, "Look out for your big bronze bell up in the foc'sle," - you know, the fog bell - and sure enough one day--we had one anchor down (she was single screw, you know, and you used to put one anchor down and work against its drag maneuvering around the harbors) - a sampan came along side and the men climbed up the anchor chain, through the hawse pipe. They were unscrewing the bronze bell when we caught them. Well I was on watch in one of the holds, to make sure they didn't steal - they'd steal the manila line out of the life buoys and things like this, you see, and tuck things under their tunics to take them off the ship. This young Japanese longshoreman was handling ingots of copper and I, of course, was posted there as a member of the crew only for the security of the ship, to make sure that nothing was stolen. As he lifted one of these little copper ingots he looked over his shoulder at me and he said, "Some day this come back as a shell, no?" And I said, "Well, if you think so, it might." So you see, the attitude was very, very different. Then we took that ship, after discharging the last of the cargo in Kobe, we took her in ballast through the inland sea and through the Strait of Shimonoseki, and beyond that to the little town of Karatsu. Now Karatsu was a coal mining town, and there the whole picture of Japan changed for me because this was a rural countryside. We were invited - they wouldn't let us in the house because we had our dirty shoes on, you know - but we sat on the front steps of the home of a Japanese student who was studying English (he wanted me to talk English with him) and we really got next to the people there. That ship was filled with coal by hand at an amazing rate. There were bamboo stagings put over the side and literally hundreds of people, men and women, with little grass baskets - there was a steady stream of coal going into all four holds of that ship. They'd sing a little chanty as they passed the baskets up, for rhythm, to carry that coal up and it just poured over the side and into the holds. We took coal to

Hong Kong, and in Hong Kong discharged the coal, cleaned the
ship out, dunnaged the holds, and we put in bagged rice.
And it's very important if you fill a ship with grain that
you allow expansion space, because if your cargo gets wet
the expansion of the grain would actually burst the sides
of the ship. So you leave a channel, dunnage at the side
of the ship to protect the grain from the cold or the
warmth or the dampness of the hull of the ship, and then
you have spaces inside the mass of cargo for ventilation
and so that, if there is expansion, you'll have some volume
in which to expand. We brought the rice back across the
Pacific (this was an oil burning ship), we refueled in
Honolulu Harbor, to the Panama Canal where we refueled
again, and then we made three ports in Cuba. This is very
interesting. We went in first to Santiago, and Santiago,
you'll remember, was the scene of a battle in the Spanish
American War. We still found shells on the beach. A friend
of mine actually picked up a five-inch shell and brought
it home with him. I don't know what had happened to the
explosive inside the shell - I hope it was a dummy - but he
brought that shell home with him. I've often wondered
whether or not it ever went off. Santiago is a very
picturesque place, you know, and it was very interesting
to us to go through a very narrow channel with high Morro
Castle on the side, and into the inner bay where the whole

Russell #1 - 17

Spanish Fleet was in the Spanish American War. From there we went to Cienfuegos, and going along that coast you could still see the wrecks of the Spanish men-of-war as they drove themselves ashore rather than sink.

Q: Were you delivering your rice in Cuba, or what?

ADM. R.: We delivered rice to three ports in Cuba, yes. Well, from Cienfuegos to Habana, and there we finished discharging the rice. And you know, it took about a week in Hong Kong Harbor for the coolies to load that rice and stow it all so carefully, and it took us about two months for the longshoremen - they were striking; they struck once, I remember, because there wasn't ice water in each hold - it took us two months in Cuba to discharge the rice that the coolies had loaded in a week in Hong Kong.

Q: That's where the element of discipline comes in, is it?

ADM. R.: Exactly, yes. And of course the Cuban was a great big fellow, too, and the coolie was a little bit of a fellow. Anyway, we then ballasted the ship with water ballast in the normal tankage of the ship, and sailed across the Gulf of Mexico to Sabine in Texas. Now the Port Arthur Ship Canal is quite a place; it's dredged out or cut out with clay banks and there were plenty of marks where a steamer which reversed course would just put her stem against the clay bank, put her rudder hard over and go ahead with her screws and push her stern around, then back away from the clay bluff. It's an amazingly simple maneuver. There we loaded the ship with raw sulphur, yellow sulphur, and it was brought aboard by mechanical conveyor into the four holds of the ship in just its loose form. It's a terrible cargo to carry. Among other things it catches fire and it burns to sulphur dioxide, and not only that but if you're perspiring and you get this yellow sulphur on your skin it itches, and beyond that the mosquitos in the Texas flat there were just - well they drove us almost insane. I remember going up and sleeping in a covered lifeboat to try to get away from them once. We had no screening in the living quarters of the ship, you see.

Q: How long did it take to load a cargo like that?

ADM. R.: Just a matter of a few days - not long at all. We sailed from Sabine, Texas, to Portland, Maine, where the sulphur was discharged to be used in a chemical works there.

Well, my seafaring by this time had - I was in the SS ROBIN GRAY for a full year and again paid off on the East Coast and came back west.

Russell #1 - 19

Q: How did you get your jobs on these different steamers?

ADM. R.: I was a member of the Seamen's Union and we hired through the Union hall. In between cruises, though, you couldn't depend on getting away so I would take odd jobs. I remember I was rivet passing on the three light cruisers that were built by Todds in Tacoma, the USS MILWAUKEE, the USS OMAHA and one other. Those were the old four pipe light cruisers, very interesting ships. So I was engaged in catching red hot rivets in a bucket, putting them with a set of tongs into holes. The bucker-up would slam the rivet home and a riveter on the other side of the plating would buzz away making the head on the rivet. I also had a job at the Tacoma Smelter where I was in the Cottrell Plant, where the process was electrostatic precipitation. Smoke from the furnaces went through tubes where a central wire applied a very high voltage. The little metal particles in the smoke would collect on the side of the tubes.

Also, on the cruise to England there was a chap by the name of Leonard Singer - he came from St. Louis - who inspired me to attend the American College of Physical Education in Chicago. He said, "You know, Socrates said you should educate the body before you educate the mind. Look, if we go to that school we can get jobs in college as instructors of physical drills, at YMCA's coaching basketball teams and things like that. Why don't you go to the school?"

And I said, "Well, I'll think about it." He went, and by the time I got to Chicago he'd already busted out of the school, but I went to school there for nine months. My grub stake, hard earned as a seaman, was rapidly disappearing so I got a job first as a bus boy in the school mess, and then catering books in the public library - I would go at the end of library hours to put books back in proper order on the shelves. I came across a book which was called LIFE AT THE NAVAL ACADEMY, by Cmdr. Earl. I drew this book and I read it on the elevated train going back to the dormitory. I thought, my God, Russell, here is a school they pay you to attend - where have you been? And it's a seafaring school. So I wrote to my father, the distinguished architect in Tacoma, who wrote to our very distinguished Congressman who spent a total of twenty years in the Congress, the Hon. Albert Johnson, who later, incidentally became my father-in-law. So father got in touch with Mr. Johnson and Mr. Johnson said he'd be very happy to appoint James to the Naval Academy but there was a slight complication. He said he'd given away not only his principal but his first and second alternates, but if I wished to take the third alternate appointment he would be very happy to make that arrangement. I said yes, and I took the examinations in the Civil Service examining room in the Post Office in Chicago, and lo and behold the three people ahead of me

Russell #1 - 21

busted, I passed and got in. So destiny sometimes hangs by a hair.

Q: Obviously during all this time at sea you hadn't lost track of an education?

ADM. R.: Not a bit.

Q: How much contact did you have with your family during this period?

ADM. R.: I always stayed at home. As a matter of fact the Shipping Board some of the time during this four years when I was going to sea off and on, four months of that time the Shipping Board saw fit to send me first to a seamen's school over in West Seattle, and then again to a four month course in navigation in the old astronomy department under Dr. Boothroyd at the University of Washington. So I had learned navigation, such as it was in those days, and it stood me in good stead on the ROBIN GRAY on the cruise to Japan because I found out standing a watch that - the first mate used to take the midwatch, because that's when the Captain wanted to get his sleep and he put his most responsible officer in charge of the ship; we seamen used to steer for two hours and stand lookout for two hours. I was steering and the first mate, who's name was Anderson, just whiling away the time, watching the horizon and watching the course of the ship while I was steering by magnetic compass, said casually, "Where are you from, Russell?" And I said, "From Tacoma, sir." "Tacoma," said he, "Did you ever hear of a school there called DeKoven Hall?" And I said, "Yes, sir. I went there." He said, "You did? So did I." Well that established right away a point of contact, and I finished up that cruise by being appointed the chief and only quartermaster - I wound the chronometers and took care of the sextants and gear of that sort up on the bridge of the ship.

Q: Well this was a wonderful background for the Naval Academy, and you must have been unique in coming in in that way.

ADM. R.: It was indeed. Well, Plebe summer, you know, was very interesting. There were a number of boys who had been out and learned a bit in the college of hard knocks; there were other boys who came directly from school and I really believe that they were at something of a disadvantage for not having had a background like this. I "starred" at the Naval Academy because I went in at nineteen and in those days if you were twenty it was the upper age, so I was well

advanced. The studying, of course, appealed to me. I liked
navigation, I liked the work we were doing, and I would
have stood a little higher had it not been for the fact
that Lt. James L. Holloway, Jr., in the far gun sheds, put
all four of the platoon leaders in our company on report for
improper performance of duty, which is a rather serious
offense. In my platoon and in the other platoons somebody
way in the rear ranks was sky larking, and we, of course,
were marching along with our command at our side and I just
wasn't looking back; I wasn't paying attention. So we all
wound up with a report against us of improper performance
of duty. Well the other three platoon leaders went around
and cried so hard on the shoulder of the Company Officer that
he reduced the offense reported slightly. It didn't bear
the onus of improper performance of duty, it was inattention
to duty, or something like that. I thought, well gee, Russell,
it happened and why should you go round and bellyache about
it? So I walked off my 25 demerits with a rifle over my
shoulder, but that Company Officer immediately took me for
being the rebel - the fellow who was holding out, you see -
and so when it came to first class year I was a mustering
petty officer. I didn't get a commissioned midshipman job.
I did stand about fifteen out of my class of about 450; had
it not been for this particular run-in on the score of
discipline, I'd have stood a little higher. But I don't
regret it a bit. We were put on report, and I just thought
it was rather unmanly to go around and bellyache about it.

It was probably my mistake.

But anyway, this background of going to sea did stand me in good stead. When we graduated and the graduation awards were being passed out I got the Daughters of the American Revolution Sword for excellence in seamanship, which I thought was rather a pleasant thing to have for a guy who was going to sea. I never will forget the little old lady from the Daughters of the American Revolution who presented it to me. She insisted on reading every word of rather a lengthy speech, and it was June Week, it was hot - all my friends in ranks were wearing (as I was) full dress uniform, you know, and it was hot as blazes, but this little old lady with her big broad-brimmed hat insisted on reading every word of her speech. But it was a very, very pleasant occasion for me, of course.

Q: Tell me about the course of study while you were there. Did it seem to meet your needs?

ADM. R.: Yes, I thought it was excellent. It was much more simple than now, of course. There were no electives; we all went through the same business. We marched to class, and I'm very much in favor of that. Practice cruises, though, we did the whole summer - away for three months. I made two cruises to Europe and one to the West Coast.

Russell #1 - 25

Q: You were fortunate to get that sort of cruise.

ADM. R.: Yes, and my class was pushed toward aviation. About a third or half of the class, instead of making the first-class cruise, the last year's summer cruise, took aviation. The Navy put flying boats and other planes at Annapolis, float planes, and we were given a course of instruction in them. I was in the half of the class which stayed on after graduating to do three months of aviation training.

Q: This was rather unusual wasn't it? I mean this was at the beginning of Navy interest in aviation.

ADM. R.: Yes, this was the push toward getting people into aviation, exactly. Then, when we were sent to the fleet, in my case I reported aboard the USS WEST VIRGINIA, and she was the latest thing in the fleet at the time - battleship #48. It was a great ship and had some very wonderful skippers.

Q: She was an oil burner, wasn't she?

ADM. R.: Yes, an oil burner, and electric drive. The Capt. Cluverius, a very wonderful fellow, was the skipper. An inspiring fellow, he spoke well in public, and was strong in leadership. Incidentally, he had two daughters whom we used to make sure were properly taken care of socially. I remember we would organize sailing parties and one thing and another and always invite them along. One, Martha, had been to either Smith or Vassar, and we didn't know this but she had been on the tennis team. So some of us in the junior officers' mess invited her to play tennis and, boy, we retired in good order and sent for Charlie Lyman who had captained the tennis team to take her on because none of us could touch her degree of skill at playing tennis.

A: Where was your ship based?

ADM. R.: Well, largely out of San Pedro, although we made some extended cruises. Anyway, we were sent down to San Diego where we had about four or six weeks of flight training. We got right up to the point of soloing, but did not solo.

Q: This was on North Island?

ADM. R.: Yes, and this was our introduction really into the aviation part of the Navy. It was determined that I was proper material to go on to flight school, but we had to put two years in the fleet first before they'd let us learn to fly, the object being seaman first and airman later.

Q: Who was in command of North Island then, Charley Mason?

ADM. R.: I don't remember. I was with Charley Mason later on. Incidentally, that chap bore the distinction of making a dead stick landing on the deck of the USS LANGLEY, our first carrier. His engine quit at altitude somewhere in the vicinity of the ship and he glided down and made a no power landing into the arresting gear on the LANGLEY, and she was a pretty small ship.

I was battery officer in the anti-aircraft division in the USS WEST VIRGINIA, and Freddie Withington was my first division officer: a very pleasant job. I had shifted over to assistant navigator for one short cruise, but when they discovered that I was no longer on the anti-aircraft battery they pulled me back again. So my entire experience before learning to fly was in gunnery, really, although we had ensign's notebooks and we had to know all about the engineering department and the boilers, the main engines, gunnery and everything.

Q: Did the WEST VIRGINIA have catapults?

ADM. R.: Yes, she did.

Q: Did this intrigue you?

ADM. R.: Very much so, and every time I could I'd get a lift in one of the airplanes any time there was a spare seat. These were two-seater float planes, UO-1s I remember, stick and wire jobs. As a matter of fact the aviators were very nice to us and very frequently we got a chance to fiddle around with the controls.

Q: What was the attitude of the officers on deck toward aviation?

ADM. R.: They saw the importance of it. So I went to Pensacola a little late because we were on a six month's deployment to Hawaiian waters, and that was a wonderful experience for me. Sam King had been the roommate of Chink Lewis.

Q: Samuel Wilder King?

ADM. R.: That is correct. Chink Lewis had been Sam King's roommate at the Naval Academy and Chink Lewis was the navigator, a three-striper, on the USS WEST VIRGINIA. So we got to Hawaiian waters and, as fate would have it, Sam King put on a great luau for his roommate and classmate. A few of us junior officers in the mess were invited along in case there were some young ladies who might need an escort. We went over across the Pali to the King country residence (he had an office downtown, too) and we watched the pig being lowered into the pit of hot rocks with Ti palm fronds all around him. We went swimming, and in due time the great feast started. There was a tremendous layout. The tablecloth was of Ti palm fronds. There were all the native delicacies; we had seaweed, and chicken, and pineapple, and papaya, and breadfruit. However, there was a staff of native servants and they were cruising up and down behind this great table with a bottle of okole hao in one hand and soda in the other. So we all had okole hao and soda. Well Sam King called on various and sundry people to make little speeches and I was very much impressed, Brad Bartlett's father (Brad Bartlett was on the COLORADO in our division, a sister ship of the WEST VIRGINIA), a retired Commodore, was out visiting at this time and he was at the King luau. Sam King called upon him and he arose and made a complete speech in the Hawaiian language. He'd been out there in the old station ship days and learned the language, and of course that generated a great deal of fanfare. He really was very proud of the fact that he could speak the native tongue.

Q: King was married at that time, wasn't he?

ADM. R.: Oh, very much so. He had a lovely wife, a beautiful wife, Pauline. Well, after the speechmaking and all the food and that sort of business we adjourned. There were two paid orchestras and hula troops. About one o'clock in the morning, however, the paid entertainment went home, and then the talent among the guests got going. Roger Scott and I were very much impressed with two little girls, one of them played the piano very beautifully and the other one did a very stately hula in the old Hawaiian style. But after several stately hulas she became a little rowdy, and she'd come hula in front of one of us junior officers and we'd have to get up and hula with her. I remember she came to me and I'd had enough okole hao and soda to think that perhaps I could do the hula, so I got up and fortunately I was in such condition that I had that degree of awkwardness which is required of a male when he dances the hula so I was a reasonable success. So the little girls brought us over to be introduced to their parents, Mr. and Mrs. Burns of Kahala. And Mr. and Mrs. Burns said, "Now you must get back down to the boat landing in Honolulu Harbor, and won't you ride with us?" So we did, and it was delightful. Well this developed a friendship through the years and just the other day my Hawaiian mother - I was adopted into their family eventually - Honey Burns visited in Seattle, and she's in her nineties. Delightful elderly lady. She was a flower girl in the court of the late Queen Liliuokalani, and her mother was a lady-in-waiting to the Queen. When my oldest son was married in the Islands, Sam King, then the first elected governor of Hawaii, gave a little dinner party at Iolani Palace, and my Hawaiian mother took me by the hand and led me to what had been her mother's apartment in the Royal Palace. It was very impressive; it was a delightful, delightful family. Now Daddy Paul, as we called him, Mr. Burns, is gone, Honey is in her nineties, one of the daughters has also left this world, but the other one, who was married, was through Seattle not too long ago. Her husband, now retired, was an official in the telephone company; he was in the Navy during World War II. A purely delightful family, and one of my most pleasant memories of life will always be knowing this engaging Hawaiian family. And Auntie Pauline (that's Sam King's wife) is still alive; Sam of course is gone. Among their five children were two, Sonny (Sam) and Charlotte. Sam (he's not a junior because they gave him a different middle name) is now a judge out there; he's active in politics. He went to Yale, and when I was at the Naval Academy Postgraduate school he came through and stayed with us. A very unfortunate thing, his daddy was opening furniture crates when he was in the Navy and a nailhead popped off and put out one of his eyes. He wears a glass eye. You'd never know it now because things are very cleverly disguised, but he has only one eye. So he couldn't go into the Navy, but he was a star student at Yale and a good lawyer. He stayed with us in Annapolis. Once he came down from Yale and called me from Washington on the phone.

I said, "Well Sonny, will you come and stay with us?" And he said, "No, I can't do it this time. I'm on the Yale debating team and we're staying at the White House!" Wonderful people, we had so many pleasant times.

Well, Jack, I was saying that my first duty was on board USS WEST VIRGINIA and I was assigned to the anti-aircraft division under Freddie Withington, but we had a very famous number two turret officer and his name was James L. Holloway, Jr. He had not only a gunnery "E" in his turret, but he had two hash marks under that which meant that for three years his turret had taken the fleet prize in gunnery. These were sixteen inch twin gun turrets, beautiful guns. But that battleship duty, and particularly the cruise out to the islands, I remember with a great deal of pleasure. We actually brought the ship up here to Puget Sound for a three months' overhaul. And it just so happened that it was in the summer. I brought the ship's rifle team down to Camp Lewis, where we used the Army range for firing, and the range officer for a time (they spelled one another) was James L. Holloway, Jr., so I got to know him very, very well. As a matter of fact, with the young officers coming to the rifle range I was regarded as the chap who should make all the dates for them in my home town, Tacoma. One of our gay young officers from the ship was Freddie Funk, a very delightful fellow. His great social attribute was his ability to play the ukulele. He composed his own songs, also, and those were very catchy. He had one, I remember, that went, "The Shore Boats Make All the Battleships Just the Same." In other words if you got down to the waterfront in San Pedro late enough to miss the last officers' boat to the ship you could always catch the shore boat, which for a dollar would take you back to your ship. So he was quite a gay blade, and very socially inclined, and among the beautiful young ladies in Tacoma was one (we'll misname her), let's call her Molly Maguire. Molly was a delightful girl but she had one terrible drawback. If anyone got very serious about our friend Molly, Mother, who was a grass widow, would step in and start climbing the individual's family tree and this would eventually queer the romance. Well, we warned Freddie about this peculiarity of this particular date and, willy nilly he was really taken into camp because she was a beautiful, beautiful girl. I remember she wore a little black crescent on her cheek, she had an attractive little mole or some small blemish which she covered up - in those days if you remember it was quite stylish. A beauty mark on her face. Well, sure enough, Freddie brought "Molly" home one night and there was Mama, and the inquisition started. Freddie seemed to be enjoying it quite a bit. Finally he let drop, very casually, a remark, - "You know, my grandfather was an Admiral," and then he went on to another subject. Well Mrs. Maguire didn't forget that at all, and she came right back to it. She said, "Freddie, did you say that your grandfather was an Admiral," whereupon Freddie said, "yes, he was in charge of all the vessels on the third floor of the hotel in Podunk, Iowa." And that ended the romance then and there. But you see we did have lots of fun on the WEST VIRGINIA.

Q: Tell me, were there organized athletics on the WEST VIRGINIA, and in the fleet at that time?

ADM. R.: Oh, yes. I was very active in sailing. As a matter of fact F.C. Sherman, then the gunnery officer of the ship, and I copped the Pacific Fleet sailing prize in Guantanamo Bay, at the Fleet Concentration there. Later F. C. Sherman became one of Mitscher's very famous task group commanders.

Q: That's Admiral Freddie Sherman?

ADM. R.: Yes, Frederick C. Sherman. I always remember him with a great deal of pleasure, although he was one of the tougher task group commanders.

Let me go back to the WEST VIRGINIA. I left her in August of 1928; I had done my two years in the fleet and was en route to Pensacola. I drove East with a very wonderful high school classmate who'd had a course in geology at Stanford. He was on rather light duty because his first job was such a tremendous burden that they, the doctors, practically ordered him to take time off. So he drove with me across country, and crossing the country with a geologist, particularly camping out in Yellowstone Park and so forth, was a great experience for me. We got to Pensacola, and he said he would take a job with a fishing fleet while I busted out of Pensacola. Well I fooled him; I didn't bust out.

Q: Why did he expect you to bust out?

ADM. R.: I don't know. The chances were, I think in those times, a little less than 50-50 of getting through, and it was a hazard that everyone undertook. Now, I had two downs. I think the final check in land planes - I got an airplane that, I don't know whether it was the instructor in the rear seat that was so heavy or the rigging of the airplane, but to snap roll I always made a roll and a quarter; I couldn't bring it out, so I got a down and got extra time and got by. This happens to many.

Q: You said Butterfield was one of your instructors there?

ADM. R.: He was there, yes, but my primary - my instructor

Russell #1-36

in primary seaplanes - believe it or not was a high school classmate from Tacoma, Al Malstrom. I just drew him by chance. He was four years ahead of me at the Naval Academy. He went directly from high school, and I had gone to sea, you know, for four years. So here he was. But flight school - our solo was in float planes. Our first instruction was in float planes, and that was very interesting, and I had Malstrom as my instructor. Of course we had other instructors to check us. The sort of the graduation exercise in the float plane was to go to six thousand feet, cut the switch, stall the plane so that you stopped your prop, and when the prop was dead, of course, you were gliding and losing altitude all the time you spiraled down and you were to land within something like fifty yards of a boat which was anchored out in Pensacola Bay. This was called the boat shot, and that was sort of the final event before you graduated from primary seaplanes. Various and sundry things happened. I remember one of our students left his wintip float in the boat, and that was disqualifying. But (RADM Rufus F.) Zogbaum, who was later skipper of the LANGLEY, was going through the flying course as a Captain. And you know King went through as a senior officer, and Genial John Hoover was a classmate of mine at flight school.

Q: And was he a Captain at that point?

ADM. R.: He was a Commander then, and I was an Ensign. But

Zoggie, who took twice as long as normal to get through the flight course, but graduated eventually, was practicing the boat shot, and he was using, in lieu of the boat, the channel buoy off the piers at the Pensacola waterfront. He did pretty well, so damn well that he took the lower wing and the wingtip float off on the buoy. It was an amazing circumstance because when the crash boat got there, there was nothing showing of his airplane except the bottom of the float, and here was Zoggie standing, dry as a bone, on top of his float. Just how he got there we never could quite understand. But you see what happened, the plane slowly capsized and the time it took the wing to fill with water allowed him time to climb over and as it turned wrong side up he just kept on going, so that finally there he was standing on the top of the bottom of his float.

Q: How did these older men work out, generally speaking? Did they get wings?

ADM. R.: Yes they did. King got wings. Halsey went through afterward, after King, and got wings. I have some reservations about King because, as you know, he was something of a sundowner, but Halsey was a tremendous fellow and I liked him very much. I was not there with him. Genial John Hoover did all the menial chores that the rest of us did, and we appreciated that.

Then we went from there to primary land planes, and these

were NY-1s and 2s at that time, consolidated training planes. They were wood wing, welded steel tube fuselage, the whole thing covered with fabric. We had radial engines. From there we went to flying boats, which was a very interesting thing - great seamanship involved in those days in flying boats, after getting waterborne on landing you had to know how to get back to the beach, and so on.

Q: Flying boats were a sort of the wave of the future, weren't they.

ADM. R.: Yes. And then we had service airplanes, a little bit of everything; we got some of the spotting planes, we did gunnery in Boeing biplanes, and then we went to fighters, and that was the graduating squadron. There were five squadrons we went through; very interesting times. And we worked hard. I lost two classmates in training. John Gotjen walked into his own propeller and split his head open that way. Irv Howell and his instructor were killed by another student actually settling on top of them in going around in the pattern; they were struck from above and behind and both of them went in. I think the student was able to land his plane although it was pretty badly wrecked. So we lost two classmates there, and every once in a while this business of aviation sort of grew on you and you realized that you were being paid flight pay for a little extra hazard.

Russell #1 - 39

Q: You had no qualms about it?

ADM. R.: No, no. I got married between squadrons. It happened this way. When Bruce Kelly, who was in the Class of '25, and I were at the Naval Academy our Congressman was Albert Johnson, who had an only daughter. Her name was Dorothy. Bruce and I used to roll the dice to see who'd have to escort the Congressman's daughter, because she was rather young and not so interesting because of her youth.

Q: You mean when she came over to a hop?

ADM. R.: To a hop at the Naval Academy. I'd sort of forgotten about this, but when I was at Pensacola our Congressman and his wife and daughter, returning from a vacation in Florida, came through Pensacola to see how their appointee was doing. By this time quarters were short on the base and we were encouraged to go out and rent places in town. Three of us rented a little cottage on the road to downtown Pensacola which we named BAD MANOR. So I was very closely tied to a couple of roommates at BAD MANOR, when appeared this gorgeous gal, the daughter of my Congressman. She'd grown up, and she was a dilly. And so my house mates nudged me and said, "What's wrong with you, Russell? Why don't you propose to this girl?" And so I did. And she accepted me; we were married in April of 1929, in Washington, D.C.

Q: Do you suppose she had anything to do with the visit to Pensacola?

ADM. R.: I don't know. But one of my house mates, Willie Watson, at Pensacola, was my best man. Willie was another casualty in the class, about two or three years out of Pensacola; he was in an airplane diving at a target and the wing folded and he was killed. So, I married the Congressman's daughter, Dorothy, and she was my first wife. We had two children in due course, Don and Kenneth, and they're still in the area here, but I lost her, as you know, to cancer in 1965.

But coming out into the fleet, among other things one of my classmates at Pensacola was Robert Burns Pirie, and Pirie had a flashy car which was a DeSoto; it was a streamlined job, looked a little bit like the modern Volkswagen but it was larger than that. One of my difficulties was that my golf clubs, believe it or not, wouldn't go athwartships on the floor of my mud-colored Ford - the longer sticks, the woods, wouldn't fit - and that was the width of the Ford in those days; this was a Model A Ford. And so Pirie, knowing of my difficulty, said, "Oh, don't give it a second thought. They'll fit in the DeSoto and I'll bring them out to you." We were to rendezvous in Coronado, you see, so I said, "Well, fine," and I left my clubs in the garage for Pirie to bring out. We got not only thirty days' leave but travel time, and at the end of this rather lengthy time I got together with my classmate Pirie in Coronado and I said, "Robert, where are my golf clubs?" And he looked me in the eye and he said, "What clubs?" He'd gone off and forgotten them. And you know, being Scotch, I've never had enough money to buy another set of clubs. So now, when I think of playing golf, I run and get my axe and cut some more wood for the fire place.

My first aviation assignment was to a battleship squadron.

Q: Was this a matter of choice?

ADM. R.: It was, because I had a great affinity for USS WEST VIRGINIA, and remembering the aviators on that ship and the aircraft I thought it would be very fine duty. I would have liked very much to have a fighter squadron, but the assignments were such that I just couldn't get one of those so I went to a float plane squadron.

Q: How many planes did she carry then?

ADM. R.: She carried three, and these were at that time O2U-1s We were in transition in the fleet from the UO-1s to the O2U-1s

Q: Now these were used for spotting?

ADM. R.: The primary mission of the squadron was to spot the fall of shot of the sixteen inch rifles of the USS WEST VIRGINIA

But, we had two 30 calibre guns in our airplanes; we would fly down on floats to San Diego, pull the floats and put on wheels and a hook, and fly off the carriers. Or we did all our gunnery on wheels rather than on floats, but yet we'd go back on floats and join our ship perhaps for a cruise. I made probably, in roughly three years of duty, perhaps three cruises on carriers - some of them short, just as far as San Francisco in a battle maneuver, some of them as long as down to the Canal Zone and so forth. I made my carrier qualifying landings, having left Pensacola in May being designated pilot number 3495 in the United States Navy. We practiced carrier landings ashore and then the LANGLEY became available, and I went out in November of 1929 and made my first seven carrier qualifying landings. I made these landings in an FU, which was related to the UO-1, but it was a single seater with a fighter designation. It had a tail skag instead of a tail wheel, and there were no brakes on the main wheels. So when you came aboard ship, a couple of things were very important; first that, as you reached the end of your arrested run, you put on full throttle, because the arresting gear was a couple of concrete counter weights over the side of the ship attached to a six part purchase and six cross deck pendants. When you came in to land and hooked a wire in your arresting hook you were transforming the kinetic energy of your forward motion into potential energy of raising the deck side weights. Now, when you came to the end of your arrested run it took a little time for a couple of burly seamen to put brakes on the cables, so the doctrine was to open your throttle wide and hold the wire out until the brakes on the counter weight cables were on. Then you got a signal from the plane director on deck that you could close your throttle and ease backward and drop the wire. And then the second point was you were not allowed to taxi forward until you had a man on each wing. The reason for this was you had no wheel brakes for directional control only the dragging of your tail skag. You parked with the men guiding you from your wingtips. The tail skag was rather sharp. It was used, of course, on sod fields ashore in those days, and it helped you in the directional stability sense when you were in your ground roll on the airfield, but if you went aboard ship with that regular skag it was rather sharp and it would gouge into what was a Douglas fir flight deck on the LANGLEY, as I remember it. So we used to put a thing that looked like a small shovel underneath the point of the tail skag to keep from gouging the deck. It was all very primitive.

Well you know that business of holding up the weights led to a rather amusing incident. We were flying O2Us off the LANGLEY and there was a scouting squadron flying similar aircraft. One of the pilots, Lanny Conn, came aboard and hooked a wire a little bit to the side, slightly eccentrically but not badly so. When you hit the wire a wave goes out to the deck sheave and back again. Well the geometry of the situation was such that as Lanny rolled down the deck, and, just as he was about to stop, this reflected wave from the deck sheaves arrived, and it slewed his airplane around, and he came unhooked. So here he was sitting, facing not fore and aft but athwartships, and true to doctrine he opened his throttle to hold the wire but there was no wire in his tail, so he slowly rolled over the side. You could see men running to grab his wings before he left the edge of the deck, but they were too late. And as he went over the side, he and his rear seat man, as the center of gravity passed over the edge of the deck and his wheels dropped down, it flipped him over on his back and Lanny Conn and his gunner were falling head down into the ocean. But LANGLEY had stacks which trained up or down; if she was not at flight operations they were up, and when she was at flight operations they were horizontal. Well it so happened that Lanny Conn fell between these stacks, and one stack caught the upper side of his upper wing and flipped him right side up just before he hit the water. So he passed down into the wake of the LANGLEY with his nose pointed toward the side of the ship, he and his rear seat gunner were like the center of a lily with the wings and the tail like the petals surrounding. We waved to them, and of course the plane guard destroyer picked them up. They were none the worse for wear

- a little bit disappointed they'd lost their airplane, and wet. In due time in a lull in flight operations the plane guard destroyer brought Lanny and his rear seat man back to the LANGLEY and they were brought aboard by high line. As Lanny descended from the high line onto the hangar deck, there to meet him was the Chief Engineer of the USS LANGLEY who shook his fist in Lanny Conn's face and said, "You snaggletoothed, red-headed aviator! You put a dent in my stack!" Little did it matter to him that it saved Lanny's life, Lanny had dented the stack and he still didn't like it. Well, the LANGLEY was a great ship.

Q: But you were still attached to the battleship?

ADM. R.: Sure, yes. Our squadron was VO-5, and we were basing on carriers, on the ships, and anywhere ashore.

Q: Now what about your duties on board battleship, I mean as far as spotting was concerned, and the use of those planes?

ADM. R.: We could either spot on wheels or on floats. When we were aboard ship we wore floats, a main center line float with a deep V, incidentally. We discovered that the way to land in rough water and not bounce back into the air was to have a fairly deep V in the float, the main float, so it would cut into the water instead of skipping off the top of it. And then there were wing tip floats. The battleships, for recovery, would steam with the wind on one bow and then turn ninety degrees through the wind and back down at the same time. This would bring them to a stop, but it would also throw up a great smooth boil of water in the sea and this was a point at which you aimed when you made your landing; you touched down in that smooth spot so you didn't have the violent effect of the waves. And then you'd taxi up and get hoisted aboard.

Q: As a junior officer, were you obligated to stand watches on the battleship?

ADM. R.: Yes, oh yes. And as a squadron officer later on, we were allowed to stand deck watches. As a matter of fact, John Sydney McCain, when he commanded the RANGER, when I was in a fighter-bomber squadron on his ship, allowed all us airplane jockeys to come to the bridge, learn what was going on, and eventually check out as officer of the deck.

Q: That wasn't the general rule, however, was it?

ADM. R.: It depended. But John Sydney McCain, of course, was a wonderful old fellow, very much a seaman himself, and he was all for passing the knowledge on down to the younger generation, which we greatly appreciated.

Well now, let's see - battleship duty. We had catapults

that operated usually with smokeless powder and that was smoother than torpedo air; torpedo air for some reason, the throwing of the valves and one thing and another, was a little bit rougher and you got more of a shock going off the compresse air catapult than you did the powder catapult. We had one catapult aft on WEST VIRGINIA, back on her extreme stern, we had one on number three turret which was elevated. The next turret abaft the main mast. There you trained the turret into the wind, into the relative wind, of course, for your shot. The after catapult was rotatable through 360 degrees, and you trained that into the wind for your catapult shot. I think you'll find in the album there a picture of Russell and his rear seat man, Archer, taking off from battleship WEST VIRGINIA. The idea was to pull your nose up to make sure that you didn't get shot down into the water as you left the ship, and if the catapult officer was wise he would fire you as the ship was beginning to come up on a roll so that would give you an upward component as you left the end of the catapult.

Q: Now these operations were all in the Pacific, were they?

ADM. R.: Yes. Mostly off the California coast, but we made trips as far as Hawaii in one direction, and to the East Coast. I've had a number of forced landings, but I have yet to have to bail out of an airplane. I've always been able to find some place to put the airplane down, which has its virtue because if you leave your airplane it's sure to be wrecked and if not, you have a good chance of saving it. One of the most embarrassing forced landings I've had, - we were with the battleships anchored in a stately row in Hampton Roads when I got permission to fly up to the Snyder Cup Races, which were to be held over the Anacostia River in Washington, D.C. The Naval Air Station Anacostia was closed to seaplanes because of the races, but I had arranged to fly into Annapolis where they'd take care of my airplane and I could get a ride down to see the Snyder Cup Races. We were well underway; I was cruising along blissfully in my 02U over land but within - always in the old days one always looked for "where do I put this airplane down if the engine quits" you know. Well, sure enough, as I got up north of Langley, Va., the engine did quit, and it quit completely. I mean, there was no question I had no power left. I could make the water by turning and making a diagonal downwind landing. I got to the salt water in Chesapeake Bay and made a normal landing, and there we were. The first thing we did was to pull out a sparkplug and see what had happened to our engine, and we found that we weren't getting any cam action to actuate the rocker arms so we had no possibility of fixing the airplane even to taxi.

Q: That was a major repair.

ADM. R.: Major repair, yes. Well, as we were drifting along

Russell #1 - 49

it was a calm day and there were a number of fish stakes around, so I stripped down and took a heaving line which we had in the airplane, made it fast to the forward struts and then led it through a chalk on the nose of the float and swam out and back around a fish stake to hold the airplane there. And then my rear seat man and I flipped a coin to see who would go and get help, if a boat came, you see.

Q: Where were you in the Bay?

ADM. R.: We were near Back River, before you get to the mouth of the Potomac - between the James River and the Potomac River - Rappahannock is the next one; it was just short of the Rappahannock River. We were out in the fishnet country, in that part of the bay. It wasn't very long before a fisherman appeared. We signaled him and he came over, and, as I say, my rear seat man and I had flipped a coin to see who'd get help and who'd stay with the airplane. I got the side of the coin that said I'd go with the fisherman and get help and get the airplane towed back down to the ship, which was in Hampton Roads. It didn't look like a very difficult job. Well, the fisherman shaved on the way to his moorings and dolled up because he was going to see his girlfriend and he was driving down to Hampton, so he was quite willing to take me to Old Point Comfort where I caught one of the WEST VIRGINIA's boats, got out to the ship, told them of our difficulty. They gave me a sixty-foot officers' motorboat to go tow my airplane back. Well, time was running out on us, although my forced landing had been fairly early in the morning waiting for assistance and so on had occupied quite a bit of the day. So we started off in the early evening to go get the airplane, and half way there one of those wonderful Chesapeake Bay thunderstorms broke. As we approached where I had securely tied the airplane to the fish stake, to my horror I saw it adrift, and a very palefaced mechanic in the rear seat. So, we maneuvered the boat, to let me get into the airplane, and the mechanic into the officers' motorboat. I told them to put him down in the engine room where he could keep warm, and I got another mechanic to join me. We took a good sized line from the officers' motor boat; it was so large we couldn't get it through the bow chock and I remember opening the lay of the line and putting one strand in the chock so we'd have a fair lead for towing.

Q: In the midst of the storm?

ADM. R.: Yes. Well then towing of course was downwind; this wind was from the northeast, and every time we started to turn downwind the force of the wind on the airplane was so great that it would submerge the wingtip float, indicating I was going to capsize if I persisted, so I'd ask them to lay off and they'd come back up into the wind. And after trying this several times and not getting the airplane turned downwind, I said well look, I'll cast off, and I had them cast off, and I took the tow line up on the airplane and I said, "I'll sail this airplane back down to a point where we can tow diagonally upwind without having to turn", you see.

Q: Treating it as a sailboat?

ADM. R.: Well, yes. You can sail a seaplane, you know. The key was, though, - say you give it right rudder, that will put you this way and that will make you go to the left as you drift backward, of if you put your rudder the other way, it'll make you go to the right. So you can sail a seaplane. It was a common maneuver, really, if you had no power.

Q: One of its virtues?

ADM. R.: Yes. So I said I will sail this airplane down to Hampton Roads; I was going out toward the sea down Chesapeake Bay, you see. By this time it was quite dark and raining and blowing. To my horror I saw a line of fish stakes appear downwind of us. I looked for an opening wide enough to sail the seaplane through and I could find none, so I headed for the widest spacing between stakes and the very tender part of the wing, the trailing edge, came up against the two fish stakes. The sea made us saw up and down, up

and down on these two stakes. Finally a big sea came along
and lifted us way up, and when we came down this time the
stakes came up through the wing, between the spars, and we
sawed up and down for a while that way and another big sea
came along and lifted me completely clear and I went sailing
on down clear of the line of fish stakes. I thought that
was fine until another row of fish stakes appeared through
the dark. I went through seven rows of fish stakes backward,
in the dark of night and finally in desperation I had them
take the line again, the wind had abated a little bit, and I
said, "Look, when I give you the word you turn downwind and
just pull like the devil, and I'll take the consequences."
I put my mechanic, who was a pretty husky fellow, on the
upwind wing to hold it down, and they jerked us around and
we got going downwind. And the farther we went, the better
the weather became, and finally we made the end of battleship row. The first ship in the row was the USS RELIEF,
the hospital ship. I was not sure whether I had holes in
some of my floats or not. I had a hand flashlight. She
seemed to handle all right but I couldn't tell whether one
of the floats - you see there were three of them, the main
float and the two wingtip floats - whether one of them flooded. So I used my hand flashlight and by Morse code called
the RELIEF and said, "Please illuminate me." I wanted to
see how we were. RELIEF had a nice little twelve inch search-
light. And she did; she illuminated, I could look around

and I was a sad looking sight. The trailing edge of the lower wing crushed up to the spar, holes in the fabric with fabric hanging down, but still water tight integrity held in my floats and I was in fairly good shape. So we started towing up the battleship line. But the battleships, seeing RELIEF illuminate my plane, turned on their big thirty-six inch searchlights, and here I was a spectacle getting towed up to my ship, the USS WEST VIRGINIA about the third ship up the line, with all these thirty-six inch searchlights on me!

Q: Home in disgrace?

ADM. R.: Home in disgrace, and that was probably the worst forced landing experience I've had in my whole naval air career. But do you know, in those days we had that airplane repaired and we flew it by the time we got to the Canal Zone during that maneuver, - that same airplane. We had aviation carpenter's mates, we had the fabric, we had the wood, we rebuilt the wings and I was flying that airplane.

Q: Were they canvas wings?

ADM. R.: The fabric was long staple cotton, and you sewed it on then you stitched it through at the ribs of the wings, and then you doped it and the dope shrunk it so it was taught. You put about five coats of dope on, the last two being of fire-

Russell #1 - 54

proofing, and by this time it was a nice smooth surface. Well, that was my experience in VO-5.

I was transferred then to VP-1. Now VP-1 was a flying boat squadron based in Pearl Harbor and they were flying T2Ds, a Douglas torpedo plane - two engines, twin floats - and as I arrived there they were just in process of shifting to a new airplane which was a pure flying boat - a big hull, bi-plane. This airplane was the PK1. One never hears of Keystone airplanes any more, but this was a Keystone flying boat, PK1, and it was a truck. It was heavy on the controls and just a regular big old clunker, but it was an airplane and we liked to fly. It was fairly long-range; we used to do our advance base maneuvers either at Hilo or up at French Frigate Shoals. You know, nothing had flown from the mainland to Hawaii at that time; this was 1931, '31.

Q: This was before that special McGinnis flight, wasn't it?

ADM. R.: Well, Rogers got part way there, most of the way, and then there was the Dole flight later on. That was after my tour though.

Well, flying boats - it's a very interesting and different sort of aviation because seamanship really comes into play. I was allowed to fly not only the PKs, but we had a Sikorsky - one of the early Sikorskys which had twin booms, twin tails, and a detached body; it was an amphian. I remember we had a forced landing in that one time and I landed in the sea off Honolulu Harbor and taxied over and up the channel into Pearl Harbor. When you had a forced landing you wondered if it was any technique on your part that might have caused it; you were very concerned to find out really what caused the thing. And in this case it was a simple thing. The fuel tanks were put together with a packing strip where the plating joined in the tanks, and this strip was sloughing off and giving a sludge in the fuel, actually a fibrous sludge in the fuel, and this was plugging up the carburetor. That was our trouble. When we got on the water we could get enough power to the engines to taxi, but if you tried to give them full power they would just quit. It was because of this sludge in the fuel which plugged up the jets in your carburetor.

Q: What was the overall purpose of this squadron? Was it reconnaissance?

ADM. R.: Reconnaissance, yes. We had a fleet maneuver I remember very well. We had the whole fleet anchored in Lahaina Roads and we did a twenty four hour a day anti-submarine patrol. The water is so beautifully clear there we discovered submarines down at depth under the water; you could fly over and see them down there. We'd wait and as soon as he'd show his periscope we'd dive on his periscope and let him know he was discovered. Otherwise he didn't know whether he was getting away with it or

Russell #1 - 56

not. But that was our prime purpose in life, to scout.

Q: What was your cruising distance?

ADM. R.: I don't remember completely, but it wouldn't carry you from the mainland to Hawaii which is 2,000 miles.

Q: What about Midway from Hawaii?

ADM. R.: Well, we went as far as French Frigate Shoals which is on the way to Midway. The longest jump that way is from the mainland to Hawaii, you know, and that's between 2,000 and 2,100 nautical miles, and we couldn't do that. We had a lot of engine trouble. I remember we had one forced landing in which the airplane lost one engine and couldn't stay airborne on the other. It landed off the windward shore of Maui, and eventually got in the surf. We recovered parts of that airplane in three different counties in Maui! That's the windward side of the island and the wind at sea spreads things along. Pete Wykoff, a squadron mate, indicated distress one time when I was flying with him. We turned back into Hilo Harbor and landed and I asked him what the trouble was. He said, "I don't have any rudder." It happened that the rudder wire came along and did a ninety degree bend through a bulkhead, for water tight integrity I presume, and then on back to the tail, and the sheave at the bottom had carried away so there was just a slack bit of wire there instead of something with which he could exert a pull on the rudder. So he had flown back with no rudder at all. His airplane was, repaired there in Hilo Harbor. we had advance base maneuvers I remember one time in Hilo Harbor when we were billeted on the commercial pier there where flour had been stored. We had a kona storm, one of those heavy, tropical rains, and you'd wade through flour paste to get to your canvas cot, you know, and then you'd take your shoes off and leave them underneath and get up on your cot just to stay out of the paste. Well, that was big boat flying and very interesting - I'm sorry that we don't have flying boats in the Navy any more.

Q: You really enjoyed them?

ADM. R.: Yes. It was a combination of surface and air that was very interesting, intriguing.

Q: What were their particular merits, I mean in naval service?

ADM. R.: You didn't have to have a field to land on. That's the primary thing, you could land anywhere where there was water. As I will explain later on, in my Aleutian campaign with amphibians, we could go all sorts of places and I'll tell you about that later. But, while I was in VP-1 orders came through. I had asked for a postgraduate course in aeronautical engineering, and I went then to the Postgraduate School in 1932. We started with thirteen people and we eliminated for the seven positions that were open; thirteen of us started and at the end of one year seven of us were selected to go on as being likely candidates to finish successfully the course in aeronautical engineering.

Q: And that was a two-year course?

ADM. R.: No, it was a three-year course. Then we specialized, the second year, under Dr. Wendell Coates at the Postgraduate School in math, mechanics, and all those things one needed to go on to a graduate course in aeronautical engineering. And then three of us were assigned to structures and we went to Cal Tech. Four of us were assigned to engines and they went to the University of Michigan. I was fortunate enough to be sent to Cal Tech. The head of the engineering department was dear old Dr. von Karman, the world famous scientist. I was allowed to do a research thesis with a powered wind tunnel model. A powered model was required to get the static stability effects of the slipstream over the airplane, which hadn't been done before. I had been working on this thesis for about two months when an Air Force officer, then Army Air Force officer, McCoy, came and together we did a thesis which was one of the papers published in the original Journal of the Institute of the Aeronautical Sciences, which is now the AIAA as you know. And that

Russell #1 - 59

won me a membership; I'm now a fellow.

Q: The use of the wind tunnel - that was something the Bureau of Standards worked with, wasn't it?

ADM. R.: Yes, but this one belonged to Cal Tech. It was something that was financed by the Guggenheims - it was known as the Guggenheim Aeronautical Laboratory at Cal Tech. Von Karman, was head of the department of aeronautics. I had only one class from him, although he advised us, he also advised me in the thesis and so on - a wonderful, wonderful old gentleman. I never will forget our experience with him. This was the only class we had of which he was the teacher; it was in the theory of elasticity. It was a three quarter course, and it was a lecture course. At the end of the first quarter, having been lectured all quarter long, he gave us a written examination. Then there was another quarter and again lectures all quarter long. As the end of the second quarter approached he said, "Well, gentlemen, what would you like? Would you like a written examination or an oral examination?" And we thought oh, what fun, an oral examination. Everyone voted for an oral examination there were about 25 in this class. So the great day came and we were being examined, and he'd get each one up before the class at the blackboard and he'd start out with something he was pretty sure you could do. Then he'd lead you along and suddenly you would fall over the precipice; you'd gone beyond your depth, and he had sounded you out. He knew exactly what your capacity was and he had an uncanny way, remember now he'd been only lecturing to us - he knew us personally and he'd been lecturing to us but we hadn't had to perform. And so, watching this performance we thought well, let's see what he does with Bill Bollay because we knew that Bill Bollay had been retained by von Karman to work out the detailed solution to some of his equations. So we were pretty sure he couldn't stump Bill Bollay. It came Bill's turn and things went along pretty well, when all of a sudden Bill Bollay found himself lost in an infinite series of vortices on two axes and he went over the cliff just like all the rest of us. This was von Karman.

Q: Sounds like a very good teacher.

ADM. R.: Yes.

Q: Tell me about the earlier phases of this special study at Annapolis.

ADM. R.: We took what was called the general line course, with a certain degree of mathematics and mechanics and the things that they knew would be required for a technical education. And based on how well we did with that, we had a class standing. And of the thirteen, seven of us were picked as being people who could go on and do justice to a proper course. And then we went intensely into math, mechanics, dynamics and things of this sort, which would prepare us for the next step which was then to go to these two civilian institutions. And I was very fortunate, I thought, in being able to go to Cal Tech. Cal Tech was a purist school. Old Robert Millikan was the head of it, and he never gave an honorary degree; anyone who held a degree from Cal Tech (I don't know whether this still holds or not) earned it. And there were questions in the class that preceded us - with one chap there was some question whether he was going to get a degree or not. They were going to make no compromises for him. I thought that was really a wonderful attitude. It happened that when old Dr. Millikan once a year would invite people to the home, he and his wife would entertain, of the three Navy people going I was the junior one - the other lads were a little ahead of me in seniority. But because I had done a little better than they had in the courses, and was standing a little higher pure learning you see, my wife and I were the two that were invited from that group. This was old Robert Millikan, a very fine old gentleman.

Q: You ended up with a degree, a Masters?

ADM. R.: A Master of Science in Aeronautical Engineering, yes. And I'm very proud of that.

Q: Now this graduate period stood you in great stead, did it not, as your career developed?

ADM. R.: Yes. I will tell you what happened to me then when I left. I went to a wonderful fighter-bomber squadron, and you'll see over there on the table a model of the airplane we flew, which was known as the BF2C-1. It was basically a Curtis-Hawk, a biplane, but here was the day when wheels were being tucked up, so we manually retracted our wheels. That was a beautiful airplane from the static strength point of view, but dynamics apparently were cast to the winds because among other things the interplane aeleron strut responded to about the same frequency as the propeller in high pitch, so it was a vibration nightmare. The airplane started shaking itself apart in the air. The engineering officer in the squadron was Doc Leach. He was killed diving on a sleeve I was towing. His wing folded back across the cockpit, and as near as we could reconstruct the thing, one of the very highly stressed fittings, the terminal for a diagonal brace wire in the wing, fatigued and failed. It took the drag load in the upper wing and without that strength member the wing folded back across the cockpit and the pilot didn't get out. I had that very sad duty of going and telling his wife that she was a widow, a duty that I would gladly pass to anyone rather than take myself, but these things have to be done once in a while.

Well that promoted me then to engineer officer of the squadron at a very interesting time. Here was an airplane dynamically unfit, and what do you do with it? As a young officer

Russell #1 - 63

graduate in aeronautical engineering it was a problem that you could really put your teeth in. Well, what we did, we eventually grounded the airplane. We sent a couple of them to then the Naval Aircraft Factory for further examination, and we shifted then to F4B4s for half the squadron and F2Fs for the other half. The F2F was a delightful airplane to fly. It was one of Grumman's very early ones. It was a bi-plane and very handy, but its main armament was only two thirty calibre guns. But it was really a beautiful and delightful thing to fly.

Q: What about the men who took this special course and came through with a degree? I mean, their careers blossomed eventually, I imagine, all of them.

ADM. R.: Yes, that's true. In my case I had two choices. I could have declared for aeronautical engineering duty only or I could have stayed in the line of the Navy. I, of course, chose the latter, to stay in the line of the Navy. But each time I came ashore thereafter I went to a technical job. My first shore duty.

Q: You were staff, then?

ADM. R.: Yes, and each time I came ashore I did something to repay Uncle Sam for the technical education I'd had. I wound up eventually in 1955 by being Chief of the Bureau of Aeronautics.

Russell #1 - 64

And then my debt was repaid and the next time I came ashore I came ashore as a Vice Chief of Naval Operations.

Well, let's go on with VB-5, this delightful fighter-bomber squadron in which I served.

Q: Well now, you grounded this particular plane, this Curtis-Hawk?

ADM. R.: And shifted to F2Fs by Grumman and F4Bs by Boeing.

Q: And what was the fate of the one that was grounded?

ADM. R.: Eventually I flew one, testing it, in Philadelphia from the Naval Aircraft Factory. We had hung weights on various places to change the frequency of wires and struts and things, and had changed the mass balance here, there and the other place, and by this time we had only 26 of them left, we had lost a number in crashes. And we had only twenty six left, we removed everything of value and took them out on a lighter off San Diego and dumped them over the side. The original order was something like thirty four; I think we had lost eight.

Q: Was the Naval Test Center in Anacostia in being then?

ADM. R. Yes, at Anacostia, right.

Q: Had this plane been tested?

ADM. R.:  Presumably it had, but you see the structural failures didn't occur until you fatigued it. Perhaps if they'd been real smart they would have detected that there were various pieces of it that vibrated in harmony to certain frequencies of the engine, but it was in service. Well, it was quite an effective airplane. We were attached regularly to CV-4, the USS RANGER, and I'd like to tell you a little more about the RANGER, but we also flew from LEXINGTON and SARATOGA which were current at that time. I never went back to the LANGLEY, although she was a wonderful ship; we used to call her the Covered Wagon and the Morale, since she was sort of an oddity, was very high and we had characters on her in the old days. Some of these perhaps you know. One was Cat Brown, one was Country Moore, one was Dutch Greber and so on, and they were forever playing tricks on one another. I remember one time - I don't know which of this crew did it to the other but let's take two of them; let's say it was Cat Brown and Country Moore. Well, Cat Brown was the victim of Country Moore. Country Moore got a hypodermic needle from our flight surgeon and filled it with oil of garlic, and he put it just under the toothpaste in the tube of our friend Cat Brown's Toothpaste - just through the top layer of the paste, you see. And so there was a little enclave of oil of garlic, and the moment you squeezed the toothpaste up came the oil of garlic. And of course it got on the brush, and Cat didn't realize until he got it in his mouth what had happened. I'm only taking Cat and Country - as two characters. I don't know who did what to whom, but I'll just use these two if I may. Well, so that left Cat holding the bag to do the next stunt. This, I thought, was very, very clever and he did it this way. He went to the flight surgeon who was a very young and ambitious flight surgeon, he'd learned to fly, you know, and he'd been through medical school, and he wanted to watch us carefully for the effects of fatigue in flying and all that sort of business. Cat went to him and he said, "You know, Doc, I'm very much worried about something." And Doc said, "What's that?" And he said, "Well this fellow Country Moore. You know, he's been acting very strangely. He acts strangely in the air and, you know, it's getting so bad I'm almost afraid to fly with him. He doesn't behave well when we're flying in formation and you know what, Doc? I think he's going nuts." "Oh," says the doctor, and this was a wonderful case for him, you see. So what happened? Cat then went to Country Moore and he said, "Country, you know what?" And Country said, "What?" And Cat said, "You may not believe this, but that flight surgeon of ours thinks you're going nuts! Did you know that?" "Oh," says Country Moore "It couldn't be. It couldn't be." "Okay," says Cat, "you just watch him in the mess tonight, in the wardroom. He'll be watching you, and he really thinks you're going nuts, Country." Well, Country wouldn't believe it, but you can imagine what happened. The eager young flight surgeon was, in fact, watching Country very carefully, and this annoyed the hell out of Country, as you can imagine. But you know this situation

Russell #1 - 67

built up, and got so bad, that Cat had to confess that it was all a hoax he had perpetrated. Well that's the sort of fun we had on the old Covered Wagon, the USS LANGLEY, and she was a lovely old ship.

Q: Well, you had to have some diversion from the tensions of flying.

ADM. R.: Yes.

Q: Did you experience tension in flying, I mean constant flying?

ADM. R.: I like best of all to fly single seaters, because you're on your own. If you had to worry about somebody else in the airplane - supposing now I had a two seater and I had an engine failure. I would weigh carefully, - could I set this thing down safely? Or should I have my mech bail out and I go out with him? - What's the safer thing to do? When you're on your own, you make that decision and you take your chances. So, of course there is some slight strain to flying, but it's such a wonderful experience. I wouldn't give anything for the experience I've had in the air; it's wonderful.

Well, we have been through VB-1, based on the RANGER, (CV-4) and on LEXINGTON, (CV-2), and SARATOGA, (CV-3). We did re-arming drills, for example; we had live bombs, we went out and landed on the ship, and we were timed from the time we touched down to the time we were refuelled, rearmed, and took off again. We took off with live bombs and we bombed a towed target. It's quite an experience. In those days you used to dive from about 14,000 feet and you'd pull out - you were not allowed to go below 1500 feet - and then watch this bomb go down and you'd see this tremendous explosion. It was a regular live bomb, and you had a feeling of power that you can't get any other way. And the fact that you'd done it gave you a feeling of, "I'm really doing something for Uncle Sam".

Q: But this was a rare occasion, because they were very careful about live weapons, were they not? In terms of expense.

ADM. R.: Yes, but when I was in VO, we fired plenty of rounds from those sixteen inch rifles on the WEST VIRGINIA. We trained very carefully of course, and we dropped many, many live bombs, although we spent endless flights training for the thing, dropping water filled bombs or the little marker bombs that had the same general ballistics as the big bombs. We spent hours diving on targets.

Q: In this period, the battleship was still supreme, was she not? And the carrier was kind of an auxiliary to the battle line, but things were beginning to change.

ADM. R.: Yes, that's right.

Q: Can you talk a little about that?

ADM. R.: Well, the attitude of the chief engineer toward Lanny Conn, who put a dent in his stack, was characteristic. And there was another thing, too. It seemed to me in the very early days when we were - incidentally I came aboard LANGLEY just after they had removed the fore and aft wires. At one time they thought that to keep an airplane in the gear it would be a nice thing to have not only athwartship wires, but also fore and aft wires. And airplanes had axles in those days, and the axle had a whole flock of little hooks like little anchors hanging down, and the thought was if the deck was rolling and you were slipping around these little anchors would hook on to the fore and aft wires. I don't know whose idea this was. The arresting wires were held up on fiddle bridges that, first of all, just came loose, but later on they were like a wagon spring and you could pull them down; you'd want the wires out of the way when you were taxiing, you see, and you could throw a lever and all these little wires would pull down on the springs and flatten the springs and the arresting wire would lie flat on the deck. These were called yielding elements, and of course they're still used, but quite differently now on the modern carrier. In the case of fore and aft wires, we found out that the arresting hook instead of catching the athwartship wire might get caught under one of these fore and aft wires, and then it would ride up and miss all athwartship wires and you'd go into the barriers. There were two fences, or more, forward of you when you were landing on the old axial deck, and the energy if you struck those was absorbed by a broach - it was a tool in a bronze collar, and the tool had increasing diameter cutters, and you'd shave that bronze block as you'd pull the broach out about two feet or so on either end of the wire, and that would absorb the energy of stopping you, but invariably you'd do some damage to your airplane if you hit the barrier. And sometimes you'd even flip over on your back, over the fences.

Q: I understand that Pride did a lot of work in this area, did he not?

ADM. R.: Mel Pride was one of the pioneers in it, yes that's true. And Frank Akers, for example. Frank Akers was doing instrument landings on carriers, or attempting to in 1929 or '30. He would practice on the deck of the LANGLEY when she was alongside the pier in Coronado. I remember very well watching him go around and around; he'd have a safety pilot and he'd be under the hood trying to land on instruments on the carrier deck. I thought it was pretty scary.

Q: How much freedom did you have to do this sort of thing when you had an idea? How much freedom did you have in developing the idea?

ADM. R.: It depended on whom you could persuade. In the old days the Bureau of Aeronautics had the whole aviation picture, including the assignment of aviation personnel. The Bureau of Personnel was a new bureau; it had been the Bureau of Navigation. But the Bureau of Aeronautics would recommend, and that was really the force of an order as where to assign aviators. So personnel, material, everything really was in the hands of the old Bureau of Aeronautics. And it wasn't until about mid-span of World War II that the Op-05, the DCNO Air, broke off and took the requirements end of the picture. Then aviation personnel assignment went first to DCNO Air, and then from there to the Bureau of Naval Personnel, where it is now.

Q: Well, that almost total control of things aeronautical was the result of Moffett's work, was it not, and later King.

ADM. R.: Well, it was Moffett. King had it for a while; Jack Towers had it my first time there.

Well, let me go on with the sequence of my duties. I had been in this wonderful dive bomber squadron only perhaps a little over a year when I got ordered to a strange assignment. I was ordered to the fitting out of a new carrier, and this new carrier was CV-5; her name was the USS YORKTOWN. And so we were shipped off to Newport News, to the shipyard, and I said

farewell to my squadron mates and said we're going back to get
a new carrier; I'll see you next Christmas. Christmas then was
about four months away, perhaps. Well we got back there in late
summer, hotter than blazes. My wife, first child and I lived
in an apartment in downtown Newport News. I went daily to watch
the construction of this ship. We had a lot of ideas. Flying
from the old RANGER, I was very much impressed with her inadequacies. She was a fairly small ship. She had two airplane
elevators that went through the center line of the deck, and
they arrived at the hangar deck level in an elevator well, so
there was only one way to get an airplane off, or on an elevator
from the hangar. Not only that but the elevators were placed
at the extreme ends of the hangar so there was no dead space,
no quiet space, in the hangar; if you were at flight quarters
there was always traffic between the two elevators and the flight
deck. So that, plus the ready rooms, - the ready rooms for the
pilots waiting to take their airplanes off were atrocious. We
used a chart toom and usually stood up on LEXINGTON and SARA-
TOGA around a big chart table, and we had these little plotting
boards of our own that we took out and put into the airplane to
do our navigation, and we'd stand there with our parachutes on.
Carrying a parachute through a bunch of whirling propellers to
get into your airplane is rather a ticklish business, because
if it gets loose and it gets caught in a propeller why, you're gone.
Well, the ready rooms on the RANGER, CV-4, were very simple things.
There was a wooden bench in our ready room; we sat on the wooden
bench and faced portholes so the light was in our eyes. Not only

that, but to add insult to injury, there was a head forward, and therefore upwind of us, and in the early morning when it was being used there was a "perfume" that came back into the ready room. So all these things built up and I became a great fanatic in trying to figure out the optimum arrangement of an aircraft carrier.

Q: It was said that there was very little attention paid to the requirements of personnel in these early carriers. Why was that?

ADM. R.: It was new, yes. And the LANGLEY was a makeshift; it was a flight deck superimposed over the length of a collier, with electric drive and her maximum speed was twelve knots. I remember in a big maneuver off San Francisco, when I was in the VO squadron, we just couldn't fly because the ship couldn't generate enough wind on her own to let us get airborne. Twelve knots plus the speed that you could get in the half length of the deck, or whatever was allowed for the take off, wasn't enough.

Q: What some of us call "human engineering" had not yet come in being.

ADM. R.: Yes, that's true. Well, so we took off and went to Newport News and we fought for a lot of things there. We put reclining chairs in the ready rooms, all facing in one direction, with a blackboard, and actually they had a teletype information system that could be operated from a central point, air plot. And we even had, underneath the seat of the chair we had a little locker with a three combination lock, so that you could lock the confidential code book in your chair. Not only that but if you were on a long alert, as they call it now, waiting for your flight you could recline and get some rest. Air conditioning came in, too, and if you were sitting for long hours in a flight suit you appreciate that very much; particularly in the tropics do you appreciate air conditioning. So we did a lot of these things in CV-5, and then in CV-6, likewise.

Q: How did you go about making an impression on the powers that be with some of this input?

ADM. R.: They were very willing to listen. We had a very wonderful flight officer, Ziggy Sprague. I remember one occasion, we used to have 24 volt circuits in the airplane with storage batteries, and if you got a pilot who was a little inexperienced with the engine he would over prime, under prime, and eventually he'd run his battery down he was a dud; we couldn't start him. So I had the idea of running a direct current loop of about 28 volts all the way around the flight deck, so that if you had a fellow who was a dud due to his running his battery down, you would run a jumper out as you do with an automobile and put it on the terminals in his airplane and get him started, in spite of himself. And then you wouldn't have to cut him out of the pack and go through all the pain of finding a place to park him while the other planes took off past him. So I got permission from Ziggy Sprague, and then the captain to fly on up to Anacostia and go on over to then the Bureau of Steam Engineering, I think it was called, to see if I could get such an installation authorized for our ship. And, guess what? I wound up in the electrical division officer's office, and this division office was manned by a chap by the name of Lieutenant Rickover, and you would have thought that every inch of copper wire in the United States Navy belonged personally to that guy. When I explained what I wanted, he said, "Do you know how much copper that would take?" And I said, "Yes. I've made a rough calculation." I had put four motor generators around the deck to reduce the i.r. drop. He said, "We don't have copper wire like that in the United States Navy! And I went away saying if I ever meet that guy in a black alley I'm really going to let him have it! I was very much unimpressed. I flew back down with my tail between my legs and admitted to the air officer I had failed in my mission. I met this gentleman later on many times, and I learned to respect him for what he'd done, but that was my first exposure to that type of treatment.

In coming back to the farewell to the squadron, "be back by next Christmas," we were back, but Christmas two years from then. In the first place, Newport News had made such profit on RANGER, CV-4, that they thought they would take a little more risk on the next one. They decided to cut the main reduction gears on their own property there at Newport News. To do so they set up the gear cutting machinery in a room with very carefully controlled temperature so that there'd be no temperature distortion in the cutting of the teeth. But apparently what they forgot was that they were on tideland, and every freight train that went by left its phonographic impression on the face of the gear teeth. So when we went to sea in our trials, the noise from the gears was just fantastic; it was 120 decibels on the engine room floor plates. This of course was not acceptable, and what to do about it - they put us in the yard after our shakedown cruise. We went down to - I remember we were going to go to South America but Amelia Erhart was lost in the Pacific and LEXINGTON went full power out there and burned so much fuel it cut our shakedown cruise short. So we were not allowed to go beyond the Virgin Islands. We had a very pleasant cruise there. But after we came back from shakedown they put her in Norfolk Navy Yard and they cut great holes in the deck and lifted the four main reduction gears right out of the ship and replaced them.

Q: With gears that were made there, again?

ADM. R.: No, no. With gears that were made by a professional gear cutting outfit. So that ship - I was detached just when she came through the canal, but it wasn't Christmas as planned,

Russell #1 - 77

it was Christmas two years later when she finally joined the fleet.

Q: Tell me about some of the other innovations which were incorporated in the YORKTOWN while she was there building.

ADM. R.: One of them was the deck-side elevator; getting the elevators off the side of the ship as far as possible. The forward elevator was pretty hopeless because of the narrow lines of the ship forward. Well I went from that job, I was ordered from there to my first shore duty in Washington, and I became, as a Lieutenant, the carrier desk officer in the Bureau of Aeronautics. There was a very interesting ship, just a few pencil lines on vellum over in preliminary design in the Bureau of Ships, and it was the ESSEX class carrier. We in Aeronautics fought to get that ship optimized for its primary mission, namely flying and servicing airplanes. We did all sorts of things to her. We asked to have the elevators put as far to the side of the ship as possible and this was done; over the side to a deck-side elevator for the mid-ship elevator, in the case of the after elevator it was displaced to the starboard side as far as they could get it. At forward elevator the lines of the ship were so fine that that had to go on the center line. Now where to put the elevators in the longitudinal direction? We figured that if we put them at the quarter lengths of the flight deck this would allow us to have two elevators available for striking below if we were landing; it would give us two elevators to bring up planes, because a plane could take off under its own power in about a little less than half the length of the ship. So you could feed handily into a take off sequence with airplanes from down below; just bring them up on the elevators, and the elevators were off to the side far enough so that you could taxi forward. In the hangar, we asked to have as much clear approach to the elevator platforms, at the hangar level, as possible. Instead of having them in a well, the forward elevator was pretty well committed but we opened it out a little bit; the deck-side elevator of course you pushed out through the side door on the hangar. With the after elevator, which was displaced to starboard, you had just about three directions in which you could put airplanes aboard the elevator there. But we insisted that the hangar have dead space abaft the after elevator where you could put a dud, because on RANGER now, with the elevators at extreme ends of the hangar, if you had a dud airplane in your squadron your poor mech would barely get his tools laid out when we'd go to flight quarters, and he'd be right in the traffic, you see. So on the ESSEX-class we had dead space in the hangar abaft the after elevator.

Q: Enough for one plane?

ADM. R.: No, no. Many more than that. And then we put the shops, the aviation shops, around that dead space, so this was really the airplane engineering part of the hangar where you could park airplanes and they wouldn't be disturbed; they were not in any traffic patterns between the elevators, they were abaft the after elevator.

Q: You say "we." How many were furnishing this input?

ADM. R.: I dealt primarily with Commander Niskern, he retired as a Rear Admiral, he was the preliminary design officer in the Bureau of Ships. And I had lots of support from the ship installations division. We had experts in arresting gear, experts in catapults, and of course we had an aeronautical engineer as the head of the division. He was very amenable to argument; he supported me in everything we did. And Niskern was delightfully broad minded in his approach, but I came against considerable resistance when I asked for rectangular outlines of the flight deck. They wished to narrow the deck as it went forward because the lines of the ship were that way, you see. And I said well, we don't want that, we want to carry the width of the flight deck right up to the bow, because when you're taking off your point of maximum error is right at the bow, and if you narrow that you're giving the aviator less chance to make a successful take off. And Niskern said well, okay we can do this, but it's going to be difficult and we won't be able to support properly, from the standpoint of the structure, those two forward corners of the flight deck. He said, if you get in very heavy weather they'll fail.

Q: You mean the overhang?

ADM. R.: The overhang was so great they would fail. And I said, "Well, until we get the ship in very heavy weather, we've got a proper flying field. How about it?" And he said, "Okay." Now you may remember that Halsey eventually got the ESSEX-class carriers in a typhoon out west, and sure enough some of them dog eared. But think of the hours and hours and hours of flight that had occurred before those failures happened.

The ready rooms were another particular consideration. We tried to put the squadron ready rooms with short access, ready access, to where the airplanes of that squadron would normally be parked. The torpedo planes were usually way aft, bombers were farther up, fighters up forward, and so forth. We tried to put the ready rooms in the vicinity of where an officer's plane would be parked when he manned it. Planning the ready rooms we put reclining chairs all facing in one direction where you had a blackboard and you had a teletype from air plot that could put the information on nearest land, all the things that you need in navigation.

Q: Sort of an early CIC, wasn't it?

ADM. R.: Right. Well, CIC for the airplanes. It was an early style ready room actually. So we got all those things in. It was very interesting to me to have had this job, and then toward the end of World War II ( I went out in July of '44) to actually serve in those ships. And by the end of WWII we had 24 ESSEX-class carriers. Of those 24, all but maybe two got into action in the Pacific.

Q: And you had one lost.

ADM. R.: There were none lost, and none that got in action came through without some sort of battle injury. I think I was aboard the one that was most severely damaged; once with a kamikaze hole through her deck, the FRANKLIN, and the second time struck by two bombs which caused her to burn rather badly.

Q: In the early designs and the development of the ESSEX-class, did Captain Duncan have any input? He was to be the first skipper?

ADM. R.: Wu Duncan?

Q: Yes.

ADM. R.: No, except generally. I've forgotten where he was on duty when we were thinking these things up, but I had been with him and we picked up any ideas we could anywhere, you know. Any suggestions were considered, and we had many good suggestions.

Q: Now how long did it take from the first concept of this new type carrier to its realization?

ADM. R.: Well, I don't know whether you remember it or not, but CV-5 and 6 were built with WPA funds, or such, and then also CV-7, the HORNET. I should explain that, just through a fluke, I happened to be the first pilot in the United States Navy to have flown off our first six carriers, LANGLEY, LEXINGTON, SARATOGA, RANGER, YORKTOWN and ENTERPRISE. ENTERPRISE was our sister and she was just about three or four, five or six months behind us at Newport News. Ziggy Sprague, our Air Officer, would never let any of those guys from the ENTERPRISE fly off our deck. I had nothing to do with this; this was Ziggy Sprague's idea. But I went out as arresting gear officer to witness the trials of the arresting gear on ENTERPRISE, CV-6, and Comdr. Allan P. Flagg was the air officer, a wonderful old friend. I was up in primary fly control observing the whole thing, and, as the exercise was coming to an end, Allan said, "Well, what do you think of it?" And I said, "It's fine. You've got a good ship here." And Allan said "Can we do anything for you?" And I said, "Yes. Let me take one of your airplanes and shoot a few landings on your deck." And he said, "Well, okay." So by that one act I beat by one day the other people who'd been in squadrons and off the other ships. I was the first one to make the first six decks.

Q: Well, going back to my question about the length of time required, I do know that the President had to juggle funds in

Russell #1 - 83

order to get a better Navy in preparation for a forthcoming conflict.

ADM. R.: I took the carrier desk in '39 and left in June of '41, and the first ESSEX-class carrier came out in 1942.

Q: Late '42?

ADM. R.: Yes. Well, there comes an end to a tour of duty, you know, and as I explained the Bureau of Aeronautics had control of everything including aviation personnel, so I could look over the shoulder of the detailer in the Bureau of Aeronautics and say, "Could I go to this squadron? or that?" We used to rotate through all styles of aviation and, having been in flying boats in '31 and '32, when '41 came along in normal rotation I was to go back into flying boats. Looking over the shoulder of the detailer I saw VP-42, home base Seattle, and I thought what could be better for a Tacoma boy than to have a squadron based in Seattle? So I said could I go to that squadron, and the detailer shrugged his shoulders and said, "You want to go to that rainy country? Why not?" So I was ordered to VP-42, and with 30 days' delay came out and was spending a delightful vacation on American Lake, where we are now. But I thought I should go over and call on the then commanding officer who was Daddy Nash, one of my instructors at Pensacola, a very wonderful chap. So I motored over to Seattle and up to Sand Poin and called on Daddy Nash. He was very kind. He showed me all through the squadron - this was a six plane Catalina squadron - and one of the airplanes was down at gunnery school in San Diego. Delightful experience, nice squadron, and I was about to bid farewell to Daddy and continue my leave when he said, "When are you checking in, Jim?" And I said on a certain date. And he frowned slightly and said, "I wouldn't come on then. I would come on this date." And I said, "Well, why? I'd lose nine days' leave. I don't want to do that." He said, "We're deploying to Alaska." So I lost nine days' leave on American Lake. I checked in at the squadron and the next morning I was underway for Alaska, and since I was not current in the airplane I served as navigator in the executive officer's airplane, 42P4.

Q: What was the speed in the deployment to Alaska?

ADM. R.: We cruised at 120 knots which was very convenient, because every minute you went two miles.

Q: But I mean, was there any special reason for hurrying up this assignment? Sending the squadron to Alaska?

ADM. R.: None, except that I would have checked in at Sand Point and the squadron would have been up north. Well, what happened, I reported in and the next morning I was serving as navigator on the executive officer's airplane. We flew a five plane formation up along the beautiful coast of British Columbia and to southeastern Alaska, where there was this new seaplane station belonging to the United States Navy, Naval Air Station Sitka. We secured our planes and spent the night there, and the next morning our beautiful weather had disappeared and there was a light rain falling. Well, we took off, joined in a five plane formation, and proceeded to go directly across the Gulf of Alaska to a new naval air station also, Kodiak, on Kodiak Island, and the farther we went the lower the ceiling got. And finally there was no ceiling at all, and we were cruising along in the fog in a five plane formation. As for radio aids, there was a surfac navigational beacon on Cape Saint Elias on which I could take a radio bearing using a loop antenna, but there was also a newly installed aircraft radio range station on Woody Island off Kodiak. But there's quite a bit of magnetic variation; - if I remember correctly it's 26 degrees or something like this, and we didn't know the direction of the legs. They had not been calibrated and we weren't sure where the A and N sectors were. You know on a radio beacon you can orient yourself because there are four legs, and on one side of a leg you hear A, on the other side it's N, and when you're on a leg it's a steady note, because of the dot-and-dash of A matches the dash-and-dot of N and you get a solid note. With a solid note you're in the beam of the particular station. We didn't know where these beams were, but I could take a bearing on transmitter you see, navigating. The signal got louder and louder and louder, as we plowed along through the fog.

Q: What kind of communication did you have with the other planes?

ADM. R.: Radio. And as the bearing started to change on Woody Island range, I called over the intercom and said to the executive officer who was flying the airplane, "Stand by. We're getting very, very close to land." So when a spruce wooded shore appeared on the port hand in the fog we continued to bore along, but when a spruce wooded rocky shore appeared on the starboard hand, that whole squadron fell out of the air like a bunch of ducks except the squadron commander, Daddy Nash. And he sailed serenely on up this fjord, and that's about the only fjord I know in Alaska where you can go up and get out the far side. He went over the village of Uzinki on Kodiak Island, and there's a big bay beyond - I think it's called Whale Island Bay or something of the sort - and it seems when he went over the little village and into this bay there was a little dome in the fog, which was probably caused by the orographic lifting of air which happens very often if you get in the lee of something, where the air descends - it's had its moisture sort of squeezed out and you'll find a little clear patch there. But the rest of us - one of them, Mike Vincent, took time enough to turn into the wind - the rest of us landed downwind. You used to pop rivets out of the hull if you landed hard, you know, and the navigator had to have a few extra sharpened pencils to plug these holes. So here we were, and we taxiied over into the lee of a little island. There was a fair breeze, not very strong, a little bit of breeze sort of on our tails blowing up this fjord, and we'd no sooner anchored and we'd started our auxiliary power plants (they made a terrible putt putt noise) than setting out from this little island was a dory. As this chap came out, I hailed him and we started a little conversation. I said, "By the way, could you tell me where we are?" He had introduced himself as Mr. Nelson. I said, "By the way, what's the name of this island here?" He smiled and he said, "Well, that's Nelson's Island." He said, "I have a fox farm on that island, and I'm out shooting hair seals as food for my foxes." And when I said could he tell us exactly where we are, he said, "Do you have a chart in there?" And I said, "Oh, yes." And we brought him aboard, took him down into the navigator's compartment, where he put his finger on our position. I had just about figured it out. We were just north of Woody Island and up this fjord that actually separates Afognak Island from Kodiak Island. You can go all the way through the Kodiak island group there. Here we were, but Daddy Nash was missing. He'd disappeared in the fog and we didn't know where he was. Maybe an hour later, here he came droning back, and landed with the rest of us. He'd been up circling in this one little open space trying to punch his way out somewhere, just waiting for something to happen. Well there we were, five planes on the water anchored in the lee of Nelson's

Island. We started our auxiliary power plants and we Morse Coded a message to the Naval Air Station Kodiak saying we are anchored in such and such a spot, and we will proceed when the weather improves. Now we had a seaplane tender, the USS GILLIS, and its skipper was Johnny Heath. If you knew Johnny Heath you'd realize he's a very energetic sort of fellow; he talks very fast and I remember one time when Johnny Heath was in one of our maneuvers off San Francisco, he pulled his fighter up from a dive and found he'd lost his engine on the way down, which wasn't unusual in those days, so he made a landing in the sea and his target, a submarine rescued him. Of course we got him in the wardroom after this experience and he was just a chatterbox about getting rescued by the fellow on which he'd made an attack. Well anyway, Johnny Heath had the GILLIS, and he said, "Stay where you are. I'll tend you for the night." And he started out from Kodiak to come join us. Daddy Nash had come back; he'd anchored with the rest of us and there we were, serenely on the water in the lee of Nelson's Island. There were a number of rocks around, and other hazards to navigation. By and by in the fog we heard the fog whistle of the USS GILLIS approaching our temporary mooring. He just about joined us when, as so often happens up there, the fog lifted about 300 feet and you could see for a thousand miles underneath it. So we all fired up and took off leaving Johnny Heath and Gillis there among the rocks. He didn't like that.

Well, we were the first squadron pulled out on the new seaplane ramp at Kodiak and we stayed at Kodiak Naval Air Station for a few days. Then we took off to the westward. The charts of the Aleutian Islands were confidential and our squadron navigator had locked them up. I think everything west of Dutch Harbor was confidential.

Q: And why?

ADM. R.: Kiska was a closed harbor in those days, you know. And our navigator had locked these confidential charts up in the safe at Kodiak. We flew off - a very inspiring flight down the peninsula. The weather wasn't too good but not too bad - and we went into Dutch Harbor. We asked the navigator for the charts and he said, "Oh, oh. I left them in Kodiak." So we navigated all the way down to Attu on sort of a road map. We wound up at Kiska Harbor where we based on the USS WILLIAMSON for about two weeks. We had the Wing Commander, Gordon Rowe, along with us. Then we slowly worked our way back. We picked Kuluk Bay and its sweeper cove, as the best harbor in the Aleutians. This was on Adak Island, and as you know the chain sweeps down to the south and Adak is about the southernmost island; it's not too far from the latitude of Seattle, actually. And it's a long, long way. It's about a thousand miles from the end of Alaska so it's the last island out, which is Attu. We worked our way back, but we did not base at Adak. There was no one there. There were five trappers' shacks a day's walk apart. There was no one on the island except in the fox season. We looked at the native village in the harbor at Atka, and then the next civilization from there eastward was Nicolski. Now, there was a tribe of about sixty Aleuts down on Attu, but we didn't get down that far. We started out for Attu and we got beyond Buldir Rock, which is about half way, when we ran into fog. I think maybe some of the planes got down there, but I didn't see Attu.

Q: Were you attempting to make something of a survey looking for island places?

ADM. R.: Exactly. We were looking for a place you might put a field on Kiska Island, for example. We were looking at seaplane mooring spots. we were looking for habitations. As I say, there were sixty Aleuts at Chichagof Harbor on Attu, there were about forty natives in the village at Atka, and in between there was nothing. There'd been a sheep ranch on Kanaga Island at one time but it failed. So we worked our way back to Dutch Harbor, and we spent some time there in Dutch Harbor. Then we went to Dolgoi Harbor in the Shumagin Islands, and here was a beautiful harbor for our seaplane tender, moorings for us, salmon running in the streams, and nobody for hundreds of miles around - just out in the middle of nowhere in the Shumagin Islands.

Q: Where are they in relation to, say, Kodiak?

Russell #1 - 91

ADM. R.: They are about, I would think, 400 miles west of Kodiak, roughly, and south of the Alaskan peninsula proper. There were a lot of little islands, and there's False Pass and eventually there's Unimak Pass, which is the first one which goes through to the Bering Sea, and is close to Dutch Harbor. From the Shumagins we came back to Kodiak.

Q: Did you recommend a base in the Shumagin Islands?

ADM. R.: It was usuable yes, of course. Cold Bay is the place that I thought was the best of all, and that's on the Alaskan peninsula. You can approach it either from the Bering Sea or the Pacific at sea level and get in. Later on when we had amphibians we found hard sand where we could lower our wheels and taxi out of the water there. So it's got a good harbor and it had flat land, and eventually we had a fighter strip there and one at Umnak Island during the war.

Well we came back to Kodiak and we based there, and we had some rather interesting experiences. A Russian delegation came through with two Russian-built PBYs, Catalinas.

Q: Russian built? After our models?

ADM. R.: Yes, they were built to our drawings. We were told these people were coming, and we wondered if our beaching gear would fit - if the structure had been accurately done according to our drawings our beaching gear would fit. Well these characters had flown over from Siberia and had landed at Safety Lagoon near Nome, spent the night there, and an interpreter from their embassy joined them.

Q: What was their mission?

ADM. R.: They were on a mission to seek aid for Russia. The Germans had attacked - remember now, this was 1941, the fall of '41 - and they were going to Washington, flying down to Seattle and from there they were going to be taken back to Washington to confer on military aid for Russia. Well, the great day came and they were supposed to be at Kodiak at 5 in the evening (the days were still long) and we gathered on the beach to receive them. And no Russians until exactly 5 p.m., when straight over the mountains, not around by sea the way we usually flew, but straight across the mountains of Kodiak came these two Catalinas. They circled down to a very nice landing in Woman's Bay, taxied up to our ramp, our men in waders went out with our beaching gear and the beaching gear fit like a glove. We hauled them out of the water, and here were these two dripping flying boats sitting on our ramp. Nothing happened for quite a little while. We put ladders up so they could get out, but only one man came out - the senior man, - then the interpreter. He asked for the Commanding Officer of the naval air station; this was Jack Perry. He said to Jack Perry, "I'd like permission to land my party."

And Perry said, "Yes, of course. You're most welcome." And then they started piling out. Our planes had a crew of eight, usually. They had 22 in one airplane and 23 in another; the 23rd man was the interpreter from the embassy. They'd been stripped of everything so they could carry as much as possible.

Well, we took them up, we knew we'd be crowded (the BOQ was not finished), we put as many as we could in the level above us which was not yet completed, really, but we put bunks up there. We hung a curtain across one end of the enlisted barracks and put beds for them down there. We put as many of the senior ones as we could in the BOQ in the new rooms. They came in on a Wednesday as I remember it, and Wednesday was the night we had what we called tactical school. By the way, I took over command of the squadron in August of '41 from Daddy Nash who then went down and became a member of the staff down in Seattle. Well, I asked the senior Russian, who was a General Gromoff, if he would mind making a speech. I told him it was my custom to hold school on the night they'd arrived, and I could gather my officers together in the BOQ, and would he make us a talk. He said he'd be glad to, no if, ands, or but's. So we invited the Commanding Officer of the station and some of the station officers to come join us for a lecture by this General Gromoff, a Russian. We'd had our dinner and this was immediately after dinner, we adjourned to this room and he made a very wonderful speech. He had been on the flight that flew over the North Pole, a very high aspect ratio airplane. They had landed in a pasture near Vancouver in

Washington State - a good number of years before. I have forgotten, it was in the thirties; perhaps you remember this flight. But anyway, he told us of this flight. He also told us of the history of aviation in Russia. He told us of the German advance and how they hoped to stall their advance. It was fascinating. And then with no change in expression whatsoever, he turned on us and he said, "I don't understand why you have built your air station as it is." He said, "Where are your revetments alongside the runway? Why don't you put these hangars under the mountain? And why do you mark this station with a steel water tower so it can be seen?" Then he sat down. Well, here I was having invited this gentleman there, and as squadron commander I had to respond.

Q: Now this was in Russian with the aid of the interpreter?

ADM. R.: Through the interpreter, yes. No change of expression but very forceful on this "why do you build your station so?" So I got up and I thanked him for his most interesting talk, the story of his flight across the Pole, the history of aviation and also the developments in the German advance into Russia. And I said, "And, General Gromoff, as far as your remarks are concerned about the way this station is laid out, you are going to Washington, D.C., are you not?" And he got this through the interpreter; he nodded his head he was. I said, "Well perhaps you could help us. This station was designed in Washington, D.C., and if you'd leave your comment there it might benefit us."

And that made him happy, and that was the end of that scene. But do you know, some of my pilots complained that they were kept up all night because there was warm water in the showers and these Russians above them in those new rooms stood and let the warm water run over their bodies practically the whole night long. There were two of them that were very gay souls. The married officers had their wives there on the base at the time (this was peacetime, you know) and Bull Dawson and his wife, Lois, were right across the road from us in a married officers apartment - we were in the BOQ - and these two Russians (they had a piano, incidentally, in the Dawson apartment) one played the piano and the other did Russian dances. They were having a terrific time, until a third party came up. And apparently he was the commissar, he was the political officer, and those two guys clammed up and the party just fell flat on its face from then on.

Now my experience was this. I had just barely turned in, and because I was squadron commander I had a sitting room, a bath, and a bedroom. Ordinarily two bedrooms would be served by one bath, but I had the corner room which I used as a conference room and my bedroom with the bath in between. Well, I had just turned in and a knock came on the door. I threw on my bathrobe, opened the door, and here was a tall, lean, cadaverous Russian jabbering to beat the cards; he just had something he had to get off his chest - with the interpreter in tow. And I said to the interpreter, "What's the problem with our comrade?" And the interpreter said, "Well it's this way. Comrade so-and-so wants you to know that he's a commissioned officer. And he wants you to know that all the officers in that party are commissioned officers, and you have placed them in an enlisted man's dormitory." I said, "Well that's correct. As you can see we don't have enough room for all of them in the BOQ. The warmest, the most comfortable place we could find on the station for you was in the wing of the enlisted barracks. We have given you privacy by curtaining off that wing, and I would hope that you would be comfortable there." This went back through the interpreter but the fellow continued to jabber, and I said, "Please, come in and have my bed." And I started out the door. He said, "Oh, no, no, no, no, no," and then he went grumbling away because he was a commissioned officer. And I said, "I thought you didn't have any caste system in your services. I thought that you were all equal and that you could get along well in such situations." He said, "I want you to know we're commissioned officers, and we're insulted that you put us in an enlisted barracks." Well, they took off the next morning.

Q: Was this a collection of experts in various fields?

ADM. R.: Presumably, yes. Plus the plane crews, you see, and just the barest - pilot, co-pilot and engineer. We bid them farewell on the beach the next morning and off they took to go over to Sitka, where they refueled and then went down to Seattle. We were in radio communication with them from Nome on, and half way across the Fulf of Alaska they reported sighting a submarine. Well, my whole squadron fired up and off we went looking for that submarine. By this time of course the sub had been alerted. I am quite sure that one of the Japanese submarines was on patrol in the Gulf of Alaska, and they'd sighted it. We didn't find the sub although we searched all that day. From Sitka they went on down to Seattle, and eventually they came back. And of course while they were parked in my hangar my intelligence officer was all through their airplanes, and they were completely stripped except for the barest essentials, radio and that sort of thing. When they came back minus all their distinguished passengers, just the plane crew, obviously they were quite heavy, and we were very anxious to see why. So that night again my intelligence officer went all through the airplanes and guess what they had? They had belted 30 calibre machine gun ammunition. Our military aid had given them 30 calibre machine guns, and they were flat out defending Leningrad and Stalingrad and these other cities, and they carried ammunition back in those flying boats. Well, that was very interesting.

Q: And the delegation remained in the States?

ADM. R.: In Washingotn. They went back some other way. How they got home I don't know. That was General Gromoff and his party.

We came out of Alaska in rotation with VP-41, about the

Russell #1 - 98

end of October in 1941. We were enjoying our time down in Seattle.

Q: How much time did you have as an interval?

ADM. R.: Well, we got out about the end of October, and the other squadron went up and took over from us.

Q: Your duty then was out from Seattle?

ADM. R.: We started training up and I went all through the course; we had a very stringent instrument flying course which I hadn't completed yet. I completed that personally, and the rest of the squadron were working up or refreshing. I had what I thought were expert pilots enough to generate twice the number of plane crews I had. Well, the war broke on the 7th of December and it was a Sunday and I was down here painting my camp. We got ordered back up and we did a frantic deployment. We opened the Orange War Plans, and we found that we were supposed to have forces at the mouth of the Columbia River, Tongue Point, where there was a seaplane base, and we were to use a Royal Canadian Air Force Base at Ucluelet Arm on Vancouver Island. I sent my exec with half the squadron to Tongue Point where we had a U.S. Naval seaplane base of sorts, and I took the other half of the squadron and went to Ucluelet Arm.

Q: You said just a few minutes ago that you broke open the Orange

Plan. Where was the copy of the plan kept in this area? You had no knowledge of its content?

ADM. R.: In the safe in the Wing Commander's office.

Q: And you did not have a knowledge of its contents until you had to consult it?

ADM. R.: That's right. I had not. But it was a fairly simple one. It was to divide my squadron and patrol the coasts of Oregon, Washington and British Columbia. So I took three Catalinas, one-half the squadron, and went to Ucluelet Arm, where we based on the Royal Canadian Air Force seaplane base. It was quite an experience. The Canadians, of course, had been at war for a long time, and they were very fine hosts. We moored out to buoys and used their boats to get aboard our aircraft, and serviced from them. We were required to be 200 miles off the coast at dawn -- not at sunrise, but at dawn -- which meant a night take off. We would man our airplanes well before daylight of course, in the dark of night, and a seaplane is sort of an unstable fellow when he's taxiing, if you get more thrust on one side than the other he just spins round and round. And we'd warm up engines by casting off from the buoy and putting power on one side and eventually test the magnetos on that engine, then warm the other one up, and when they were up to stuff we'd head for the phosphorescent surf and take off. We'd come to at dawn having navigated, usually because of the low ceilings prevalent over the ocean here, on dead reckoning, and our navigation was far from precise under the circumstances. If it was a nice clear starlit night, we'd go out and there would be frost on our wings. And frost is a very dangerous thing because it breaks the circulation of air around your airfoil, and you won't get airborne. So we would bend a bucket onto a piece of line and dip up salt water and sluice down the wing. The salt water would melt the frost off the wings and clean them off before we'd warm up and take off.

Q: No such marvel as a defroster in those days?

ADM. R.: No. We had our de-icer boots, but those don't help you when they're frosted, you see. Or it would be a blustery blowing night with driving rain and we'd go out, take off under a low ceiling, all lights out as we went over the surf, and we'd begin to live again when the dawn started breaking 200 miles off the coast. We went out 500 nautical miles, and then across something like between 25 and 50 miles, and then across something like between 25 and 50 miles, depending on visibility, altitude to which we could climb and so forth, and then fly back again.

Q: Why the requirement 200 miles out by dawn?

ADM. R.: This was the Wing Commander's idea. You see, where the Japanese went after Pearl Harbor was a great question. A lot of people thought they were going to make an immediate landing

Russell #1 - 101

on the west coast of the United States and all that sort of nonsense. Well, this went on vigorously, and my planes became in need of considerable servicing. So I flew down in my airplane one afternoon to Seattle and told the Wing Commander if he wanted three airplanes to stay in commission he would have to give us some time for maintenance. He agreed to this, and we had an engineering maintenance crew assigned. We pulled out of Ucluelet Arm and concentrated the squadron at Tongue Point at the mouth of the Columbia River. From the moment we came back off patrol (and we'd fly for about eight hours or so) we'd turn our aircraft over to this maintenance crew, which included some non-flying officers, and we'd turn in, rest, and have some time to ourselves while the airplanes were being put in top shape to take off the next morning.

Q: It was around-the-clock for the planes, then?

ADM. R.: Yes. Well, Tongue Point was no bed of roses, either. The water of the Columbia River is fresh, and in December we would have freezing temperatures and the spray just from take off would freeze on the windshields so that even though it was night, you wouldn't see too much anyway; you were completely blinded as far as your take off was concerned. We had a lighted sea drome runway and we had a boat patrolling it because there were logs in the river. I remember one morning watching one of my airplanes head directly for a log that had roots sticking up - apparently he didn't see it. I was afraid to call him for fear that I'd get him excited right at the crucial point of getting airborne, and those roots actually passed between his wingtip float and his hull. When he took off I called a halt in the operation while the boat went out and towed this thing off the course.

Q: What were the Canadians doing meanwhile with their PBYs?

ADM. R.: They didn't have PBYs, they had Stranraer Flying Boats. They were very happy to see us because we had much longer legs; we could do a better job of scouting than they.

But this just put life more or less in order down at the mouth of the Columbia River. Then as the days went by, and the date for our return to Alaska to relieve the squadron that was up there approached, we flew down our six planes to San Diego and turned them in. We multiplied the squadron by two and we drew twelve Catalina Amphibians, PBY5As. With the personnel I had I could splice out twelve crews -- actually maybe fourteen crews because we tried to have at least one or two spare crews. So we flew back up to Alaska and relayed the first planes up there at the end of January, and I got the entire squadron of twelve completely up there about the first or second week in February of 1942. VP-41 very happily left and flew back down to Seattle to get themselves in shape, having been deployed from the time they relieved us up there at the end of October of '41. And there were some amusing incidents. I made the squadron headquarters at Kodiak and put two planes at Sitka on the eastern side of the Gulf of Alaska, four to the west at Dutch Harbor, and six at Kodiak. Four at Dutch Harbor was about all that the facilities there could conveniently take care of at the time. The place was under construction; the ramp was usable, but we actually lived in the contractor's housing when we went down there, we made BOQs of the little cottages and things. And that's the way the situation more or less stabilized until...

Q: And this was the dead of winter?

ADM. R.: Oh yes. The Wing Commander remained in Seattle - he started up one time and turned back, then he came up in perhaps early April and I flew him down to Dutch Harbor. I said, "Commodore, you would really do wonders to the morale here if you would pick, not a special crew, just put your finger on any plane that's going out on patrol in the morning (this was at Dutch Harbor) and take that patrol with them. Ride with them while they'r on this patrol and see for yourself what the conditions are." And he said fine, he would do it. Well we got up the next morning to make an early take off, had breakfast in the contractor's mess, and we were walking to the seaplane ramp at Dutch Harbor. It was a fairly calm morning, a light breeze blowing toward the sea, and we were half way between the mess hall and the seaplane ramp when I heard a Catalina's engines start to roar on take off. I looked at my watch, and this wasn't right. The flights were governed by the staff at the air station. Billy (Wm. N.) Updegraff was the station commander and he had a little operational staff. Well, I listened to these Catalina engines roar, and they roared, but all of a sudden they stopped. And the echoes came back from the mountains, until there was dead silence, and then the hiss of fire. I left the Wing Commander and ran to the beach. There was a standby airplane, I got in it and I saw one of my airplanes burning on the spit across Dutch Harbor. We taxied over. I put over a rubber raft and jumped in it right after pulling the inflation bottles, and it was so cold the raft didn't inflate to its fullest and it sort of came up around my armpits. We paddled ashore, two of us, and I immediately looked for the bombs. We had two 500 pound bombs on one wing and two 500 pound depth charges on the other, and I found all but one bomb, which had dropped off on the impact of this plane striking the spit. Then I saw the last bomb very close to the fire and we ran in and got a line around it and pulled it clear. So that took care of the ordnance. Meanwhile the station fire department were making their way around the spit, which was rather a long drive around, and came on the scene and got the fire out. I got in and looked at the cockpit. The armored seats had torn loose and there were the black charred corpses of my plane commander and his co-pilot staring at me from the depths of the front end of the airplane; the armored seats had come off and turned 180 degrees so they were facing me, looking at me up through the hole where the cockpit had been. I recognized that this was Andy Smith, and Andy Smith was headed for a crash, there was no question about it. When we based at Dolgoi Harbor we routinely used seaplane sea anchors. We used to trail one out of the waist of the airplane and work the engines against it on a beach approach. And because of the weather and the strength of the wind up there we had both oversized anchors and oversized sea anchors. At Dolgoi Harbor Andy Smith got airborne, took off, with one of these great sea anchors on the turtle back of his airplane. We looked out of our airplane and here he was with this thing on his back. We called to him and told him to fly slow and get back down to the water as fast as he could because if this thing had torn loose it would probably have taken his tail off, you know. Here it was just lying on the back of the airplane, between the blisters. And here was the same Andy Smith, dead on the spit at Dutch Harbor. And he wasn't supposed to take off at that time anyway.

Q: It wasn't the right time?

ADM. R.: It wasn't the right time. Well, the Wing Commander was helpful to me in all the dispatches we had to make out. We had three survivors, and they were all from the after part of the airplane; their backs were to the bulkhead when the collision with the ground came. One was on fire, and he was rolled in the tundra and the fire was put out - not too badly burned. They were taken over to the hospital. Then we got the corpses out; there were five dead people. And then I started reconstructing what had happened. The station aerographer had pronounced the weather not good for scouting (we had to maintain contact with the ocean in those days) but operations said they would appreciate it very much if we would patrol the passes between the islands from Unimak Pass, Atkutan Island, Unalaska Island, and over to Umnak. Andy Smith, hearing this, was tremendously annoyed because we were all set to take our Wing Commander out on a regular patrol, and here the patrols were cancelled. But knowing that this one patrol was required, he said, "I'll take that," and jumped in an available plane. Out on the little porch of the quarters that morning there was frozen snow so I realized that we'd need to clean our wings. He got in an airplane with ice on its wings and tried to take off. He shaped his course to pass the end of the spit (there was a mountain beyond but plenty of room to turn). Every time he tried to lift off the water - the wind was from the side, it was toward the sea from the mountains, cold air settling down - every time he tried to lift off he'd be drifting sideways so he'd kick a little down wind rudder, and finally his take off course, his path, was inside the spit. And instead of chopping his engines and going back, cleaning his wings, as he should have done, or at least before making another attempt to get airborne, he tried to jump the spit. Kept full power on the engines and tried to jump it. He never got airborne. That was our first casualty up there, and it was due to the stupidity -- I warned our gang time and time again, never attempt to take off unless your wing is clear, never attempt to take off unless your wing is clear.

Well, with all due respect to the Commodore, the next day he put his finger on a patrol we had to do and he went with them, for which I admired him.

Q: In a case like that, the other members of the crew had no voice in what happened?

ADM. R.: The co-pilot might have advised him, or could have even chopped the throttle, knocked his hands off and chopped the throttle. It was just too bad. You could tell, that lad was just like a classmate of mine who eventually went into the ground on a dive bombing attack, some people are that way, you know, they're just headed for a crash.

Anyway, things were quite reasonable and quite quiet. We rotated these various duties; the four planes that were at Dutch Harbor would stay there maybe two weeks and then come back and another would go down for two weeks and so on. So things were fairly quiet until May.

Q: No Japanese submarines in evidence?

ADM. R.: Nothing that we discovered. A little bit of excitement occurred when Commander Paul Foster, who was a friend of President Roosevelt, came up, with a letter from President Roosevelt. I was going to fly him over to Siberia. But as intelligence started building up the Japs were coming that way we gave that up. I flew

him down the Aleutian chain.  General Buckner, who was the
Commanding General of the Alaska Defense Command, Simon Bolivar
Buckner, knew everything that was going on of course and when
we were scheduled to go down on a reconnaissance of the Aleutian
Islands he would usually show up and say, "I am going with you
guys."  He was a lot of fun; he had a lot of stories.  But he
came down there in May, and I was a little annoyed because I
thought he was sticking his neck out unnecessarily.  This is when
Foster was there and we were going down to Attu, and come back
and base  at Kiska Harbor for overnight and then come back to
Dutch Harbor.  General Buckner said that he would go.  I had lost
another airplane; I'm sure he let down and Hit the water because
of weather and perhaps inexperience.  I had multiplied the squadron by two and some of these people were not as ripe as others.
This was hugh Wingers, and I'm quite sure that he just let down
in a fog and thought he could level off before he got to the water
to get through the islands.  I'm pretty sure he flew into the
water.  We never found a trace of him.  I had been down searching
and investigating when Paul Foster and General Buckner arrived at
Dutch Harbor.  So Sammy Coleman took one airplane, I took another,
and we flew them down to Kiska.  We tried to make Attu; we got
almost there and started running into weather. We turned back
to base at Kiska and maybe go down the next day.  We were tended
overnight by the tender WILLIAMSON, and the next day we had fog,
rain, snow and an offshore breeze in Kiska Harbor maybe 30 or 40
knots.  This meant an instrument take off heading toward the moun-

tains of Kiska Island. If it had been any sort of a light breeze or if the wind had been from the other direction, I could have taken off toward the open sea and gone on instruments, you see. But taking off in Kiska Harbor toward the cliffs - and you were in sort of a horseshoe there, you see - just wasn't healthy. So there we were, weathered in. And the storm got worse rather than better. At the end of the second day, Knappy Kivette had the WILLIAMSON, he and I persuaded General Buckner to take the tender and get away -- scram. He didn't want to do this and we argued with him most of the day. Foster was there of course, and also Lieutenant Commander Bill Miller, who was on the District Commandant's staff down in Seattle and had been in the squadron before, a very good friend of mine, a classmate - we'd been to flight school together. Finally toward the end of the second day, Buckner said, "Al right. If you want me to, I'll take this boat and go home." So Knappy Kivette left me a whaleboat with a coxswain and an engineer, he left me a Chief Barbo, a chief aerographer's mate, and he steamed away with the Commanding General of the Alaska Defense Command. Theta Combs and the USS CASCO had been down to Chichagof Harbor on Attu, and coming back he came into Kiska Harbor and found me there with two planes by myself (we spent the first night alone). He had a little survey to do and he said, "I'll stay until you get off, get airborne. My ship is a seaplane tender." Well we were the last, Sammy Coleman and I, were the last people to see the weather men on Kiska before the Japs moved in on us. I went over with them. Their plan of escape -- we had food caches at three different likely spots, where we thought we could land on the sea, taxi and pick them up, and get away with them.

Q: Some sort of an invasion was anticipated then?

ADM. R.: Yes. There was in the wind the Midway operation, which included the Aleutians. And we expected the Japs would come up that summer. I mean, it was more or less an obvious thing that they were going to hit us.

Q: And we were reading their messages so we had some idea.

ADM. R.: Well, I went over with those ten men what to do if the Japs came in.

Q: This was a weather station?

ADM. R.: Yes. Go to the hills, and then try to meet us at one of these three points where they had the food caches. Now there are no trees on the Aleutians; there's fairly tall grass, moss, heather and rocks - that's it. CASCO stayed with us, and we got out on the fifth day. One of the problems was once the storm had passed us it went up the Aleutians, and the places we were to go closed. That was one of the hazards of flying in the Aleutians, your alternate bases were all in one line and if it was bad weather at one it would go on up the chain. You either had to beat it or to be far enough behind it to have decent weather for flying. Well we got out on the fifth day and went back up the Aleutian Chain. I had a very fine co-pilot on that trip, Clark Hood, a Naval Academy man, a Lieutenant, quite a senior officer, and we'd been training him up. He was very good on instruments. We were then ordered to come back and join up with the Wing Commander in Kodiak. Now I found out in Japan after the surrender that, before we went to Kiska, we'd had a visitation from the Japanese. Kimikawa Maru, I think it was - (this is written up in the interrogation) - and the KISCO, a light cruiser, had come to a spot south of Kiska, maybe 75 miles out, they had photographed all of Adak, which we had flown over with Buckner, and they tried to photograph Kiska. Now, if they'd photographed Kiska we'd have known about it because we had ten men there. We had nobody on Adak. The flight that was to photograph Kiska turned back because of weather. Here I had the Commanding General of the Alaska Defense Command down there, and just a few days before we'd had a light cruiser and a seaplane carrier, as they called them, in the same area. We could have delivered the Commanding General of the Alaska Defense Command on a silver platter to the Japs, even a submarine could have taken us. All we had were three fifty calibre guns and a thirty calibre gun aft firing through a hatch under the tail. So I've often thought that we were sort of lucky; if they'd really known we were there and if they knew the passenger we had, they could very well have pulled the clever stunt of capturing our good general.

Russell #1 - 112

Q: Where did you say the General was based?

ADM. R.: Anchorage, at Fort Richardson. Wonderful companion, he kept us amused the whole time he was aboard ship but you can imagine that we were under some strain trying to get him out of there. This was absolutely unplanned, the fact that the weather would turn sour like this. That was one of the problems, you never could be sure; you had to know what the weather was off to the west of us and we just had no way of knowing that.

Q: As it turned out eventually, Buckner was somewhat difficult to get along with, was he not, as far as the Navy was concerned?

ADM. R.: Well, it was absolutely uncalled for, truly. That was sort of a sad episode.

Q: That was Admiral Theobald?

ADM. R.: Theobald came up and adopted the attitude that this was a naval war, and you folks in the Army don't know how to fight a navy war, and all that sort of business, and it was very unfortunate. Buckner was a good guy; he had the courage of his convictions. He was killed, you know, by being in the forward lines on Okinawa when a shell arrived in his forward observation post.

Q: That's why they named it Buckner Bay, was it not?

ADM. R.: Yes, that's right. I admired him very much, and I thought it was rather small potatoes of Theobald to come up there from Pearl Harbor and quarrel.

Well, VP-41 flew up from Seattle and joined us, and because my boys had been up there all winter I tried to give them a little rest. I wanted to put them in Cold Bay where we could have a tender and so on, but the Wing Commander split us up into little detachments - he put the skipper of VP-41 in Dutch Harbor and he put me at Cold Bay. After all I was very interested in getting the then Army Air Force in on this. We had a very wonderful bomb commander whom we knew as 'Wild Bill Eareckson', Colonel Eareckson. A wonderful guy. I knew we would have to do something about their (A.A.E.) communications because they just didn't have any down the chain. So we used a portable radio we had in the squadron. We set it up at Cold Bay, and Eareckson and I slept in the tent with an operator from my squadron on the circuit all the time. I slept so the operator could kick me in the foot in anything showed up from our scouts, my planes and those from VP-41, and sure enough came the day Dutch Harbor was attacked.

Q: That day was the 7th of June?

ADM. R.: No, no, it was the third of June, 1942. It's important to note that the Japanese hit Dutch Harbor the day before they hit Midway, which is a good military tactic, a feint on the flank and strike in the center. The raid occurred about 7 o'clock in the morning - there were two carriers, RYUJO and JUNYO - and it was a pretty devastating raid although the planes from JUNYO on the first day never got through to the target; it was just the RYUJO's planes. The horizontal bombers, I learned since, were led by ADM. Samijima, who's now Chief of Maritime Staff. Of course the moment this happened all the dispersed planes, all the Catalinas, took off to look for the enemy. We had one very good piece of evidence as to where the Japs were because Cusick in VP-41, in a sector to the southwest of Dutch Harbor, didn't come back that morning from his overnight search. And that's a story in itself, which I'd like to relate for the sake of history. One of my people, Campbell, who was an excellent plane commander - he was a former CAD, Chief Aviation Pilot, (we commissioned the Chiefs, Lieutenants junior grade, and the Aviation Pilots First Class as Ensigns from the moment the war broke) - he was in dispersion point at Akutan Harbor on Akutan Island, from which he took off. By this time we had radar. My squadron was the first squadron to get radar in the Pacific. We got the old British ASV which had hayrakes and dipoles all over the darn airplane. You looked like a porcupine, and the quills would collect ice, too; we'd watch them get heavy with ice and break off.

Q: How effective were they?

ADM. R.: Well, you'd be surprised how well they'd work with a goodly number of quills missing from some of these hayrakes and things. Well there were side searches and on ahead search which were very useful, but the presentation was that of an "A" scope; you didn't have a plan position indicator, there was just a vertical presentation, but you could tell if you had an airplane target because the pulse rate from your radar would synchronize and de-synchronize with the propeller of the airplane, and that meant that the image would wax and wane. You had range vertically, and an image to the side. If it was a steady image it was a ship, you were getting a steady return, but if it was waxing and waning it was an airplane because of the radar reflection from its propeller. Campbell, who told me this story later, saw by radar an airplane coming at him. He ducked down, and he had found the Japanese Fleet. He was getting out a radio report, which unfortunately was garbled, but we knew he'd made contact with the fleet. He saw this airplane coming at him, and he thought, "Well I'm in a cloud here and nothing's going to happen." The first thing he knew a Zero was on his tail spitting bullets at him. He did a quick turn and lost the Zero in the cloud. Then severa more times after that first encounter he saw airplane images identified by the waxing and waning of the radar image, and he'd always make a turn in the clouds and he'd lose them, which led us to believe that maybe since this contact was made in the clouds that the Japanese had radar. They didn't at that time; they did later, on Kiska, But instead, their vision was keen,

their listening was keen, and they vectored this plane with only
a quick glimpse of the Catalina, they'd gotten the fighter on
course and into the cloud, and they'd found Campbell. Campbell
said he sent off his contact report. He had a number of bullet
holes so he started back for his dispersion place, Akutan Harbor. When he got within about 50 miles of the island, he ran
out of fuel. He had had his rudder wire shot away so he had
no rudder control. There were various and sundry holes in
his hull from the fighter bullets, and he had climbed on top
by this time to have a fairly comfortable flight back to
Akutan - he said he was at about 6,000 feet on top of an
undercast. When his engines quit he lowered his nose and
started an instrument let down, minus rudder, through the clouds.
He broke out, he said, at about 300 feet and he said later,
"Skipper, I forgot to cut my switches when my engines quit."
And he said, "When I lifted my nose to land on the sea there was
gas in one tank which went through to one engine, and one engine caught briefly." He said, "It didn't matter too much because it was the downwind engine. It kicked me around into
the wind a little more." You see, he hadn't time to turn into
the wind, he was landing crosswind, but it was the downwind
engine that took for just a minute and kicked him around a little
bit into the wind. They got on the water, they patched their
holes, and it was sometime later that a Coast Guard boat was
directed to them. A Catalina looking for Cusick, or our missing
Catalina, discovered him adrift at sea. The Coast Guard boat

went out and took him in tow. Campbell and his crew left the airplane and went aboard the patrol boat. It wasn't very long until their patches and one thing and another loosened and the airplane filled up, and they cut the line and let her go. We didn't know that crew was alive for three days. We had a wonderful deal with the cannery watchmen; they were on short wave radio and we would check in with them. We had bombs and drums of aviation gasoline stashed at all the canneries all around the Alaskan Peninsula-Aleutian Islands.

Q: These were salmon canneries?

ADM. R.: That's right. Well, on the third day (we'd given Campbell and his crew up for lost because my squadron had had two other planes shot down) a cannery watchman at Sand Point in the Shumagin Islands came on the radio and said, "I have one of your crews." And I immediately said, "What name?" And he said, "Campbell." Well I got in a PBY and flew over to Sand Point and here was Campbell and his whole crew. The skipper of that Coast Guard boat was under radio silence orders and he didn't open up to tell us that he had the crew. You can't blame him for that, he was not supposed to. We picked them up and I flew them back down to Cold Bay, and Campbell told this terrific story of letting down with no rudder and getting away with a landing at sea and keeping his plane afloat until he was rescued from the sea.

Russell #1 - 118

Campbell's plane was one of my casualties and we were fortunate to get his entire crew back. I've forgotten, I think one of his men was slightly wounded but not badly at all. Of course he lost his airplane but under the circumstances we were delighted that he was able to survive the brush with the Japanese Fleet. The other two airplanes were rather interesting. One of my pilots, Marshall Freerks (he's now a Ph.D. chemist with Montsanto in St. Louis) discovered the Japanese Fleet the next morning, which is the morning of the 4th of June, and he tracked them. I sent Stockstill out to relieve him, and it was fortunate for Freerks that he made contact with the fleet when he did because they had considered that the weather was too rough to fly and they had no fighters airborn at the time. Stockstill came out and took over the trailing of their fleet, Marshall Freerks came back, but the Japanese launched fighters and shot Stockstill down. There was no trace; he was just shot down and he and his entire crew were lost. The otherplane I lost on the 4th of June was Ensign Mitchell. I was very sad about this, he had had a very tough time. He had been patrolling overnight as usual on a southern sector out of Cold Bay, and he had received some bad gasoline from the tender (there was rust and salt water mixed up with his gasoline) and his engines were running rough but he kept airborne and managed to get back to the base. We looked him over at Cold Bay and we cleaned out the un-self sealed side of his tankage, but the other side where we had our bullet-proof fuel cells we just couldn't clean out. So we closed those off and filled him full of good clean gasoline on his good side and sent him up to Kodiak, and I told him not to show up again until he had an airplane that he was satisfied he could fly. He got to Kodiak and there was a lot of excitement up there, and the Wing Commander had an operation order that he wanted to send down to his squadrons. Instead of getting Mitchell's plane back in shape, cleaning out the tanks on the bullet-proof side, the Wing Commander sent him back still flying on the one good side to deliver operation orders to me at Cold Bay, to Foley at Dutch Harbor. He landed at my place, I was very much annoyed to think that he didn't have his airplane back in shape, and he took off to make the delivery at Dutch Harbor. We always radioed in to any base before we landed to find out if the place was under attack and whether it was fit to land there, and he followed this procedure. He radioed in to Dutch Harbor as he approached, and they said, "No, we're under attack." And instead of going out into the Bering Sea and staying clear until Dutch Harbor was open, or coming back to us at Cold Bay (and these two bases were fairly close together) he elected to go into Beaver Inlet. It's a very deep fjord on the eastern side of Unalaska Island, on which Dutch Harbor is located. He was very familiar with the country because he had flown the Dutch Harbor detachment; he'd had the four weeks of duty down there and knew the country extremely well, and he remembered that this particular fjord led into rather an open bay - completely surrounded by mountains but open water - and he decided he would slide in there and wait until the attack was over. What he didn't know was that the RYUJO's air group was coming around that side of the island, and they spotted him in there and a section of fighters peeled off and shot him down. There is every evidence that his waist gunner, who's name was Rawls, got in a lucky shot on one of the Zeros, because this Zero was found on Akatan Island, on its back, in a marsh. The reason that I believe that it was Mitchell's waist gunner who winged the Zero is this: the bullet that brought him down went in from the top and severed the oil pressure gauge line behind the dash of the Zero. This cut off the oil pressure from the gauge and flight petty officer Koga, who was flying the airplane, saw his oil pressure drop to zero, and radioed in to the RYUJO saying, "I expect my engine to freeze up momentarily. I've lost my oil pressure, and I will make a forced landing on Akutan Island. Please send a submarine to pick me up." His plan was to land on the island, destroy his airplane by burning it, and walk down to the beach on Akutan Island to be picked up by a submarine which they had cruising in the vicinity of Dutch Harbor. What he didn't realize was this lovely mountain meadow which he picked out to make his landing was a bog, as most level places in the Aleutians are, and he lowered his wheels. If he'd left his wheels retracted I think he would have gotten away with it very handily, but he didn't do this. He lowered his wheels, these immediately caught in the bog, flipped him over on his back and he broke his neck and was killed. We found this airplane

Russell #1 - 121

thirty days later. The airplanes were out looking for a missing Catalina, and, flying over Akutan Island, they were amazed to find this airplane with red apples on its wings bottom up in the marsh on Akutan Island. A salvage party was put together at Dutch Harbor. They went over to Akutan Island to the scene of the wrecked Zero and disassembled it enough so they could get it down to the waterfront and get it on a lighter. Towed back over to Dutch Harbor, it was put in a freighter, and brought down to the naval air overhaul facility at the naval air station at North Island, San Diego. It was repaired and flown beginning in early October of 1942. It was a Zero Mark II, one of the early Zeros, a beautifully put together machine. I saw it at Dutch Harbor. Repaired, it was used to develop tactics against the Zero. Now the pilot who was assigned to it was Boogie Hoffman (Melvin Hoffman) who was a former enlisted pilot, fighter pilot, and his sole duty was to become completely familiar with that airplane and all its maneuvering capabilities, and to dogfight against our pilots.

Q: Where were these exercises conducted?

ADM. R.: Around San Diego, and actually it was flown to Wright Field, it was flown all over the country. Jimmy Thach, who developed the Thach weave against the Zeros in the early days of World War II, flew against it. And it is interesting, and I have this first-hand from Boogie Hoffman with whom I've talked He lives up here in Everett. He said they discovered that the built-in incidence of the vertical surfaces of the Zero, which were designed to help meet the tremendous torque on take-off, which you get normally with a big swinging propeller like that on the Zero. You know you must carry a lot of right rudder as you make your take-off run because of the torque of the prop - and some of this torque load was relieved in the design of the Zero. But if the Zero got going at very high speed, (and you know the force against an airfoil varies as the square of its velocity) the airplane would roll very fast toward the right and very slowly toward the left. So the tactic was, if you got in a brush with a Zero get him at high speed and roll to the left, which was his slow roll direction. Now I think I'm right, right and left, but at least you'd roll very fast one direction and slow the other, at high speed. And this tactic was, of course, used. Now, Okumiya, who wrote the book ZERO, which is the best history written of naval aviation in Japan, attaches a great deal of importance to the fact that the U. S. got early on in the war, June of 1942, a Zero, and could try it out themselves and find out what its foibles in the air were. He attaches great importance to it, and rightfully so.

Q: Now this was the sort of thing we hadn't acquired by intelligence before the war broke out, and yet the Zero in some sense, wasn't it a copy of one of ours?

ADM. R.: No, that's quite wrong. The Japanese did a terrific job in designing that airplane. The nearest approach we had to it was the F4F; you see, the F6F had not come along yet. Actually it looks quite a bit like the SNJ, which the Army at that time knew as the AT6. I have a photograph of the Zero if you'd like to see it, and you're certainly welcome to copy the photograph.

Q: I saw the photograph of it in the marsh.

ADM. R.: Yes, but I have one of it in flight with U. S. colors on it after it was overhauled, and I also have one of Boogie Hoffman with the airplane in the background. Well, we lost Mitchell and his entire crew, and Rawls, the waist gunner who probably got in the lucky shot, was apparently the only survivor, but he was machine gunned to death in the water in his life jacket. So you can imagine this didn't make us feel very kindly toward our Japanese enemies. After the plane crashed apparently there was still life in it; one person got out - Rawls - and our tender, which went around to the scene, got the corpse of Rawls with bullet holes in it from the water, free of the airplane.

Q: In your postwar inquiries in Japan of naval people, did you touch on this subject? I mean, their facility for shooting our men who were down in the water?

ADM. R.: Well, it wasn't brought up but you can imagine that this is not unusual. I daresay perhaps some of our own people would do something like that. The lad who was piloting the Zero was flight petty officer Koga, and I went into this thing rather thoroughly with the Japanese at the end of the war.

Perhaps we should go on with the story. The Japanese hit Dutch Harbor in the early hours of the 3rd of June, and then went west, and, for reasons unknown to me, they thought they were going to make a strike against Adak. We had nothing there. But they found the weather was not good there and, steaming back, they still didn't have fighters airborne when Marshall Freerks raised them and trailed them, but when Stockstill arrived they shot him down. They made an attack about one o'clock in the afternoon against Dutch Harbor on the 4th of June, the second day, and that's the day they struck Midway of course. On the first day, as I said, about the only indication we had early on as to their position was the fact that Cusick and his crew didn't come back off their patrol. They were shot down by the task group and, I have this story, there were three survivors. The senior one was the navigator, Wiley Hunt, and he was then an ensign or, I guess, a lieutenant junior grade. His story is very interesting; I have written it up in "The Interrogation of Japanese Officials." I interrogated him after we came back from Japan on the bombing survey and his story is a part of the official record. When they were shot down they landed and got out the big rubber boat which held seven men, and the little one which held two, in the water -- perhaps I'm wrong but anyway there were three men in the little one and the rest of the crew, the five men, were in the big raft. The big raft was riddled with bullet holes and it didn't float too long, and the men swam over and hung on to the little raft when the big raft was no longer usable. Hunt tried to get them to come aboard but they wouldn't because they knew that it wouldn't support all of them, and he watched them slowly get numb, expire, lose their grip and drift away. The three of them who were in the raft survived, the two enlisted men and Hunt. They were picked up by the heavy cruiser MAYA, and immediately the commissioned officer and the two enlisted men were segregated. They were so far gone that the Japanese had to put a line on them and haul them up, get them up on the deck; they couldn't climb up under their own power, they were that far gone. Hunt was interrogated, but not severely, until the second day. The second day of attacks, the JUNYO's air group, which had not made it to the target the first day, had attacked Dutch Harbor and they had chosen as their rally point a rock which was known as Ship Rock, because it looked like a sailing ship, in the passage between Umnak and Unalaska Island. And it was on that end of Umnak Island that we had a fighter strip, and there were P40s on the ground. When the attack occurred they immediately got airborne and they were able to take on JUNYO's air group at that very embarrassing time when they were rallying, forming up to go back to the carrier after making the attack on Dutch Harbor. Four of the Japanese dive bombers were shot down, but the Zeros accounted for two of our P40s, and I believe that the pilot walked away from one of them. But the Japanese were very surprised to find that we had fighters in the air; they didn't know there was a strip at Umnak nor at Cold Bay when they made the attack. The air group commander from the JUNYO was infuriated to be hopped by fighters at this embarrassing spot, and having lost four of his airplanes, and he came over to MAYA and set about beating Hunt, and asking questions. They rigged a device to make him open up which was pretty cruel. They tied his hands behind his back and a deep sea lead, which weighs considerable, around his waist (you couldn't swim with it around your waist, particularly with your hands tied) and they put him out in the leadsman's chains, took the life line down so he was on the platform over the sea -- and this is Hunt's story now, to me, at the end of the war -- and a burly seaman had his hand on his shoulder to push him over the side, when the interpreter thrust a paper at him saying, "Answer these questions or you will die." They were about Umnak, from which he'd taken off with his amphibian that morning, but he was so imbued with the idea that you said nothing but your name, rank and serial number, that he generated a cock-and-bull story that he had flown up in forced marches from down in the States, he'd taken off from Dutch Harbor that morning (he knew they knew all about Dutch Harbor) and he didn't know anything about this fighter field. But the air group commander was in a rage and he wouldn't take that for an answer -- if a pilot was flying from Dutch Harbor he must know more than that, he must know where there are fighters. I said to Hunt at this point, "What did you do?" And he said, "Well, I thought pretty fast, I said I have told you I flew up in great haste from the United States, I flew out of Dutch Harbor, and I don't know anything about this field that you mentioned." They they thrust the questions at him again. "This time," he said, "I thought maybe I had better stall a bit, and I said to the interpreter, "Is there a priest or minister on board?" (The idea of administering the last rites.) The interpreter didn't know "minister" and "priest" so he ran down to his stateroom to get his English-Japanese dictionary. Meanwhile, Hunt was standing there with a hand on his shoulder ready to be pushed over the side. The interpreter came back up and said, "No, no priest or minister on board." And he stood there for some time and then finally they said, "Okay, you will live," and they pulled him in and after that he had a pretty fair time. But what a terrific ordeal to go through. You know, when I learned this story from him, and actually it was borne out by the two men who were with him, he never could tell what the other men had said, you see; they separated them right away. Well, when I learned of this story from Hunt himself I recommended him, after the war of course, for the Silver Star for gallantry, and the Navy

Board of Awards in their wisdom cut it down to a Bronze Star. As far as I'm concerned I'd give him the Navy Cross, but that's the way things go.

So, Cusick's disappearance, the contact by Campbell on the first day, the finding of the fleet by Freerks the second day, and so forth led Wild Bill Eareckson to attack -- I sketched out the position and everything and we sent Eareckson on his way with his B-26s, and those were the old Martin B-26s. Each one of them had a Navy torpedo strapped to its belly. He took off with about six airplanes for an attack against the Japanese Fleet, but they never found it. One of them continued on course and speed, he got separated in the fog and weather from the rest of his squadron, he continued course and speed and he hit them right on the nose. He attempted to make a torpedo attack, but he said, "You know, Commander," when he got back to Cold Bay, "they kept turning so the ships were endwise to me. That made them very poor targets and I decided that I couldn't make a hit with my torpedo." He said, "You told me that if I dove the plane too fast the torpedo might arm itself." This was because there are little arming propellers near the nose of a torpedo, which turn as the torpedo begins its run in the water, you know, and I had told him that with the high speed of the B-26 it might be possible to arm the torpedo in the air. So he took his airplane up to altitude and dove it as fast as it would go, then he came down and flew over the length of the flight deck of RYUJO and let his torpedo go as a bomb. He told me he didn't know what had happened to it.

This chap's name was Thornborough, and the field at Cold Bay was later named for him. He came back, Eareck went into Umnak. Thornborough came back, he sat down with me, I sketched out what he told me (he described the ships and their formation, and put it on the wire back up to headquarters at Kodiak. Thornborough was like a little boy who'd been to the candy store; he wanted to go back and get some more candy. He'd been in contact with the Japanese. So he loaded his airplane with 500 pound bombs and took off. And the last we heard from Thornborough, he was 10,000 feet on top up over Cold Bay. I had a field telephone set in my tent where I had my radio and monitored the scouting circuit. The telephone wire ran through the salt water out to Theta Combs, C.O. of CASCO out in the bay, where his ship had radio direction finding equipment. I called him on the phone and I said, "Do everything you can to get this guy down, he's a hero. Try to nurse him down through the overcast and get him into Cold Bay," and Theta said he would do everything he could. We never heard from Thornborough again, but several days later someone flying along the north shore of the Alaskan Peninsula said there was some airplane wreckage on the beach. We went up, and the body of Thornborough's radioman, still strapped to his chair, was awash on the beach. His squadron mates were very much concerned because there are bears there, and they asked if I could take them up for a burial party and bury the corpse so it wouldn't be eaten by the bears. Now I had Campbell resting from his brush with the Japanese and I had one spare airplane, so I asked Campbell if he would fly this party up, take no risks with this new airplane, but put them ashore and let them bury the body and see if there was any more evidence (they'd found also the nose wheel of Thornborough's airplane). And I didn't hear from Campbell. So I got in an airplane and flew up there, and I could hardly believe my eyes. Here was our brand new replacement Catalina (for the ones that we'd had shot down) sitting in the surf with two gaping holes where the reduction gears in the nose behind the propeller were, and I could realize that both propellers had come off. Well, here was the party - I had taken survival gear and everything with me - but I wrote out a note to Campbell and I said answer these questions in the order that they're given, and use these symbols with a piece of white cloth I dropped; you know, you can fold it one way, you can fold it another way, and so forth. The first question was, "Are there any injuries in your party; do you need medical help?" And, about the last one was, "Do you need food?" So, the party was all together, I zoomed the party and I dropped out my message and the piece of cloth, and circled. I saw them go over and pick it up and read the message, and lo and behold instead of answering the questions in order, the very last one, "Do you need food?" Was the symbol that appeared on the ground. Well this made me furious. I dropped the emergency rations to them, and immediately they attacked the emergency rations and started sitting down and eating. So I just about brushed their hair with my airplane and I dropped another note and said, "For God's sake, answer the other questions!" They went back, picked up my note, and they did answer the other questions. They were all in good shape and things looked okay. So I then drew a chart of the terrain from there to Port Moller, which was a walk of maybe fifteen miles, showing them where to ford the rivers and so forth, and dropped that on them. Then we kept track of that party from the air -- I was darned if I was going to lose another airplane. One of the YP boats went up, took that airplane in tow, and by the time it reached Dutch Harbor it was practically a complete loss, because of the weather, surf and handling. We landed at Port Moller and picked up Campbell and the crew, his crew and the boys from the bomber squadron, and got them all back to Cold Bay, and then the story unraveled as follows. Campbell landed in the sea, the Bering Sea. Bristol Bay was quite calm, but with the surf running of course. They inflated the rubber boat and put the shore party in it, who paddled ashore, dragged the boat up on the beach, buried the body and picked up the wreckage (identified it thoroughly). Then they manned the rubber boat and tried to get back out to the airplane which was anchored out beyond the surf waiting for them. Every time they got in the surf with this light rubber boat, the surf would pick them up and put them back on the beach. So Campbell, seeing their difficulty, hauled up his anchor, took off from the sea, lowered his amphibious wheels and landed on the beach. I could see the tracks on the beach where he landed. He got them all aboard, and when it came time to take off (the thrust of the Catalina's engines is rather eccentric as far as the amphibious wheels are concerned) with the thrust up high and the resisting force on the main wheels low, the more power he gave resulted only in driving his nose wheel further into the sand. He figured then that he couldn't get off, but they found some driftwood and built sort of a causeway which allowed him to taxi, along with their help, onto the wet hard sand and out to the sea. Then he got them all aboard and he said, "We will taxi out and take off from the water." Well, the first sea that came along broke over the top of his cockpit, which was enclosed, and that got him a little excited so he poured a little more coal on, and he had quite a bit of power on the engines when the next sea passed over the top of his fuselage. And when those two props took solid water instead of air, they just went "poof" and left the airplane. You see the reduction gear is in the nose of the engine and the thrust was through this casting, and it just took the two props off

Russell #1 - 133

like that, and there he was with no propellers. So he sailed the boat back up into the surf and they got out, and that's the way I found them.

Q: That could have been anticipated, couldn't it?

ADM. R.: Oh yes, of course, He was a very ashamed Catalina pilot for a while, but we got him back to battery and everything went all right.

Now, the Japanese, after attacking Dutch Harbor, raiding it, let us say - appeared about the 7th of June -- that was the date of the first indication we had in Kiska Harbor. We looked around for our men, and of course the enemy landed in very considerable strength, and I found out after the war that two of the men, of the ten, were taken right away, which was bad. The senior man was a second class aerographer's mate by the name of William Charles House, a very wonderful guy; he and one other man stayed behind to burn the code books, which they did, and then they took to the hills. Two men were taken immediately. The rest, except for House, were taken by coming down to the food caches. The Japanese had established a man-to-man scouting line and raked the whole island of Kiska, and found our three food caches.

Q: Had they been aided by the man whom they'd taken?

ADM. R.: We don't know about that. Two of them, Turner and Winfry, told me this story, which was apparently typical. Those two had come down from the hill to a food cache, and they found it empty, the Japanese had been there. The two men were sitting wondering what to do next when they heard the "putt-putt" of a Japanese motor launch coming around the point into the cove. No place to hide, so they dropped into the tall grass alongside the food cache. A small platoon of Japanese landing force got out of the boat, and they'd been out and started up the hill behind, looking for our people. I think it was Winfry that told me things were going pretty well, they hadn't been discovered, until the leader of this small platoon looked back to encourage his men to climb faster and he saw them lying in the grass at the foot of the hill. He said they were surrounded, they cocked their rifles, and they said well, what the hell. Who are we against twenty Japanese, and they dropped their rifles and held their hands up.

Now House, William Charles House, got separated from the rest of them. He went over to the western side of Kiska, he lived in a cave, he subsisted on grass roots and shell food, gathered moss for his cave and so forth, and he held out for fifty days.

Q: No heat?

ADM. R.: No heat, no nothing. Eventually he figured he was going to starve to death or die of exposure, so he picked up a piece of driftwood on the beach, tied his handkerchief to it, and walked into the camp with the symbol of surrender. It was fifty days after the Japanese had made their first landing, and they had forgotten all about him. He became quite a pet in the camp according to their landing force commander, who survived the war and with whom I talked in Tokyo after the war. The other men had already been sent back to Japan, and he was in due course sent back also. All ten of those men came back, and one of them had a 13mm machine gun bullet in his thigh which the Japanese operated on. Once they got through the interrogation camp at Ofuna it was pretty easy, they said. House himself told me about working in a shipyard, then in the steel mills. You remember when Halsey's battleships shelled the steel mills north of Tokyo on the beach? They were in there and the Japs wouldn't let them out, so they went down in the foundation of the big steel rolls and they watched these sixteen-inch shells going through the steel mill above them. But they all came back alive, fortunately.

The landing force was discovered on Kiska on the 7th of June, if I remember correctly. Then there began a war of attrition against them. The Catalinas were used for early bombings, and then as the Army Air Force built up its strength they were used. The first B-24s flew up from I believe March Field, somewhere in the south, and came to

Russell #1 - 136

Cold Bay. They were very eager to get at the Japanese and they were quite green at flying in that area. My flight officer, Clark Hood, volunteered to go with them to identify the Japanese ships and assist them in finding the way for their very first bombing of Kiska. The B-24s stopped at Umnak, refueled, and went on down over Kiska. I was very sorry to learn that the lead plane, with Captain Todd at the controls, was shot down over Kiska. We lost Clark Hood and of course the B-24 crew. In Japan after the war although there were very few records available to us, we did find records of the Japanese Navy Board of Awards. And in those records were the accounts of all those units which had been cited for their actions at various places around the world. Among those cited was Kimikawa Maru, the seaplane carrier which bore the float planes which photographed Adak, as I explained before. KIMIKAWA MARU was in Kiska Harbor, and she had actually a photograph of Capt. Todd's B-24 down in flames over the pass to the west of Kiska Harbor. I would presume that Lt. Clark Hood, my operations officer, had suggested that they make the approach not from the direction of the U.S. but from the opposite direction, namely from Japan, where they might gain greater surprise. We'd many times flown through the pass. The mountains on Kiska, except for Kiska Volcano itself, are not very high, but there is a break in the hills to the west of Kiska Harbor proper. Apparently the B-24s flew under the ceiling, above the pass,

Russell #1 - 137

to drop their bombs on Kiska. The story from the remaining B-24s was that when their leader was shot down the explosion was such that it jammed the bomb bay doors on the next B-24 in line, so it really put two of them out as far as offensive action was concerned. But only one of the B-24s was lost, and with it we lost Clark Hood, much to my sorrow.

Q: What was the chance of survival if a man fell into the ocean there?

ADM. R.: We figured about twenty minutes if he didn't have an exposure suit, and we didn't use exposure suits. We did wear woolen underwear, which was a great help because even though the water penetrated to your skin the wool gave you a degree of insulation which, even though it was wet, was helpful. I imagine the water temperature was somewhere around $35°$ or $40°F$, somewhere around there, so we figured about twenty minutes.

With the occupation of Kiska, things settled down then to bombing. There were great plans to go down the Aleutian chain and get closer because after all the distance from Umnak, the very closest field we had, to Kiska was quite great; it was on the order of 550 nautical miles, and beyond fighter range until we got some P-38s up there. P-38s could make it down and back, but in the uncertainty of weather a good many airplanes were lost just due to the fact that they'd come back to the base and run out of fuel trying to get in. One of my pilots performed a rescue; he found a whole B-24 crew in the water, Bob Donley. He landed and picked them up and flew them back to the base.

Q: How valuable were the weather reports that were furnished you?

ADM. R.: Well as I said, the weather to the west of us was something of a question because the Japanese were over there and very few of our ships, so it was very difficult to get really reliable weather beyond our own search sectors. The weather in the Aleutians is generally, in the summer, low overcast, showers of drizzle, and it's quite calm. But the fog is generated by the mixing of the colder Bering Sea with the warmer Pacific along the Aleutian Islands. In the winter there's a succession of great storms. There's a permanent Aleutian low and these storms seem to peel off and rage along. Many, many times these storms would, well they're quite destructive really. One time I remember there were Catalinas, not the amphibious kind, but they were on their beaching gear and they were lashed down in revetments at Dutch Harbor. The wind was strong enough to blow the tires on one side, and once that loosened the lashings they'd start wobbling around, and eventually there were two or three of these large flying boats just rolling down the little strip we had there like pieces of paper. I remember also one time there was a lumber pile which was not lashed down at Dutch Harbor, and as the wind picked up these timbers started taking off and flying through the air. And there was a very famous picture of an airman after we got down to Adak who was leaning over almost at a 45 degree angle just being supported by the force of the wind.

Well, plans were made and the first move was to go to the island of Adak. General Landrum was the Army officer in charge of the operation, and of course the Navy put him ashore and in preparation for that two of our submarines took Castner's Alaska Scouts down to the island and put them ashore by rubber boat. Although we observed the island very carefully, we just didn't know where they were. They were concealing themselves when they heard an airplane of course, and they had hidden the rubber boats. However we waited for a signal from them; they were to comb the island and find out if there were any Japanese present. At exactly the appointed place and time there appeared a cloth strip signal on the ground saying there were no Japs on the island. By this time Gen. Landrum and his amphibious party were underway for the island. One of the casualties was due to the weather. A lighter which carried half of the marsten mat strip, which was to be on the order of 8,000 feet long, capsized and the marsten matting was lost. The Army engineers were in conference just after the unopposed landing, discussing how they might make a strip in the area. One of the old sourdoughs from Castner's Scouts (we had given them a name; we called them Castner's Cutthroats) stroked his long beard and said to the Army engineers in conference, "There is a natural flying field on this island." The engineers were incredulous and they said, "Where?" (They'd found very little horizontal real estate.) He pointed to the lagoon out in front of the tent and he said, "When the tide is very low this lagoon drains and there is a very smooth hard sand bottom. I think it would be suitable for a flying field." Well, the engineers were rather unbelieving, but they manned a rubber boat and went out to sound the lagoon and, sure enough, it was only a few feet deep. They took bulldozers and diverted Sweeper Creek, which flooded this flat, and they put a tide gate at the seaward end (the seaward end drained into Sweeper Cove), and when the tide came in they closed the tide gate and when it went out they opened the tide gate. It wasn't very long until the flat was bare and hard and perfectly okay as a flying field. We operated aircraft within eleven days of the initial landing, on the field, which was quite a record. Although 4,000 feet of marsten mat arrived and was laid on the field, it really wasn't necessary because with our amphibious Catalinas we could land any place on this flat. Of course fighters, the liberators, moved in and we set up operations. Mine was the first squadron, VP-42, first Navy squadron to base on Adak after the occupation.

Q: Were the Seabees involved in this operation at this time?

ADM. R.: No, Army engineers. Seabees had done yeoman work in other places, like at the Naval Air Station Kodiak. Much of the work, however, originally was done by contract.

Well, Adak became quite the paradise of the Aleutians. It was in fact, as we had estimated in July of 1941, the best harbor in the Aleutian Islands. And strangely with the flying field being on the northern side, the moist sea air drifting in from the south would rise over the low hills on Adak, and settling would have lost some of its moisture, and you'd get visibility on the north side of the island and over the field when the rest of the island might be fogged in. This was not the case at all as we knew from our previous experience up there on Amchitka Island, because Amchitka has a flat portion which is the sort of east-west bit of real estate, which projects down into the ocean; it's perfectly flat. There's nothing there to break the weather, and it's constantly foggy. Later on, as we moved on down, we found that Shemya, which was a small, flat island, had its weather somewhat broken by the fact that the mountains of Agatta and Attu were to the westward of it and broke up the weather, so they'd get some ceiling and visibility there when Amchitka would be fogged in.

Q: Did we realize that Attu had been occupied also by the Japanese?

ADM. R.: Yes we did, because we'd flown down there and we knew there were troops on the island.

Q: That didn't concern us very much at that point?

ADM. R.: Well, we were concerned about both Kiska and Attu.
Let me continue then with the occupation of Adak. I had the honor of leading the first Japanese plane into the field at Adak, unbeknown to me. This was a month, at least, after we'd made our landing and I couldn't believe that they hadn't found the place already, because the raids had been intensified of course over Kiska. Once moved down there it was a much shorter distance, it was roughly 220 nautical miles from Kiska, much shorter distance to fly. It happened this way. I took one of the sector searches off to the west-northwest from Adak, and when coming in from the search sector I landed on the field to find all hell breaking loose. There were fighters taking off into the wind and downwind. And somebody came out from the operations tent and very excitedly

said, "Which way did you come from?" I gave him the designation of the sector I had searched that morning, or overnight, and he said, "Did you know a Japanese plane followed you in?" I said, "No, I didn't." And he said, "Well there he is," pointing overhead. And sure enough there was a Japanese plane over the field. The fighters took off, searched for him, formed a search line and flew in the direction of Kiska. So this fellow went on down to the island of Atka, to the east. Well all the fighters were off to the west, and when they came back and landed he'd gone down and dropped a single bomb, I believe, on Atka village, which by this time was abandoned, and when he passed Adak going home to Kiska the fighters were all back down refueling. So he got away with it.

Then the Japanese launched some rather weak bombing raids nuisance raids, at night, but this was actually after I left. As October came along, we were relieved on Adak and we were settling down on Umnak Island for the winter. By this time I had made three stripes, Commander, and I was then too senior for squadron command. The Wing Commander asked for me as the Headquarters squadron commander, which was a three-striper's job, a Commander's job, and I thought that's where I would go. He appreciated very much my knowledge of the islands because I had been up there so long, and he wanted me to stay but Washington took care of that, and I wound up with a set of orders to report to Washington, D. C.

Russell #1 - 144

Q: May I ask at this point, what value were the various places in the Aleutians to the Japanese other than the initial diversionary effort?

ADM. R.: Well, if I could divert from my story and tell you the information we acquired in Japan I think it would be illuminating on this point. When the Japanese made their great thrust to the south, they established an eastern perimeter which ran through Wake Island, Marcus, up to the northern Kuriles, and then on down through the Marshalls, the Carolines and so forth. This was merely a holding line, a line to scout and know what military penetration there might be of it so that a concentration could be made if a penetration was made, to thrust it out. But it was a holding operation while they took the Philippines and Indonesia. They were very anxious to get the oil which was in Indonesia and the raw materials, rubber and so forth, from down in that area and French Indo-China. The perimeter went down to short of Australia, actually. They did not plan to occupy Australia, in the original war plans. Then something happened which made them change their minds a bit. They had had tremendous successes. They'd gone all the way over and raided Ceylon, you know, with their carrier striking force; they'd gone through the Philippines in short order; they'd taken Hong Kong; they'd taken Singapore. And success sort of went to their heads. They were mortified when USS HORNET carried the Doolittle flyers to a point in the Pacific Ocean and a raid against Tokyo occurred. This gave them cause to think, and to decide that they would extend their eastern perimeter, advance it in the direction of the U. S. They would take Midway and Adak. Midway and Adak are on the same meridian and about 1400 nautical miles apart, and the idea was to establish a barrier patrol across the north Pacific which would detect any movement of hostile forces, such as the Doolittle raiders, across that part of the ocean. And they also were looking for a decisive battle with the U. S. fleet. They knew that we were fairly weak and that the carriers were engaged down around the Solomons and that area-Coral Sea that is, (they were not). You will remember Guadalcanal was August of '42 if I remember correctly. So as the spring came along, and early June was their target date, they were going to take Midway and they were going to take Adak, establish the barrier patrol to close off and avoid the humility of having an undetected raid against the home islands.

Q: Had they determined the origin of these Tokyo raiders?

ADM. R.: I'm sure they must have, because some of the Doolittle raiders were taken prisoner, you know, and there were picket boats which were destroyed by our force, and so forth. That raid was made by HORNET, which carried B-25s, and ENTERPRISE, to provide fighters protection.

Q: Morison seems to think that they didn't really know where they came from, that the picket boats were destroyed before they could possibly send messages back.

ADM. R.: I am not sure of this. In our interrogations in Japan I don't know whether we really asked that question directly, but I can't imagine that they wouldn't know, really, whence they came. Really it was the only way they could get there.

But when the main body attacked Wake -- as I explained, the raid on Dutch Harbor was a feint; it was a feint and a probing to determine our strength in the Aleutians, preliminary to occupying the island of Adak. When the four Japanese carriers were sunk at Midway, Adm. Yamamoto, who was in overall command of the operation, gave up the Aleutian part of his venture, told the Aleutian force to concentrate on the main body and return to Japan. Vice Admiral M. Hosogaya, who had the Fifth Fleet up in the north, sent messages to Adm. Yamamoto asking him to permit the northern force to proceed with their operation, pointing out that American territory could be taken, and that although they'd had a reverse at Midway he was positive they could have success in the Aleutians. Incidentally, during that time we could hear Morse Code on high frequency, many Japanese messages. You could tell a Japanese message from a U. S. message Morse Code because of the forty-odd characters as against our twenty-six letters in the alphabet; you'd hear these odd sounds so we knew it was Japanese being transmitted and there was much chatter on the radio circuits at that time. So Yamamoto was persuaded and he told Hosogaya to proceed with his operation but to stand by for a modification in his operation order. Perhaps you saw the chart which I obtained in Japan, a copy of it is in my photo album there, where the amphibious force heading for Adak reverses course, and during this time Hosogaya pleads with Yamamoto to reinstate his operation. Yamamoto says yes, the amphibious force turns again in the direction of Adak, but then the modification to the operation order came through and Hosogaya was told not to take Adak, but to take only Kiska and Attu. And you see the amphibious force turn to the west and eventually go up and go in only to Kiska. They thought of course that since they hadn't Midway, there was no reason now to have Adak as a scouting base, and they thought it would be easier to hold Kiska and Attu. So Hosogaya was told to proceed with that modification to his orders and that's exactly what he did; he went into Kiska and went into Attu.

Well, to sort of conclude, after I left up there our forces in the north went on and established a base on Amchitka. The amphibious thrust against Attu was made and troops were put ashore of course, and there was a very bloody battle on the island of Attu. I had the honor, having come out of the Aleutians and now on duty in Washington, D.C., of going out to the West and talking with the planners. They wanted to know the geography of Kiska and Attu, and they wanted to know

Russell #1 - 148

the general conditions of weather and all that sort of business and I was able to help them. Although I was assigned to advance bases in the staff at naval operations, I was actually in on the planning and I remember Bob Dennison was in that planning group.

Q: Were these Nimitz related planners?

ADM. R.: Oh yes. And, of course, King's planners. Well, I didn't know until the actual operation began that they'd elected, in higher echelons, to take Attu -- bypass Kiska as being the stronger of the two and to take Attu. We had quite a concentration of force; there were old battleships and they even had some escort carriers up there.

Q: The PENNSYLVANIA was up there?

ADM. R.: Yes. And it was very difficult flying for the carriers. There was a lot of air activity supported from Amchitka and from Adak, but there was a very bloody battle. I found out in Japan that the whole Japanese Fleet had concentrated in preparation for going up to knock off our amphibious force at Attu. And I said, "Why was this not done?" And they said, "Well, by the time we had concentrated and were ready to sail, Col. Yamazaki, who was the commander on Attu, sent us a message that he was making his final charge," as they say. The final charge was their suicide charge and they overran the American lines on Attu and got way back into the command territory before they were finally all killed off. It was a banzai charge, you know, and they overran field hospitals and all sorts of things. It was at the Attu affair that Squeaky Anderson (Commander Charles E. Anderson) gained his fame as a beachmaster. He had come for the Navy to Alaska early on as the skipper of YP-72, which was a halibut boat converted into an auxiliary for the United States Navy, and a very picturesque character he was.

Q: He originated in Denmark, did he not?

ADM. R.: He was from Sweden, and he was known as rather a hard trader. He'd been down in the Aleutians many times. He put into Dutch Harbor - this was Christmas of '41, I guess - and he had a famous entry in the log of the YP-72 which read as follows: "I, Lt. C. E. Anderson, Commanding Officer of YP-72, have this day exchanged one coil of manila line for a case of scotch whiskey, this for the morale of the crew on Christmas Day, 1941." He was port captain at Dutch Harbor when the carrier raids of the 3rd and 4th of June, 1942, were in progress. In the occupation of Adak he was on the staff, advising. But he was beach master at Attu and gained fame there, and he was beach master at practically every other amphibious operation we had in the Pacific, throughout the central Pacific, not down in the Guadalcanal area. His last beach master job was the hottest one, and that was on Iwo Jima; he came very near being eliminated in that. He told me that he was riding in an LCVP, which was a little amphibious boat with a ramp, and he was way up forward on the ramp looking at the beach as they approached to find out where the best spots were to place provisions and one thing and another, ammunition and what not, and suddenly there was a great blinding flash. He couldn't remember just what happened but he found himself on all fours on the beach. He felt his body and he seemed to be all whole; no real damage but he was slightly bruised, and he looked back for the landing craft and she'd disappeared completely. They'd hit a beach mine, and the boat was literally blown out from under him and he was catapulted onto the beach. And as you know, Iwo Jima was a very difficult action. The Japanese were well dug in, and our losses were very heavy. Squeaky was a very interesting character. I could tell you many, many stories, but I think we should go on with my story.

Well, as I explained, I was detached from VP-42 in the latter part of October in 1942, and I came home with proceed orders, which meant I had four days to get underway for Washington, D. C.. While I was at home a messenger from the 13th Naval District arrived. Incidentally, I had left my family here at American Lake in the old camp while I was in the Aleutians. The messenger from the 13th Naval District had a message that said my orders were changed from proceed to immediate, which meant I had to take the next available transportation. I felt rather badly about this. Because I'd been in the Aleutians for so long I thought I rated a little rest at home, and this was not to happen. I headed for Washington, D. C.. I arrived on a Sunday. I checked in at Naval Operations and they had no idea where I was supposed to go, and suggested that I go to my hotel and rest and come back Monday morning. I said, "But you have changed my orders from proceed to immediate and I want to know why you wanted me back here." No one could tell me. And Monday morning I found the chap who'd done it, and he said, "Oh, I thought you were on duty in Seattle, and we couldn't understand why you were taking so long to get here." I said, "Sir, I was fighting in the Aleutians. I left Dutch Harbor in a windstorm; I was detained in Kodiak by the Wing Commander while he pumped me for some detailed information of the Aleutians before I could leave for Seattle; and I was at home hoping to spend at least one night with my family when I was ordered to proceed on the next available transportation." I guess he felt a little badly about it perhaps, I'm not sure. I saw him later on in the war. Well, I spent a month planning the organization of advanced aviation bases in the Pacific. The theme was to have OAKS and ACORNS -- the OAK was a big base and the ACORN was a little base. We were concerned with all sorts of things -- the equipment we put ashore, how the marston mat strip would be laid down, the control people we needed for tower, radio aids to aerial navigation, Seabee equipment which would be used on the bases and so forth. I thought that was a very dull way to continue with the war as far as I was concerned, but the thing to do was to find a place on the West Coast where the ACORNS could be trained. I had a friend, Marshall Gurney, a classmate who had been in the business of expediting freight of various sorts to the forces in the Pacific. He had a Beechcraft, one of those old bi-planes with negative stagger in the wings, and we flew the length of the West Coast from San Francisco down to San Diego looking for a place where we might set up a training site for ACORNS. In the vicinity of Oxnard in California we discovered Port Hueneme, and a maritime school for training officers for the Merchant Marine. I said to my friend Gurney, "That looks like a likely spot." We investigated further and sure enough. Eventually we took it over; the maritime school was sent out to Catalina Island, I believe. We took over; it was a training place for Seabees. Of course, Port Hueneme is still a Seabee stronghold, as you know. And that's where the ACORNS were trained. There was a Commanding Officer of the ACORN, who had all the elements of a forward aviation base under his command. Personnel were trained there and they were sent out as units to the Pacific. And as we'd take one atoll after another we'd set these units up to establish bases.

Q: Who determined where the bases were to be located?

Russell #1 - 153

Adm. R.: That was a war planner out with Admiral Nimitz. All we did was provide the unit. He could order an ACORN here, there or the other place, anywhere he liked. He knew the composition of it, the training of the officers and men, their requipment, what their capabilities were, and it was up to him to plan where he'd put them down in places like Eniwetok, and various islands and atolls.

Q: This means that you obviously had to work very closely with the men like Ben Moreell, did you not?

Adm. R.: Oh, yes indeed. I knew Ben very well. But, this was not my dish of tea and I got Marshall Gurney to take the base at Hueneme, while I checked in at OpNav and told the director of the Advance Base Division that I had completed my job and I wanted to go to sea. And he said, "Well, okay, but the Bureau of Aeronautics has something they want to tell you." I discovered that there was a section in planning in Aeronautics called the Aircraft and Equipment Section under then Commander Harris, and I was to be his relief. I said, "But look, I don't want duty in Washington, D. C.." And John Sydney McCain was then the Chief of the Bureau of Aeronautics. I took my case to him, and he was a delightful old gentleman who had false teeth, and who rolled his Bull Durham cigarettes with a great deal of flair and not too well and usually spilled them down his front as he rolled them. But a delightful fellow, a fellow I admired very much because he'd been my skipper on RANGER, CV-4, and it was he who allowed us airplane jockeys to come up on the navigating bridge and learn how to be officers of the deck and get the entry in our records that we were qualified as officers of the deck; he'd let us handle the ship. He was a great fellow. He listened patiently to my great plea to get out from under and get back to sea. He had a strange habit of clicking his false teeth, sort of putting them in place. And after my great harangue he said, "You've got to stay, son." And I said, "Well, Admiral, that's very bad news indeed for me." He said, "But I'll tellyou what I'll do. I'll let you out of here in 18 months. Now go on about your business."

Russell #2 - 155

An Interview with Admiral James S. Russell, U. S. Navy
(Retired)

Place: Tacoma, Washington

Date: November 23, 1974

Subject: Biography

By: John T. Mason, Jr.


Q: Well, sir, it's good to have another session with you this morning. When we broke off last night, you were returning to Washington for a reluctant tour of duty in the Bureau of Aeronautics. But before you tell me about that, I wonder if you'd relate the incident that involved Admiral Paul Foster when he was up in the Aleutians, while you were on duty up there.

Adm. R.: Yes. I think he was then a commander, Naval Reserve. We heard that this important person, who had a special relationship with President Roosevelt, would be coming north. And if I remember correctly, I flew to Sitka and picked him up and brought him to Kodiak where we briefed him on the area and our activities. Mine was still the only Catalina squadron, the only Navy squadron, in Alaska.

He said he'd like to see all of the Aleutian chain, that he would like to call on General Buckner in Anchorage, and he even suggested that he might want to fly over to visit with the Russians in Siberia. I told him we were at his service. He showed me a letter from President Roosevelt. I flew him to Anchorage. We called on General Buckner, and spent a day there very pleasantly, and then we started down the chain.

Meanwhile, I had lost one of my aircraft. The plane commander was Lt(jg) Edward R. Winter. He apparently let down short of the island of Unalaska, and we never did find a trace of him. I presume that he let down, there was no ceiling, and he flew in to the water. It can happen, as you know.

So, I took off and left Paul Foster at Kodiak, but the next thing I knew, he appeared in Dutch Harbor and General Buckner was with him. And we prepared to go on down the Aleutian chain. Sammy Coleman and I each took a plane. I took along Lieutenant Clark Hood, my flight officer, who was later lost in a B-24 over Kiska. And we flew down and we almost made Attu, but we were weathered out just short of the place, and went back to Kiska where the storm that was brewing overtook us, and, as I explained, we were weather bound there for about five days. Paul Foster, along with a classmate of mine, Bill Miller, from the 13th Naval District, who was escorting Commander Foster, were in the party.

On the afternoon of the second day, when we persuaded General Buckner that it was a better part of wisdom for him to take the tender and leave us, because the intelligence we had of the Japanese coming up our way that summer, Paul Foster and Lieutenant Commander Bill Miller joined the skipper of the Williamson, Knappy Kivette and off they went, leaving me a whale boat and a chief aerographer's mate, Barbo, and an engineer and a coxswain for the boat. As you remember my story of yesterday, we got out on the fifth day. Meanwhile Foster had gone back up. And I rejoined him either at Dutch Harbor or Kodiak. And by this time, intelligence got warmer and warmer that the Japanese were, in fact, coming up our way. The wing commander arrived, and Paul Foster just slipped into the background, because of the great rush to make a deployment and establish very extensive search patterns against the arrival of the Japanese up our way. So I then lost track of Foster.

But when I got back to Washington on duty, first in the Office of the Chief of Naval Operations and then in the Bureau of Aeronautics, I joined up with Paul Foster, who, if I remember correctly, had an office in Washington at this time. And he showed me a film which he'd taken. He had a hand-held movie camera - 16 mm film - and it was a very complete record of his trip up to the Aleutians, including motion pictures of the departure in the whale boat from the side of the Williamson of Jim Russell, Sammy Coleman, and our respective crews! As a matter of fact, he showed me that several times in Washington, and one time he offered to give it to me, I believe, to give me a copy of it. So that, Jack is my association with the then Commander Paul Foster.

Russell #2 - 158

In looking back on Paul Foster's visit, I believe that word had gotten as far as the White House that there was some disagreement between the command ashore and the visitor from Pearl Harbor, Admiral Theobald, and I believe that one of Foster's purposes was to analyze the problems up that way. As a matter of fact, though, Theobald had not yet arrived, and it may have been because he was on the scene, that he looked in to it later on. But in my conversations with him and reviewing the film and so forth, I believe that was one of his purposes in life.

Now, there's a very amusing incident. I've told you of Wild Bill Eareckson who commanded the bombers, who took off with navy torpedoes on his B-26's. He failed to find the fleet. Thornborough, one of his pilots who had separated from the flight did find them, made an attack, and went off the second time and was eventually lost on his return. Bill Eareckson was in a tent very close to mine. He had a dog, which had been given to him. It was a white Siberian husky with blue eyes, a beautiful dog whom he called Scootch. And Bill Eareckson and Scootch lived in a tent sort of by themselves very close to his command B-26, very close to the runway. It so happened that the six-holer, the latrine tent, was down the way, down the prevailing wind away from our main camp, and the trail to it from my tent went by Bill Eareckson's tent. And I was walking down one morning to do my morning's morning. I heard a typewriter typing away in

Russell #2 - 159

Bill Eareckson's tent, so I threw back the fly, and I said, "Bill, what are you doing?" "Oh," he said, "I have been directed to write a report about the noncooperation between the Army and the Navy in the Aleutians." And I said that sounded interesting, that it was a good subject, and that I'd like very much to read the report when he had it done. He said, "Yeah. I'll give you a copy, and it will be on that flimsy paper." And seeing my course set for the latrine, he said, "And you can do with it what you like!"

Q: Well, let's go back to Washington to the Bureau of Aeronautics, when you returned there with Admiral McCain.

Adm. R.: Well, when I left my home in American Lake to go back to Washington, I had arranged a code with my wife, Dorothy. It ran something like this. If I said, "Well, today I met Lieutenant Smith," that meant I was going to North Africa. If I said, "Today I met Lieutenant Jones," I was going to England. I was sure I was being groomed for some exotic job overseas. And you can imagine my horror when I arrived in Washington, D. C. on a Sunday under immediate orders, and the duty officer in the office of the Chief of Naval Operations didn't know where I was supposed to go. That was terribly deflating. But when I did find out that I was to stay there and plan advance bases in the Pacific, I found I had no code word with my wife. It never occurred to me that I might be staying for duty in Washington, D. C.. But I got out of that job in naval operations in about two months time by turning it over to my classmate, Marshall Gurney, who set up the ACORN-OAK training establishment at Port Hueneme.

Ready to go back to sea, I went to the Bureau of Aeronautics, which at that time controlled the assignment of aviation personnel. And the detailer had very depressing news. He said, "You're supposed to relieve Dale Harris who has the aircraft and equipment section in the planning division of the Bureau of Aeronautics." And I said, "Oh, no, you can't do this to me!" But he said, yes, that's the way it is, chum! So then I went and had my little interview with Admiral John Sydney McCain, who was Chief of the Bureau of Aeronautics, who said, "You must stay eighteen months." Well, I looked the situation over, and the Bureau was expanding, the responsibilities were increasing, and it was quite evident to me that in the planning section there needed to be some one to set up true military requirements, people who were experienced in battle. I was directed to form the Division of Military Requirements in the Bureau of Aeronautics, and I selected an experienced squadron commander in each type. I asked Roy Simpler, who had flown F4F's off the strip at Guadalcanal to come join me.

Q: Did you have carte blanche in this to get anybody whom you wanted?

Adm. R.: Very much so, anyone who was returning, you know. For the Marine Corps, Joe Renner, who had the very first F4U squadron. The F4U, which was a competitor to the F6F, had a bad habit of bouncing on landing, it would bounce and float in the arresting gear. It was a bad actor on the flight deck in this respect. So we gave it to the Marine Corps, but they were going to fly it from ashore, where it didn't matter so much - the landing characteristics. It also had a habit of dropping a wing if you stalled it close to the ground. These oddities were corrected eventually. The tail-wheel oleo was lengthened, the main oleo was softened so that the plane wouldn't bounce back in the air, and so forth, but Joe Renner was squadron commander of one of the very early Marine Corps F4U squadrons which had been in action in the South Pacific in the Guadalcanal area. So he knew the characteristics of this new fighter we had.

For dive bombers, I got Dave Shumway, who had been flying SBD's, the old Douglas _Dauntless_. For torpedo planes I got Clare Miller. Clare had had experience in TBD's and also in the new Gumman TBF, which became the TBM when the building in quantity was turned over to General Motors.

And finally, I got Paul Foley, whom I'd known in the Aleutians, who had a sister squadron of mine up there, to join as an expert in patrol aviation. This division of Military Requirements was a very interesting task. Unfortunately, the fruits of our labors were not apparent in

World War II particularly, except for the improvements we had made to existing airplanes, such as making the F4U carrier suitable. The only new airplane we got was the F8F, a beautiful airplane, but unfortunately too late to see action. As a matter of fact, it was an old gentleman's airplane. I used to delight in flying it.

Q: This, then, was future planning, was it?

Adm. R.: Yes. It was planning and also taking care of the airplanes that were in service, correcting them. We had troubles with the Sb2C-3. It was rather a bad actor. We took a turret off that airplane and put an ordinary gun mount in it, and so forth.

Q: This involved you with the test center, did it?

Adm. R.: Well, this was headquarters, you see. It was testing, design, in effect everything that pertained to the performance of aircraft, both those presently in service and those planned for the future. And as I explained, the one for the future which we planned was the F8F, which was a delightful little fighter. It was built to out-perform the Zero. It had many interesting features. One was if you really pulled the wings off, just the outer panel was supposed to leave, and you could still fly on your inboard sections!

Q: Had it been based on the Zero you captured in the Aleutians, or had others been taken by this time?

Adm. R.: That was on the performance of the Zero as developed through the capture in the Aleutians but that was only one ingredient in this. Grumman was out to get something that would be a super performer. And it was a very delightful little airplane. It was used in the fleet for a good number of years after that, but it was replaced eventually by heavier, larger, more powerful aircraft.

Well, that was the Division of Military Requirements, a very interesting job.

Q: Talk about your relationship with the manufacturers, for instance.

Adm. R.: Well, the principal manufacturers - of course, Grumman, I think, led the field. He was making the F6F, and we got an R-2800 engine in it. George Anderson had the quantity planning, and he was interested in getting the numbers of fighters up, which we needed, and I remember one time if they got the thousandth aircraft out for that month, he volunteered to go up to the Grumman plant and push it out of the hangar himself!

Russell #2 - 164

Q: How were these numbers calculated?

Adm. R.: Well, it was almost maximum capacity by the manufacturer, really, and expanded. I think that the Bureau of Aeronautics got up to some unbelievable rate, maybe 25,000 aircraft per year, toward the end of the war.

Q: So, FDR's original statement - 50,000 planes - wasn't too fantastic.

Adm. R.: It was done. It was actually done.

Our relationships with the manufacturers, of course, were excellent. There was already an interesting shift in flying boats. Martin in Baltimore and Convair in San Diego were competing. Convair had developed the CORONADO which was a four-engine flying boat, and it was so large that we in the Aleutians much preferred a two-engine, smaller, handier aircraft; because in poor visibility making approaches in mountainous terrain, for example, you wanted a rather short turning radius, and the CORONADO was a rather big, stately airplane something like the Boeing Clipper, which PanAm used.

So, we got the PBM's out, the PBM-5, I remember, and then there was a P2M, and so on; a steady, continued production of the Catalina, which was a rather slow, blundering airplane, but it could stay aloft and cover vast reaches of the ocean, and equipped with radar it turned out to be

Russell #2 - 165

a pretty good search airplane.

Q: How did the Navy happen to build its own flying boats, the PBN's?

Adm. R.: Oh, the Naval Aircraft factory, you know, at one time was supposed to build airplanes as sort of a check on the industry. I remember the aircraft factory when they were doing goldbeater-skinned bladders for the helium in dirigibles, in competition with Goodyear. They built a training plane there to make sure that the Navy understood how to build airplanes and what might be a reasonable price for them from commercial manufacturers.

Q: Were they prototypes then?

Adm. R.: Not necessarily. They developed their own airplanes, and they also manufactured an occasional quota of airplanes that were in production by commercial manufacturers. And that was the case with the PBY. Did they call this the PBM? I've forgotten.

Q: The "N". Yes.

Adm. R.: Well, strangely enough, the engineers got a little fancy up there, and they said, "You know, this airplane is directionally unstable." Well, we'd been flying Catalina for thousands of hours, and unstable as they were perhaps, they'd been no particular bar to operations. So we thought it was sort of silly, but the aircraft factory did make some changes. They put a bigger tail on it, which meant that we had a small quota of Catalina-style airplanes that were oddities in the fleet. And we had a commitment to the Russians to provide them with PBY's, and we thought, "Ah hah! Here's a way of getting rid of the oddballs. We'll let the Russians have these." And it was rather odd that during World War II, President Roosevelt gave orders which said in effect, "From all this military assistance, don't ever short-change the Russians on their quotas." I have the feeling that President Roosevelt thought that by kindness - getting next to the Russians, that he could persuade them from their ideas of turning the world into a communist camp. And one of these was we would always make our commitments in military aid to them.

Well, the problem then was to sell the Russians the PBN. I flew a party of Russians in a Cessna, a little twin-engine plane, up to Philadelphia, and this chap who was a pilot I put in the co-pilot's seat, and I asked him if he didn't want to try the Cessna, and he just folded his arms and shook his head. He didn't care to fly. I did the same in the PBN, taking off from the Delaware River. I asked him if he wished to fly the airplane, and again, no.

And why? I never could understand whether it was that they didn't want me to know their piloting skill, or just what it was, but they wouldn't handle the controls of the aircraft. I turned the airplane over to another pilot and went back and fired the .50 calibre machine guns in the waist, and my Russians friends went with me. They did everything except fly the airplane. It was a great mystery to me why they wouldn't actually man the controls. I flew them back in the little Cessna down to Washington, and again, offered to let the Russian fly the airplane. And he just shook his head and crossed his arms and sat there. It was an oddity. Well, that was my experience in the Bureau of Aeronautics.

I made great friends during that tour with Ralph Davison. He shoved off to sea. He had a division of CVE's first, and chose John Crommelin as his chief of staff. And finally, my eighteen months drew to a close in June of 1944. I was to go back to sea, and I was in a very awkward position as far as rank was concerned. I was too senior to get an air group to fly from the carriers, and I was too junior to get a combat carrier. I probably could have gotten - just possibly could have gotten - a transport carrier, ferrying airplanes to the forward area. But, a wonderful thing happened. Ralph Davison asked for me as his chief of staff. John Crommelin had had a lot of combat. He was with Mullinnix, if you remember, when the Liscomb Bay was blown up, and he actually went over the bow of the ship with a sheet of flame behind him and had a badly burned back, and so forth. He was getting a little war-weary and in the normal tour of duties, he was overdue to come ashore. So Ralph Davison asked me to come out and join him as his chief of staff, and that was really a wonderful event in my life, because it put me back in the fast carriers where I could be in an effective job in spite of being in this rather awkward position of being too senior for an air group command, and too junior for a combat carrier.

Q: This would be a point to ask you to comment on the necessity for these desk jobs in Washington. The war had to be fought, and it was a coordinated effort, so intelligent men had to serve there as well as in the fleet.

Adm. R.: I should probably acknowledge that I'd had the post-graduate course in aeronautical engineering in the Navy, and it was my due as somebody had to do it, that it was natural that a fellow who'd been technically trained as I had would be forced to take this sort of duty. So I felt it was just, that I had repaid Uncle Sam by taking a technical job of that kind.

Q: And that post-graduate course is what qualified you for that particular job.

Adm. R.: Yes, generally yes.

So I bade farwell. Oh! I found out another thing about duty in Washington at that time. The way really to get clear was to find someone who was willing to take over. And I found, much to my delight, Bob Dixon, who had had a long, long tour, and he had come back for a rest and one thing and another, and was thoroughly experienced. He'd been in many battles, flying fighters, and I told him what a wonderful job this director of the Division of Military Applications was, Military Requirements, I mean. And he said he wouldn't mind doing a tour there. So Bob Dixon was available, and when I went to the detailer, I said, "Let me loose. Here's my relief." He said okay.

Meanwhile, John Sydney McCain had gone to sea. He got a task group of fast carriers, and his relief, of course, wasn't aware of this compact I had with Admiral McCain to get clear. Well, I flew out to Eniwetok where the fast carriers had come in for a breather. They came in the day after I arrived. I remember shaving in my reflection in the water in a steel helmet. I used the surface of the water in the steel helmet as a mirror to shave, and I used the water therein for lathering and softening my beard.

Well, the fast carriers came in and I reported aboard. And John Crommelin turned over to me and went home, and we prepared for the next exercise, which was to be the assault on the Palau Islands.

Q: What was the flagship?

Adm. R.: The flagship was the <u>Franklin</u>. And I believe Ralph Davison was in the <u>Franklin</u> when I joined him. He could have been in one of the other ships in the division, but we made most of those early cruises in the <u>Franklin</u>.

Before we went down to the Palaus, however, we made one raid against Iwo Jima-ChiChi Jima. This was a repetitive series of raids, which were designed to keep the Japanese from sending down aerial interference at Guam, Saipan, and Tinian, which we'd taken over. And Iwo Jima was not too far away, you remember, and they could fly airplanes there and come down and attack Guam, Saipan, Tinian.

Q: And catch them on the defensive.

Adm. R.: These raids were scheduled at the proper times to clear out the aircraft which were coming down to Iwo in preparation for attacking the Guam group.

Q: Were these dawn raids?

Adm. R.: Well, most of the raids had occurred at dawn, so my very first operation as chief of staff we struck Iwo Jima at 1 o'clock in the afternoon, and we sneaked in unobserved apparently. Their night searches, which were supposed to develop where we were, failed, as we were far enough out not to be detected. We ran in at high speed and launched, and it was a veritable slaughter. Most of the fighters were down. The very few in the air were shot down by our fighters, and we got most of the other airplanes taxiing from the revetments out to the runway and taking off the runway, actually destroying them on the ground in that fashion. It was a revelation to me the power of those fast carriers. It was just terrific. And once we'd disposed of the aircraft, it was just repetitive strikes against the military targets and ammunition dumps and fuel dumps and all that sort of business on the islands, ChiChi and Iwo.

ChiChi didn't have a flying field on it as I remember, but they had a lot of seaplane activity. But Iwo, of course, was very active. There were something like five fields on that island - five strips, and we just plastered the place.

Well, we came back and rested up a bit in Eniwetok, refurbished, and sailed for the Palaus. And again, at that time there were about four carrier task groups. These were comprised usually of two *Essex* class, two CVL's. Some of the groups had three *Essex* class carriers. We'd have two or three battleships and four or five cruisers. We'd have an anti-aircraft cruiser usually at the pivot point in formation or a leader of the screen, and usually twenty-four destroyers in a circular screen.

Q: These were all in the 3rd Fleet under Halsey.

Adm. R.: We were alternately the 5th or the 3rd Fleet. We used to say, - we'd watch Halsey go back to Pearl to start planning the next operation, while Spruance came out with the 5th. We would be 58. something, and then he'd go home, and Halsey would come out, and we'd be 38. something. And we used to say that they changed the jockeys, but not the horses!

Q: Who were the other task force commanders in the carriers?

Adm. R.: F. C. Sherman, Montgomery for a time, although he went shortly after I joined; Jerry Bogan, Jocko Clark, of course. He was the aggressive type. He liked to go up and burn airplanes on Iwo! He kept score. He wanted to keep his task group well ahead of all the other task groups in the number of airplanes they shot down, preferably in the air, on the ground if he had to. He didn't go so much for hitting the ordinary targets. He wanted to knock down airplanes.

Let's see who else. I gave you Montgomery, and Ralph Davison, of course. Mitscher was fast carriers. At this time McCain came out and took a task group under Mitscher. He took this as sort of a mak-e-learn job, so that he could in time spell Mitscher. Mitscher had been there for a long time, as you know, been through many, many battles, and it was high time that he get some rest. McCain was training up. Actually, he didn't take over until, I believe, after the Leyte Gulf action.

Well, the Palaus was rather a simple thing for us, because we put an Army infantry outfit ashore on Angaur, a rather detached island with very little resistance. And our job was to give them air support after we'd made very thorough strikes against the place first, you know. Peleliu, Angaur, and so forth. The tough spot was Peleliu itself, where the Marines had a pretty bloody battle on that island, and as Angaur got secured, we moved over. And then we were left to give close support there when Mitscher made his first assault on the Philippines proper with the other three carrier task groups. And that changed the whole course of the war, really. He found out that the Japanese were weaker than we thought, and he had a very successful raid over there and not nearly the resistance he thought there would be.

The war plans up to that time had put us ashore in places like Mindanao to slowly work up the Philippines. But he decided, and it was his advice, I believe, that persuaded Nimitz and King that we could strike the center of the Philippines, anyway Leyte Gulf, and do it fairly soon. So, as the Palaus became secure, we retired again to Ulithi atoll, and prepared for an assault on the Philippines.

Now, in preparation for the assault on the Philippines, we went as far north as Okinawa, and we struck Okinawa, and we struck Taiwan, and then there was a field up at Luzon that we gave attention to, but the idea was to cut off the

Philippines from air support from the home islands. This we did with the fast carriers. And then we started working our way to targets in the Philippines.

Q: Did you meet much opposition in Okinawa and places like that?

Adm. R.: Yes. One of the very best attacks against the fleet that I saw in the war was off-shore in the Okinawa-Taiwan area. It was an attack by Betty's, and they rendezvoused and took their positions for attack over the horizon from us. There was a rain shower which they used to particular advantage, and the attack was beautifully coordinated. They came in from about three directions, and it was amazing to watch. They got through our screen, and we could see the tracers, for example, on these Betty's. They were flying so low that you could see the wash of their wings and props on the water. And you'd watch tracers shooting at a Betty, and as they'd concentrate on him, he'd lift up a little bit, and the bullets would go under him. And as they moved up to him, he'd duck under them. And when they came down again on him, he'd come up. We had five Betty's burning in the water inside our screen in our task group. It was miraculous that there wasn't more damage than happened. From the flag bridge looking over the side, I thought, "Gee! There's one that hit us that didn't go off!" But it missed the stem of the

Russell #2 - 175

the ship by a matter of feet, and the bubbles from the torpedo were rising as the ship passed through the wake of the torpedo.

Q: Was there any night fighting at this point?

Adm. R.: Yes. Our night fighters were pretty thoroughly trained, and I remember one time when we were up off the north of the Philippines, there was a pattern of patrol search coming down, because we raised a bogy off on one side and then the other. It looked as if our task group was right in between these two. And I asked Ralph Davison if he'd like to launch a night fighter, and he said, "Let's see if they really find us or not." And these planes passed down either side of our task force and disappeared to the south of us. But then they stepped over a half space, you see, in coming back. There was one coming right for the task group. And Davison said, "Okay. Launch night fighters." We launched two night fighters, one from each of the two Essex class carriers, and very quickly there was an orange flame over the horizon and down went an Emily flying boat - a beautiful piece of work.

Q: What about the Japanese ability to illuminate at night?

Adm. R.: Many, many times we had lone scouts up there dropping flares, and we were never quite sure that they saw us, of course. Our task group was always in a darkened ship condition, and the task group commander was the only authority, unless they were under immediate attack, of course, who could give permission to open fire. One of our screening destroyers might call in and say he had a good solution, "Permission to open fire," which meant that he had his 5-inch .38's all ready to go, and he had a good fire control solution, and we'd say, "Permission granted," and he'd fire only a few rounds, and the influence fuses, you know, the VT fuses were extremely effective. You could see this stream of 5-inch shells go out, and those next to the plane would burst, and the plane would flame and fall. It was an amazing performance. The combination of waiting until your fire control solution was good, the fellow was close enough for your fire to be truly effective, and you wished to remain "at darken ship" and nothing to disclose your presence until that time, it was obvious that you could shoot this plane down, and the commanding officer of the ship would be allowed to release his guns, and it was just short work, very snappy, quick fire, the airplane would flame, and then again we'd impose silence on the guns.

Q: Did the Japanese develop something similar to the VT fuse?

Adm. R.: To my knowledge, no. They did not. Their anti-aircraft fire, of course, from their ships was quite intense. I didn't have the opportunity to make any attacks myself, but the reports of our pilots, for example, when Yamato made her suicide charge, the aircraft fire was very intense.

Well, may I go on then with the campaign of the Palaus. My first taste of action when returning to the war zone was the raids against ChiChi and Iwo Jima and the Palau operation, and we had to stay behind and cover while Mitscher took three task groups off on over to the Philippines. And when he found the resistance there was much less than he expected, he passed advice up the line and we shifted our war plans from going to Mindanao to an amphibious landing directly into Leyte Gulf. Then we started preparing for that.

As I say, we struck Okinawa, Taiwan, and the fields in the Philippines. And when the amphibious force actually came in, we could see that it was going to be a very great battle. Now this was October of 1944. The Japanese scheme of battle obviously was to bring their forces through the passes in the Philippine Islands where they would have the benefit of land-based air to screen them and make attacks on the opposition, and then to come through these various passes and take on the fleet. By this time it was the 3rd Fleet. Halsey had taken over from Spruance, and Mitscher was still in command, but he was now Task Force 38, instead of 58. If I remember correctly, we had five carrier task groups, one of these, under command of Mat Gardner, was a night carrier task group. And I believe it had Saratoga and two of the CVL's in it.

Well, we were 38.4, I believe, in the southernmost task group. And we found the enemy force which eventually came south around Leyte. We started hitting them way over the other side of the Philippines, in the Sula Sea.

Q: Was that Ozawa's?

Adm. R.: That was Ozawa's. No. Excuse me, it was not Ozawa. Ozawa was to the north. Kurita came through the San Bernardino, and this other outfit was the one that was actually stopped by Oldendorf and company eventually.

Well, we were having pretty good luck, although we were flying at the extreme range of our airplanes, but their forces were approaching, so we worked them over for a time, and we were a little bit disappointed when Mitscher told us to knock it off and concentrate on him up to the north. Meanwhile, he had lost Princeton, a light carrier, and he told us to come north, and we went up and joined up. We had then something like four - excuse me, McCain was off with his task group refueling, replenishing, so that left four task groups, if you counted Mat Gardner's, which was a night task group. And we concentrated on Mitscher up north off the island of Samar.

He had been working over the Kurita outfit, which came

through the Straits of San Bernardino eventually. And we joined in, we got off about two strikes against that force, and one of our flight deck strikes, that from the Enterprise, was the last to leave the scene before dark, and they reported that Musashi, one of the two great, big Japanese battleships with 18-inch guns was sure to sink. They reported that her forecastle was awash and that she must be doomed, that she would go down. This report was not believed. We passed it on and it was not believed in higher echelons, by Halsey and Mitscher. But, in fact, she did sink. It wasn't until collateral intelligence proved this point that we could claim that she actually went under.

Well, strangely enough, Kurita's force reversed course and started steaming away from the scene of action, but then he re-reversed, and meanwhile we all formed up as the 3rd Fleet, orders came from Halsey. It was dark by this time. He said, "Steam west at 25 knots." And we turned our ships west. The carrier task groups were formed on a line of bearing which was normal to the direction of the prevailing wind, which was from the northeast. We steamed west at 25 knots, which seemed to be an interminable time, and finally, I said to Ralph Davison, "Admiral, at about 1 o'clock this evening, we will run aground on the island of Samar!" Admiral Davison smiled and said, "Well, Jerry Bogan will run aground first, won't he?" He was to the west of us, and I said, "Yes, sir, that's right!" So, there was no more conversation. Suddenly in the black of night came the order from Halsey, "Steam north at 25 knots."

Meanwhile, we were getting reports that the enemy forces were coming south around Leyte. Oldendorf's battle had started, and here we were steaming north at 25 knots. The night scouts from Mat Gardner's group had reported that the navigational lights were on in the Straits of San Bernardino. And they also reported that there was a Japanese force there. Halsey came on the voice tactical and asked Mitscher, "What do you make of it?" Halsey didn't talk himself on the voice tactical, and Mitscher seldom did, but I detected the voice of Arleigh Burke, then commodore and chief of staff to Mischer, in an immediate response, and the response was this. "I recommend you form LEO." LEO was the voice call of the old battleship lineup if you had a surface engagement. There was silence, and then the order from Halsey came out, "Form LEO."

And that was Admiral Lee's command, and we watched our battleships, certain of our cruisers, and certain of our destroyers, on the plan position indicator on the radarscope it looked like an amoeba. We were shedding and generating a different force, you see. All our ships carefully threaded their way out through our formation and joined up with the old battle line, the battleships and cruisers in the van and in the rear, destroyers screens and all that, and they formed up off to the east of us. And to our great surprise, they kept steaming north with us. Meanwhile, the night scouts had discovered there was a force to the north of us, and that was Ozawa's force. And as we steamed north, the battle line kept going with us, and we just couldn't believe it! And Davison looked at me and said, "Jim we're playing a helluva dirty trick on the tranports in Leyte Gulf!" And I said, "Do you wish to say anything to Admiral Mitscher?" He said, "No. They have far more intelligence than we do, but this doesn't look right to me." So we steamed north, and we launched a search and a strike practically simultaneously at dawn, and sure enough! Here was Ozawa's force with four carriers, two or more battleships, and a whole flock of smaller ships up north of us. And about that time, in plain English, came through I think from Ziggy Sprague, "I am being shelled by a Japanese battleship!" And this was Kurita's force, steaming south from San Bernardino Strait, which we'd left unplugged, and everybody thought that the Lee's battleships would stay and plug the San Bernardino Straits. But here they were.

Immediately, they were told to steam at maximum speed to San Bernardino Straits, and away they went. Meanwhile, we in the carrier task groups had started working over this force to the north, and it looked like the airplanes, what there were of them, were float planes, and practically no carrier planes. It looked like a cinch, nothing except the antiaircraft from the ships themselves. Now there was Gerry Bogan, F. C. Sherman, and Ralph Davison in those three task groups. McCain, you remember, was off to the east replenishing. Much to Gerry Bogan's disgust, I know, he was told to give air cover to the battleships as they ran south to plug the gap. The wind was from the northeast, and the battleships steaming at maximum speed to the south-southwest were gaining decidedly on Gerry Bogan's task group, because he had to turn his ships into the wind to launch and recover his fighters, which was to the northeast, and the battleships, the big ones, had the same speed as the carriers and they were getting farther and farther apart. Lee sent word over the voice tactical through two linking destroyers - in position for line of sight transmission - "Close up on me." Well, this infuriated Bogan. And it's alleged that Bogan made a remark over the voice tactical which has never been recorded in history to my knowledge, and that is, "You are running away from me. I suggest you retire to the protection of the carrier's guns."

Here was Lee running south with the New Jersey, Iowa, Washington, Massachusetts, Alabama - all these great big battleships, but he had to have fighter cover, and Gerry Bogan was furious because he knew there was pie and cake up to the north, because there was Ozawa's force with no air opposition and just all sitting ducks, you see.

Well, we continued to work this gang over up north - fortunately, we didn't have to attack through fighter cover - and we sank that day the Zuikaku, the Zuiho, Chiyoda, and Chitose, four carriers. And we were hot after Ise and Hyuga, which were running away to the north. We nailed a few lighter ships like cruisers and destroyers, of course. But Ise and Hyuga got away from us. As the wounded carriers got disposed of, the two battleships were steaming at high speed, and they got separated, so it was more and more difficult to cover them with strikes, and when they got up into waters which were reserved for the action of our submarines, we gave up the chase. And they got away, and they were later sunk in Kure Harbor. I saw them on the bottom at the end of the war.

Well, of course, these were very exciting days, and we were very proud of the part we had to play in it, and we were sorry for Gerry Bogan, who had to leave the scene of action to provide air cover for Lee's battleships. Kurita sortied from San Bernardino, attacked our forces off Samar where we lost two CVE's and four destroyer types. Strangely, he broke the action off and went back up to San Bernardino Straits and out before Lee's battleships ever arrived on the scene. His retiring was a great enigma to us until I had the honor of being present when Kurita was interrogated in Tokyo at the end of the war, and that's a story in itself.

Q: Now we'll hear Kurita's story as told at the end of the war.

Adm. R.: We were very anxious to insure that in any interrogations we would get straight information. We found in our interrogations that the Japanese were very polite and very obliging and if you asked them a leading question, the answer was usually yes. For example, Major de Seversky said in effect, "The B-29's were great airplanes," and, of course, the answer was "Yes." "And they won the war, didn't they?" and the answer to that was "Yes, and so on.

Q: No elaboration!

Adm. R.: Well, no. They would dress it up a little bit, but you had to be a little careful. If you asked a leading question, you would probably have an accommodating answer, although they tried to be straight-forward, and, particularly the professional naval officers, were quite interested, like Okumiya, to get the straight story across as to what they did and why.

So we interrogated Kurita, and we interrogated important members of his staff separately. Kurita's story was this. He said, "In the first place, you sank my flag ship." I think it was Atago. You remember the Darter and the Dace over off Palawan had sunk Atago. That was Kurita's flagship, and he shifted his flag to the Yamato. He said, "You knew we were coming. Certainly you would have left none of your transport in Leyte Gulf. You were certainly not that rash! I had sunk four of your Essex class carriers, possibly six." These were battle reports as he received them of the

the sinking of the CVE's. These were not the Essex but as they were reported to him, they were Essex class carriers.

He said, "Having dealt that blow and knowing there was a big battle raging to the north, I went north to join them." He said, "However, when I got opposite the Straits of San Bernardino, I found that my fuel was limited, my destroyers would have run out of fuel by the time we could join the battle, so I gave the order to retire.

Now, we checked this with his staff officers, the stories agreed, they all thought that Kurita had done the right thing. And that's just how far wrong one can be in battle, if you don't get the correct intelligence. He said that they launched float planes from their cruisers to try to scout Leyte Gulf and find out actually what was there, and he said the planes would disappear. Of course, they were being knocked down by our fighters. So he was without information, his assumption was there would be nothing left in Leyte Gulf, he also understood that there were a couple of active airplane strips quickly installed in Leyte, so that he'd have land-base air, as well as our sea based air opposition, and certainly the transports would have gone.

Q: Would have gone where, did he expect?

Adm. R.: Oh, knowing that the main Japanese fleet was coming, they would have scrambled east and all gone to sea. But they were there, of course. The whole amphibious force was there. But he was sure, that knowing the Japanese fleet was coming, we would have dispersed them to the east.

Q: So that was the story and it was verified by his staff members.

Adm. R.: Now Ozawa, on the other hand, his four carriers by this time had become so short of really skilled pilots that he had depended on one strike, and they sank the Princeton, you know, and he put them ashore in the Philippines. Just the skilled pilots were left. It was sad that they had these carriers without proper air groups to go with them. They'd gotten so far down on the reverse side of the power curve on supplying airplanes and pilots that these Japanese carriers were reduced to almost impotency.

Q: In these postwar interrogations, was there any indication that they knew the "jig was up"?

Adm. R.: Ozawa was to lure the 3rd Fleet to the north. Once he'd made his strikes, as he did, (he sank the Princeton) he was supposed to stay around long enough to let the U. S. forces get the scent and start to chase him north.

Q: That was part of the SHO plan. And this was to help

the units coming up from the south.

Adm. R.: That's right. Now this has been pretty well - a chap that was in on the interrogations was Jim Field, and he's written a book on this, and he's quite accurate. If you're interested in it, it's worth reading.

Let me return, then, to Leyte Gulf. After these big battles, things settled down. MacArthur was ashore, and George Kenny, who was MacArthur's air man, said that he wanted the shore-based air, the Army Air Force, to take over all targets ashore, and that the Navy could hit shipping, et cetera. Up to the time, Kenny announced that he was ready to take control of the air over the Philippines, he had been cleaning out methodically all the fields, from the north of the Philippines on down, of Japanese airplanes. Now, I remember one time Dan Smith as air group commander in the Enterprise Air Group, was flying along, over Luzon. He'd always had a penchant to explode a locomotive. And he and his three division mates flying F6F's off the Enterprise were flying low along a railroad track looking for locomotives to blow up. He was so low in fact that he could see under the palm trees! And to his great surprise he saw a large aircraft park. He said hundreds of airplanes under the palm trees concealed by the vegetation from the view overhead, but since he was so low flying over the railroad track, he could look under. He came back, flashed the word, and we set up a big fighter-bomber strike, and went in and burned the vegetation, and burned the airplanes. Our task group was credited with something like one hundred and twenty airplanes on that one strike. These were the sort of things that were going on.

Q: They were stored, they weren't operational at that point.

Adm. R.: They were non-operational due to lack of spare parts, little things. They were hidden under the palm trees there, as a park, until the Japanese could get what was necessary to make the airplanes serviceable.

Q: Were you using napalm at that time?

Adm. R.: Oh, anything. We used bombs, napalm, machine guns, incendiaries. That was one of the strikes, but after Kenny had taken over, we didn't hit fields, and it soon developed that the enemy was getting enough airplanes through to develop some strikes against our forces. We were acting alone as a single task group one day, and our oiler group, which was well off shore, reported being under air attack. We figured that we could just reach the oilers with some fighters, so we set off a flight of fighters for their protection.

About this time, a sizeable kamikaze attack developed against us. Our fighters knocked down all but six, but these six got overhead, and down they came in long slanting dives. The first wave of four took one each of the carriers. The one which dove on the flagship, the Franklin, hit the ship. He dove through the flight deck, burst in the after elevator well, and, of course, set fire to the ship. San Jacinto knocked hers down, Belleau Wood knocked hers down, Enterprise knocked hers down. Then the next two came down, and the first one was shot down by one of the carriers - I've forgotten which. The second one dropped a bomb on us on the Franklin, and we thought, ah hah! he's the fellow who goes home to tell the tale, because usually in these kamikaze attacks, there was one plane that went back - at least one plane to tell the tale.

Q: Oh, really! I didn't know that.

Adm. R.: This had happened to us over in Ulithi atoll when we were attacked by Betty's.

Q: Now this was a predesignated pilot, who was to report on the success.

Adm. R.: That's right. But having dropped two bombs on us and missing us, instead of pulling up, he went at low atltitude across the formation and took Belleau Wood in the fantail. He apparently was aiming at sweeping the deck in a kamikaze attack, but they killed him before he got there, so he dropped down below the flight deck and struck her in the stern. Unfortunately, he hit the ready room of San Jacinto's TBM squadron, and some of the pilots were lost. And there we were with two carriers on fire in the formation, the Belleau Wood and the flagship itself, the Franklin. The Franklin did a very creditable job. She had her fires out, and patched her flight deck using steel plates secured by spike-driving riveting guns. These guns were specially developed to drive a spike that would go through the plate into the deck and secure the plate. Plates covered the hole through the deck, and Franklin was operating airplanes in about twenty minutes!

The fires were put out in the hangar. The body of the kamikaze pilot was recovered. It was held together by his flying suit sufficiently so that you could recognize it was a human; and there was actually a letter in his pocket, which we pulled out and had translated eventually. It was an amazing circumstance. But the damage was done, and although not too serious, it put the after elevator out of commission, because there were long, slender hydraulic plungers damaged, that were used to hoist and lower the elevator, so eventually we had to send her home to get repaired.

Now, the Belleau Wood put her fires out and remained operational. Her flight deck was intact. She did have a fire aft and that was extinguished in short order.

Q: Was any attempt made to examine this body of the kamikaze pilot to see whether he was under the influence of drugs or anything like that?

Adm. R.: No. We recovered a kamikaze pilot, believe it or not, from the water once.

Q: Alive?

Adm. R.: Alive. He was a big, burly fellow. He had bailed out. His plane was loaded with explosives and one thing and another, but he was shot up by a fighter and his plane broke up in the air. He found himself free in the air and parachuted down. One of our destroyers picked him up.

Q: They were equipped with parachutes then.

Adm. R.: This fellow was. And it was a very strange circumstance. He had one wound, a .50 calibre crease across the back of one of his hands, and we put him on sulfa drugs to prevent infection and sent him over in due time to Halsey's flagship, where he was interrogated. Eventually, a carrier leaving the formation took this man back to prison camp. Although he'd been in the fleet quite a long time, perhaps a month or more - much to the surprise of the doctors who examined him on the carrier, it was found that he had just broken out with a case of gonorrhea. So this led to a bit of banter between the skipper of the carrier going home and the commanding officer of the New Jersey. A message passed saying, "Your little yellow man has just come down with a case of gonorrhea. What sort of a brothel do you run on your ship? We understand the period of incubation is nine days!" We had put him on sulfa drugs, which suppressed the disease, and when on New Jersey they took him off, there was time for the disease to get the better of his system, and develop.

Q: Well, was there any information of any value obtained from him?

Adm. R.: Not very much, not very much. We took other POW's. After a Betty attack once, we picked up three survivors. They were picked up by a destroyer. In refueling, we were alongside the oiler, the destroyer was on one side, our carrier flagship on the other, and the three POW's were transferred from the destroyer to the oiler. However, when the first fellow got in the boatswain's chair to come across on the high line to us, he got halfway between the oiler and our carrier, where he slipped his safety belt, slid into the sea, and committed suicide right in front of us. So the next two we lashed into the chair so they couldn't get loose, to bring them over to the flagship.

The kamikaze business, of course, was a strange development and one that really had us worried, as we were receiving hits that we wouldn't have received if it had been any other style of attack.

Q: Was that your introduction to it on the Franklin at that point?

Adm. R.: Yes. That was in November of '44, I believe. Later, when Admiral Davison was out for a brief leave, during the time of the Lingayen Gulf affair, the Japanese really developed their kamikaze attacks. And that's also when the fast carriers went over into the China Sea. We missed that exercise, and our next effort was then against Iwo, and ultimately against Okinawa.

Q: You missed the battle of the Philippine Sea, too?

Adm. R.: Yes, I came out to the Fleet just after the Philippine Sea. That event was in early June of '44, and I got there late June or early July of '44. I missed the "turkey shoot."

Well, it was wonderful duty. Ralph Davison was very considerate of his captains. He usually engaged in a bit of banter with them when they would join up. Every once in a while he'd send us to the dictionary to decipher what his words in a personally drafted message really meant. He accused, I think, Tex Weller of meretricious conduct, when Tex tried to get an extra night fighter from the replenishment group and we looked up "meretricious". One of the meanings we found was "of or pertaining to prostitution." And in another case he accused someone of a "retromingent act". And do you know what "retromingent" means, Dr. Mason?

Q: No. Retromingent - no, I don't know that.

Adm. R.: It's the ability to project excretion forward like a skunk! Well, you can see what fun we had with Ralph Davison! A very learned man, cool as a cucumber in battle and very considerate of his commanding officers of ships. He had me fly a TBM three hundred miles into Manus one time, when our next task group replenishment was to be in Manus. We got requisitions from all the ships of our task group as to what they needed, and I took all these requisitions in, flew in to the field at Manus, and got the logistic authorities there to have lighters arranged at each ship's anchorage. Thus when our task group arrived the next day there were lighters waiting when a ship anchored, and what that ship ordered was on a lighter ready immediately to come alongside. It was really a tremendous show. Sort of the ultimate in consideration for the forces under your command. Unfortunately, this was not the custom. Ordinarily a skipper was left to fend for himself in these logistic arrangements. But not so with Ralph Davison. He was a very considerate man, a very wonderful man. He had one fault. He liked his whiskey.

And in Ulithi, for example, he'd go ashore and he would be mellow most of the time we were in port. But we'd get him out to sea, and he was terrific under attack, cool as a cucumber, a really wonderful, wonderful commander. Many times he'd come back to the ship, and I'd have the operation order for the next sortie all written out and ready to go, and I would say, "Admiral, here's the operation order." And he would smile at me and say, "Where do I sign?" And I would say, "Admiral, this is going to be a very serious operation. I would strongly recommend you would read at least part of this operation order before you sign it, the main part of it." And he would smile at me and say in his pleasant alcoholic euphoria, "Oh, what's a chief of staff for?" And he would sign it! He'd read it after we got to sea. A wonderful fellow! I just can't say enough for the way he conducted his job at sea.

Q: Well, this sort of let-down was a necessity for men under such great strain, was it not?

Adm. R.: Yes, I suppose so, I suppose so.

Well, let's see. There was the battle of Leyte Gulf. Then there was Iwo Jima, which was a pretty hot affair. And then, eventually, Okinawa.

Q: Well, tell me about Iwo Jima.

Russell #2 - 196

Adm. R.: Well, Iwo Jima, of course - the job was to get the Marines ashore safely. We raided the islands to the north. We raided the home islands.

Q: Standing off how far?

Adm. R.: From the home islands? Oh, about one hundred miles, maybe, something like that.

The heavy raids against the home islands were made in preparation for the landings on Okinawa. But I'm quite sure, and I'd have to check these dates, but I think we raided the Kanto plain around Tokyo prior to Iwo.

Q: Now, sir, you were going to tell me just a bit more about the kamikaze phenomena in the war. You said that you recently, last year, visited the museum in Tokyo, dedicated to them.

Adm. R.: A museum, indeed. I had visited the old Imperial Japanese Naval Academy when I had a small task group in Kure Harbor in 1954, and I was very desirous of showing my wife, Gerry, the place. And Admiral Samejima, the current Chief Maritime Staff, very kindly arranged a trip for us. He loaned us his aide, Commander Inoue, and we went to Hiroshima. We were to go by air, but the weather was such that we had to go by train.

We were met there by a Japanese naval car and taken to

the ferry and crossed to the island to Eta Jima, which is the site of the Japanese Naval Academy. Vice Admiral Mogami, who was commander of the First Service School, gave a dinner party for us in his quarters - a very nicely planned dinner party at which he and his wife were present, and also Vice Admiral and Mrs. Ishikure. Vice Admiral Ishikure is in command of the officer candidate school. The young officers in the Japanese armed services all go through the Defense Academy, which is south of Yokosuka on Tokyo Bay, and those who are going into the Navy attend the old Naval Academy for a year of training in naval things. This is the school which Vice Admiral Ishikure commands.

In addition, they train technical petty officers there, and they have a boys' school, so-called. It's a recruit school. So there are three activities there now - a great point of interest. Well, after the dinner party at Admiral Mogami's quarters, which was beautifully done, we were billeted that evening in the Eta Jima Club, and were told that morning formation would be at 7, and the admirals would be very happy to have us join them to witness the morning assembly.

We did that. Incidentally, we were wakened at about 6 o'clock in the morning hearing what I thought was a mob scene, shouting voices and a confusion of noise, which lasted about five minutes, and then there was the toot of a bosun's pipe, and it stopped just as suddenly as it began. So I asked Admiral Ishikure at morning formation what had happened.

I thought perhaps there was a mob assembled at the gates. He said no, not at all. He said, When our young officer candidates rise in the morning, we have them drill for five minutes giving commands." And this was the hubbub we heard from our billet!

Q: Similar to the plebes in plebe summer, who shout all over the place.

Adm. R.: Well, we went back to our quarters for breakfast, and then visited the Japanese Naval Academy Museum, a beautiful old building, where we were given the great privilege of visiting the shrine of Admiral Togo and Admiral Yamamoto. The shrine is in an alcove. Steps covered with white canvas lead up to the shrine. We entered the shrine and the upper half of a bronze sphere was unscrewed from its base. Inside the sphere were two vacuum tubes, a lock of Admiral Togo's hair in one tube and a lock of Admiral Yamamoto's hair in the other. These relics were treated with great reverence, showed to us, and restored to their position. Then the bronze hemisphere was again screwed down over them.

Q: Admiral Yamamoto was lost at sea, was he not?

Adm. R.: No. He was shot down over the jungle, but his body was recovered. He was shot down by two P-38 pilots, who at an appointed spot at an appointed time shot him down.

Well, there is much in the way of art work and memorabilia from the Russo-Japanese War of 1905 - many scenes from that in one room.

Then there was the Kamikaze Room. The Kamikaze Room is a sizeable room, which had at one end on the wall the personal flag of Vice Admiral Arima, who was the leader of the Kamikaze Corps. It was explained to us that he committed suicide by diving his airplane into a carrier on 15 October, 1944, which began the kamikaze movement. The room was filled with memorabilia of the various pilots who sacrificed themselves for the Empire - photographs, letters, even flight equipment, and things of this sort.

Q: These were all officers, were they?

Adm. R.: As far as I know they were officers. There were a number of enlisted pilots in the Navy, too, but I don't know whether kamikaze was an exercise restricted to commissioned officers or not. I don't know.

The other end of the room, however, was devoted to the kaiten, the little submarines that, you remember, got through the nets and inside Pearl Harbor at the time of the attack on Pearl Harbor. And out in the museum yard is one of the little submarines, which was apparently raised by the U. S. Navy in Pearl Harbor and given as a gift to the Academy for the museum.

It was quite obvious that the Japanese hold in great reverence those men who sacrificed themselves as kamikaze pilots, and their acts are held up as examples to the young officers in training as being the supreme objective of service to their country. It's a greatly respected activity.

Q: Did you have any conversations at that time or when you were a member of the survey team with Japanese officers who indicate the psychology of this whole thing?

Adm. R.: Yes. It's quite simple. They were rather desperate. Japan was in great danger, and sacrificing their lives for their country was considered the thing to do.

Q: These were all volunteers for these missions.

Adm. R.: They were volunteers, yes, but I can imagine that if one was available for such a mission and refused it, he would be in great disgrace. I do know from interrogating our prisoners of war, particularly the submariners, whom we captured from the RO-61, in the Aleutians, that they were quite willing to talk, because they figured they'd never be accepted again in society in Japan. It was just unthinkable that they would surrender.

As a matter of fact, I had an interesting experience with a major in the Japanese army. My interrogations in

Tokyo at the end of the war were largely with the Japanese naval officers, because, after all, we were in the naval analysis division of the U. S. Strategic Bombing Survey. I was interested in reconstructing the size of the garrisons on the various islands. We knew that there were about 2500 Japanese men, soldiers, on Attu. On Kiska, it was reported that the Japanese had a garrison of 5400 men. They were the ones who disappeared in the fog, who had already evacuated when we landed on Kiska with some 35,000 troops in August of 1943.

But I was interested in reconstructing the strength of the garrisons - Kiska, Attu, and in the Kurile Islands. The chap who was recommended to me as knowing these numbers was a beautiful specimen of humanity - a Japanese major in the Army - a handsome fellow, large for a Japanese, and husky. And he came in to be interrogated, obviously a little bit disturbed, not knowing what might happen to him, but when he discovered we were very friendly, he unlimbered a bit; and when it was explained to him what I wanted, he said, "Well, if Captain Russell will permit, I will return to the War Department and I will have those figures tomorrow." So I bade farewell to him and away he went.

The next day he came back and his figures were so perfect I was a little suspicious that he might have invented them, or "gun decked" them, as we would say in the Navy. When the garrison on Attu came, to a total of about 2500 men, I thought perhaps I had best let him know that I had a means of checking his figures. So I said, "Well, this looks quite right in the case of Attu, because there were so many counted dead and twenty-four prisoners of war for a total of almost the same figure that you have." There was no change in that man's facial expression whatsoever, but that statement bounced. He said did he understand the captain to say correctly that there were twenty-four soldiers of the Empire captured on Attu? Talking through the interpreter, I said yes, that was correct. And again it bounced. And this time he said, "Well, would the captain please not say that were not all those who were captured very severely injured?" And I saw what he was getting at. He wouldn't believe that a soldier of the Empire would surrender. He just wouldn't believe it. And knowing his problem, I said, "Hell, tell him yes, and let's get on with the interrogation." But that was the Japanese Army - absolutely uncompromising. No surrender, and if they did surrender, they were forever disgraced in their home communities and never to return to Japan.

Q: Well, now, the kamikaze attitude doesn't stack up with our concept of duty to country, does it?

Adm. R.: No. We would like to at least give a man a chance to survive his action. It's a much more comforting feeling to know that you have some chance of coming away from it.

Q: Is that not why it was so difficult to comprehend their mission and to deal with it?

Adm. R.: It was extremely serious, and the picket stations, you know, when the Japanese started taking on our ships on picket stations off Okinawa, it was a very serious thing. We were losing ships, and it was very tough. As a matter of fact a great number of our carriers were kamikazed. Clare Miller, who served as my torpedo plane officer in the Bureau of Aeronautics in 1943-'44, was killed when a kamikaze struck the superstructure of the carrier in which he was on duty.

Well, perhaps I should go on. You asked to have a little more information on the Iwo business. We did raid the home islands, and many attacks occurred against us, and frequently we had a ring-side seat, because if I remember correctly we were 58.3, and we had Radford in 58.4 on one wing, and perhaps Jocko Clark or some other task group commanders on the other side, so that we were spared in their attacks. They attacked the ends of our formation. And I saw some beautifully executed attacks. You just couldn't believe that a Betty, for example, would survive under the fire that was concentrated on it. He'd get so close to the ship, and finally he just "creamed" himself, and wound up in a cascade of fire along the surface of the sea, but very close to the ship. And we had casualties, actually two, shooting across the formation and striking our own ships. So your tin hat, and decks and bulkheads with light armor were desirable things to have. I'm sure that at the time of the great fire on the Franklin, when we eventually shifted Admiral Davison and his staff, those of us who survived, to the Hancock, I'm almost sure that Admiral Mat Gardner, who joined the task group in Enterprise, was burned off his flag bridge by one of our own rounds of ammunition. As a kamikaze took on the Enterprise in a practically vertical dive and you could see the guns leading the target. I saw one shell land on the water half way between us and the Enterprise. I actually think it was one of our own shells that set fire to the ammunition locker that burned him off his bridge.

Q: About this time, units of the Royal Navy joined the fleet out there.

Adm. R.: Yes. They were in a task group or task force to themselves, and when we were going in to Okinawa, I'm not certain just when they arrived on the scene, but they covered the Taiwan side of the picture. They took one flank and we took the other. We raided the home islands and the chain of islands going down to Okinawa, and they operated down to the other side, so if any reinforcements were coming up from Taiwan, they could intercept them.

Q: How did they meld into our operation?

Adm. R.: Very well. They were flying our airplanes, you know.

Q: What about the logistics of the units in the Royal Navy? They were so accustomed to land-based refueling.

Adm. R.: I believe that they developed underway refueling just as we did. I have exercised with Canadian destroyers, Australian destroyers, Dutch destroyers, and except for occasionally having to have a special fitting on the other end of an oil hose, to fit their plumbing, it was done well and in an alongside method. I was not privileged to operate with them, to be in their ships, but we did have Commander Dick Smeeton, who retired as a vice admiral in the Royal Navy, with us in many of our operations. He was very astute in forecasting the outcome of our battles. He's now the head of the Farnborough Air Show which is held every other year - Vice Admiral Sir Richard Smeeton. He and Betty, his lovely wife, were in residence in the States when I was in the Bureau of Aeronautics in '43, '44, and we also had Commander Frank Hopkins, and Casper John, who retired as Admiral of the Fleet, Sir Casper John. He eventually became the First Sea Lord. All these, incidentally, were naval aviators in the Royal Navy. Another one, Dennis Campbell was a very fine fellow. He'd been in ordnance test at Boscombe Down. We enjoyed their company very much.

Well, now, Iwo Jima. We were in support. We interposed between the home islands and Iwo. We raided ChiChi and other places to the north, and we struck the Kanto plain for the first time. That is the plain on which Tokyo lies. All in all, it was a very successful operation. The casualties ashore were heavy, because of the dug-in positions of the Japanese forces on the island. As a matter of fact, even after the island was announced as being secure, there were people coming out of caves, making raids on our people.

I remember one incident at night when we were cruising along, and task groups were operating independently, but we could hear over voice tactical radio what was going on in the other task groups. F. C. Sherman was under attack and did some very adroit maneuvering. He passed out a compliment to his task group units congratulating them on their expert maneuvering to avoid attack. Meanwhile, we'd been under attack, too, and one of our destroyers had announced that he had a good fire control solution, - also, one of our cruisers. We knocked down two airplanes. So, not to be outdone by Admiral Sherman, Admiral Davison came on the voice tactical to our task group and, giving the voice call of the cruiser and the destroyer, said, "Congratulations on your shooting!"

After Iwo Jima, the next exercise was preparation for the amphibious landings on Okinawa. If I remember correctly, D-Day was the first day of April, 1945.

Q: Did you have conferences with the other task force commanders in preparation for an operation of this sort?

Adm. R.: We did. We were at anchor in Ulithi atoll and Mitscher sent for all his task group commanders and chiefs of staff, and we reported to the flagship. We were given the general lay of the land and what was about to transpire and details of that sort, intelligence, our own operational plan, and so forth. I remember particularly on that meeting that I had a conference with Arleigh Burke, who was Mitscher's chief of staff, and I told him what we would do, knowing there were going to be pretty hot battles, what we would propose to do if we had one or more of our carriers on fire in our formation.

Burke impressed me very strongly with Mitscher's desire that he lose no more aircraft carriers. He had lost Princeton, and he wanted that to be the last loss of an aircraft carrier in World War II. So I explained to Arleigh Burke our plan, which was first of all, if a carrier was on fire, that we were counselling our skippers to put the carrier into a tight turn to starboard. A carrier of the Essex class lists outboard in her turn, and putting her in a tight turn to starboard would slope the decks to port away from ship control on the island, the conflagration control stations in the hangar and the repair lockers on the flight deck which were on the starboard side in those days, the main intake for air to the machinery spaces which was below the island on the starboard side of the ship. Listing a ship in that way would carry any flaming gasoline over the side of the ship away from the part that was more useful, you see.

We had two cruisers paired off for each carrier, depending upon their position in the task group formation, one to go to the aid of the carrier to assist as possible with fire hoses and repair parties from alongside, the other cruiser to take the cripple in tow, if she had lost power. In those days, we had a circular screen of about twenty-four destroyers, which was the anti-submarine screen, the outer screen also against aircraft, but primarily against submarines using their underwater sonars. Four destroyers, assigned according to whatever position they had in formation, had the duty of screening the cripple.

I explained all this to Arleigh Burke and he said, "This looks good to me, Jim. I think that's the best you can do." Then he reiterated that Mitscher wanted to lose no more aircraft carriers.

Q: I interrupt at this point to ask, and perhaps this is the logical place to ask you to discuss preparations for damage control in these carriers other than what you've just said. I mean the training of men, and so forth.

Adm. R.: Yes. Damage control training, of course, was heavily stressed. We had damage control schools ashore. We had firefighting where they actually set fire to various structures. We had gasoline fires, we had oil fires and whatnot in the schools, and the men were drilled on how to put fires out.

On the carriers one of the most vulnerable commodities, of course, was the high-test aviation gasoline which we carried. Gasoline was carried in saddle tanks, so-called. A saddle tank was constructed with a central, more or less cylindrical tank, and then a saddle around that, and again a saddle around the saddle. In no case was their air and gasoline in the same compartment together. The gasoline was displaced by salt water, which was pumped in and provided the pressure to force the gasoline up to the refueling stations on hangar and flight decks.

Q: And how many gallons would one of these saddle tanks contain?

Adm. R.: I used to know. The amount of gas was computed for rather intensive operations and it was a balance between the amount of ammunition you had, the gasoline for flying and your own fuel, and so forth. Just how much, I've forgotten - a goodly number of tons, of course. But, as I say, the aviation gasoline was displaced by salt water, and displacement occurred first in the outer saddle. So that as you drained down your gasoline, you wound up with a salt water blanket around the interior tank. And then the inboard saddle tank was next to be exhausted of fuel, and finally, you got down to the core. You never got below about 5 percent of fuel, because you began to get a mixture of gasoline and water, if you got too low, you see. But the gasoline was very carefully filtered at the outlet to prevent water from getting into the aircrafts' fuel tanks. It was very necessary, of course, to have a pure supply of fuel for the aircraft.

So that was one protection, but the whole vertical trunk where the pumps and piping were, was protected. Electric motors drove pumps through stuffing boxes in a bulkhead, so that there would be no electric motors to make sparks in the trunk. But also the whole trunk, which contained the fuel system, the aviation fuel system, could be flooded with CO-2 gas. There were big storage cylinders of the gas, and if you pulled the right ripcord, you would just flood the whole trunk, and fill it with the inert gas, CO-2.

Also, when we fueled aircraft, the moment we finished refueling, the gasoline which was up to the hoses was put back into the system. By pumping water out, you sucked the gasoline down all the risers back into the tanks, so there was no gasoline above the storage space. Flight deck and hangar crews were also very careful; if there was any gasoline spilled on the deck it had to be swabbed up immediately.

Then as far as firefighting was concerned, there was foam, fog, and regular salt water through fire hoses on the flight deck. In the hangar there were water curtains which were just a sheet of water, and then, of course, later we started having hangar doors to divide the hangar into spaces, but overhead in the hangar there were sprinklers that gave a regular tropical rainstorm in the hangar if they were cut loose. And here in the hangar again, you see, there were conflagration stations, sealed in cubicles with thick glass ports, from which all the firefighting devices in the hangar could be controlled. Of course, there was form and fog and whatnot in the hangar, too, which could be applied manually. Each bay of the hangar had its conflagration control station. The men stationed there could see what was going on in the hangar and by remote control could turn on the valves which would do the sprinkling. Curtaining and so forth.

Magazines, of course, were floodable - could be sprinkled or flooded. These were the principal damage control features. The training of the men, of course, as I say, was intensive, and this all paid off.

Q: How large a crew would you have on an *Essex* class carrier devoted to this particularly?

Adm. R.: Devoted only to this? I really can't say. But

the total crew in those days ran somewhere between 2500 and 3000 men.

Q: I was thinking of the damage control element.

Adm. R.: I really wouldn't know. As a matter of fact, any man was a damage control man. There were specialists, but the entire crew were also trained. Damage control was one of the standard drills. Fire on the flight deck, you know, and you'd run everything out and test everything, make sure you'd got fog and foam, you'd put the foam over the side to keep the ship clean, and you'd be timed as to how quickly the foam arrived at the scene - many drills.

Q: Well, thank you for that picture, because I think that's interesting.

Adm. R.: It's of interest, because, as I say, we explained to Burke what our task group plan was with a carrier on fire. And that very exercise we raided the whole coast of Japan, really, and our sector was down around Kyushu and Shikoku. We started attacking airfields on the island of Kyushu (Izumi, Kagoshima, and Miyakonoji). We hit Kobe and the Osaka area from an area at sea south of Shikoku, on the second day.

Q: Were there any verboten targets?

Russell #2 - 213

Adm. R.: Not that I remember. Of course, the intelligence officer set up the target list - there were no just city targets or anything like that. They were all military targets.

Q: You spoke of the Kanto plain attacks around Tokyo. Were those firebomb attacks?

Adm. R.: Aircraft factories, usually largely bombed. I remember there was an automotive factory, oil complexes, fuel storage. Aviation facilities, of course, had the primary attention. We always aimed at securing as nearly as possible control of the air first before we hit the other targets. But I remember there were many plants, industrial plants on the Kanto plain that were our targets.

Q: In these latter-day raids, from what you learned later with your survey team, were you being more effective than you had been previously on some of the hit-and-run raids on the mainland?

Adm. R.: Well, let me say this. There were certain places that were not damaged very much. I was surprised, for example, that the First Naval Air Technical Arsenal at Yokosuka didn't have more damage, but it was explained that the place was usually under cloud cover, whereas other places like

Kisarazu and places to the north, which had much better weather as far as bombing was concerned, were thoroughly plastered.

Leaving Ulithi, in preparation for the Okinawa affair, we had back our regular flagship, CV-13, the Franklin. And with her, Hancock (CV-19), San Jacinto (CVL-30), and Bataan (CVL-29); plus two battleships (Washington and North Carolina); three cruisers (Baltimore, Pittsburgh and Santa Fe); and 17 destroyers. We were Task Group 58.2. We hit Kobe, as I say and I had the experience of looking at one of the strike photographs and recognizing the pier alongside which I had been in 1920 as a merchant seaman in the harbor of Kobe.

There were two large ships which we believed to have been aircraft carriers that we sank. They were finishing up construction at buoys out in the harbor at Kobe. And generally, it was a pretty satisfying plastering of the facilities of Japan.

Q: What kind of opposition did you meet from land-based defenses?

Adm. R.: Sporadic, sometimes pretty heavy. I remember on the Kanto plain raids in February, we lost Phil Torrey, the son of the Marine general. Phil was shot down probably by an enemy airplane.

Q: And batteries of anti-aircraft guns as well.

Russell #2 - 215

Adm. R.: Yes. There's some question. It may have been anti-aircraft that got him, but he obviously was killed in the cockpit, because the plane, as observed by his wing man, did various gyrations indicating that he just wasn't there. He was killed or inoperative. Strangely enough, we found his ashes in a village east of Tokyo Bay, where they were enshrined in the local Shinto shrine with a simple label. It was translated as Phil Tolley, and I couldn't be sure that it was Phil Torrey until I got a good translation of it, which said, "Here lie the ashes of a brave American flyer."

Q: And the name.

Adm. R.: And the name, yes. But it was translated to me as Phil Tolley.

Well, we had done a strike against the island of Kyushu, the fields there, and on the morning of the 19th we were up and more or less hitting the island of Shikoku. At 7 o'clock in the morning, our first flight deck strike was returning to the ship, and unknown to us it was being accompanied by a Val, I believe, a two-seater dive bomber, who was trailing the flight deck strike back to the ship.

Q: A kind of a sneakthief effort, was it?

Adm. R.: He was all by himself, and there was a 2000-foot

ceiling, and apparently he was stitching in and out of the clouds. He'd duck down just to make sure he was still with the air group and come back up again. And we changed our tactics as a result of this thing quite a bit, and I'll tell you about that later - such things as keyholes and tomcats, pickets, and one thing and another.

We were half way through the launch of the second flight deck strike at 7 o'clock in the morning, and suddenly this lone plane started a dive on the Franklin. The Franklin didn't pick up this fact. You see, they were fairly green. They'd come back from Bremerton Navy Yard, as a matter of fact, and this was their first action.

Q: Was it a different crew from what had gone back?

Adm. R.: Oh, yes, quite. Quite a turnover. A new skipper, had taken her back, injured, to the Navy Yard, when the old skipper, Jimmy Shoemaker, was relieved out in the forward area. Gehres had taken her back to the Yard, and he was with her coming back. He was very anxious to do a good job.

Hancock, across the formation from Franklin, came on the voice tactical and said in effect, "Hey! You're being dived on!" Then a Val came zipping across the flight deck and released two bombs, about 250-kilo bombs. They didn't miss the centerline of the flight deck by more than ten feet, went into the hangar, and burst, at least one of them, at at the optimum height above the hangar, to split the light armor on the hangar deck. This meant that the ship was exposed down to the second deck. Of course, the sprinkling system was cut on right away, and this made a tremendous deluge of water, part of which drained down into the second deck spaces.

The skipper did put the ship into the doctrine turn to starboard to list her to port and they started fighting the fires. The captain made the mistake, however, of steadying down on a course directly to the south, and the wind was from the northeast. This put the burning airplanes back aft, those that were still remaining to be launched, upwind, which enveloped the ship in choking black smoke. The air group commander, Commander Parker, and his fighter wing man, who had just been launched, streaked across and knocked this fellow down. He was shot down. We were on the flag bridge when the skipper steadied down with the wind on his port quarter. Davison observed this for a while, and finally he said, "Well, Jim, would you present my compliments to the skipper and suggest that he put his ship into the wind, so that he can get his fires under control." I wasn't sure whether the gasoline system on the ship was leaking and causing the big fires or whether it was just from the ruptured tanks of the airplane, because by this time the ordnance on the airplanes had started blowing up. Later I found out that the crew had properly secured the gasoline system. It was down to the tank tops, and the fires were all being fed by the gasoline which was in the aircraft.

Various pieces of ordnance were exploding - there were 1000-pound and other size bombs. Also we were using Tiny Tim's that day for the first time; Tiny Tim's were 12-inch diameter rockets with explosive warheads just like 500-pound bombs. I remember as those things cooked off, you'd hear a whisht, a 12-inch rocket would go by the bridge, and you'd see it splash in the sea way up ahead of the ship - fortunately, on the flight deck the F4U fighter armed with Tiny Tim, in a three point attitude had his nose up a bit which accounted for the harmless trajectory. However, we had about four of these F4U's, with Tiny Tims on them, down in the hangar, and when 12-inch rockets are ricocheting around the hanger, it's quite another matter.

Well, we had advised the skipper when he was in Bremerton, to get a number of fireproof ladders - chain with metal rungs, and metal doughnuts to keep the hand grip away from the side-plating of the ship. He had these stowed at various places along the side of the ship and around the island structure. So, with this direction from Admiral Davison, I cut the stops on one of these ladders above us, and it unrolled down over the side. Using it, I climbed to the navigating bridge, presented the Admiral's compliments to the skipper, and suggested that he turn the ship to put the wind on the starboard bow. He did, but he turned the long way 'round, and it seemed ages before the smoke began to clear the island.

While I was still on the bridge, the engine room reported that the ingestion of smoke through the intakes of the machinery spaces was so heavy that they figured they'd have to abandon. The captain, I remember, told them to set their throttles and abandon the engine rooms. She burned and exploded for some time. The four destroyers which were cut out to screen her joined and two of them set about rescuing people, in various odd places around the ship, where they were cut off or enveloped in fire.

One of them, for example, the Marshall or the Hickox would put her nose right in against the side of the ship, and trapped men would jump aboard from the hangar deck or from the side of the ship leaving all behind them enveloped in flames. Many of the men went over the side. They'd come up from down below, find themselves surrounded by fire, and over the side they'd go. A destroyer was combing the wake, picking them up out of the water. The cruiser to render alongside aid was Sante Fe. Santa Fe came in with great gallantry, put herself alongside almost like a motor boat, started hoses and began taking the injured across between the two ships.

Q: How were you involved during this period?

Adm. R.: We were up on the flag bridge, the radio circuits all went dead, and we were just useless appendages. We had only a fraction of the staff there. We didn't know what had happened to others of the staff. I knew that our intelligence officer had been killed, a bomb blast had broken the door down and he was killed at his desk just below the island. There was smoke welling up through the island structure into the spaces, and we were just spare parts, really.

What we didn't know was that a good number of people were down on the forecastle. They worked their way up and started to help fight the fires on the flight deck eventually.

So, after about an hour and a half of this, Santa Fe was alongside rendering aid, and Pittsburgh at hand to take Franklin in tow. This evolution went off very well, and I suggested to Davison that he should go over with what staff he had, put his flag in the Hancock, and get fighters in the air to protect Franklin, because she was a regular beacon with all that smoke going up to high altitude.

Q: Was there any danger from submarines?

Adm. R.: Yes, but as I say, the task group was reformed and we had four destroyers around us as an anti-submarine screen, and the two cruisers. The Admiral was a little loath to leave. However, he went up and said farewell to Gehres, came down, we got a line over, and went over to the Marshall, and the Marshall took us over to the Hancock, our other Essex class carrier in the formation, and we regrouped the task group. Mat Gardner joined in Enterprise,

Russell #2 - 221

because Mitscher was not sure that Davison was still alive, looking at all the explosions going off on the Franklin. Mitscher called off all the strikes except those against air fields and airplanes in order to concentrate on getting the Franklin out.

She was in tow and in pretty good shape and started slowly to head south toward Ulithi. A number of attacks developed against us. I remember one kamikaze attack aimed obviously at Hancock. We found one of our destroyers, the Halsey Powell, was a little low on fuel, and we always tried to keep the destroyers up to 65% fuel. Halsey Powell was alongside refueling from Hancock when this kamikaze attack developed. She'd just broken away, was accelerating, and had seven degrees left rudder on. She had been alongside the starboard side of the carrier. The kamikaze which aimed for the deck of the Hancock missed the Hancock, obviously was killed somewhere in his dive, but he hit the Halsey Powell in the fantail. Halsey Powell's rudder was jammed at seven degrees left, and as she accelerated, she came right across and we watched her disappear under the forward end of the flight deck. We all held our breath while the skipper of the Hancock backed emergency full, until she came out in one piece over on the port side.

We were tremendously relieved. She found she could make 14 knots steering with her engines against her jammed rudder, but if she went any faster than that, all she did was make circles. So we told off one of the other destroyers in the task group to escort her and head for Guam, and we put a fighter patrol over her until she got well clear of our action area.

Well, there were many events like that, and as I explained, Gardner had taken over temporarily the command of the task group. Davison, who was senior, told him to continue with control of the task group until we could get reorganized on Hancock. But meanwhile, in a kamikaze attack, he was burned off his flag bridge. So Davison then took over. And I didn't explain that Davison was in the process of turning over his command to Jerry Bogan, who had been on leave and had just come back, and he was with us. Both our fighter director officers, for example, were killed. It was too bad that we had the two staffs, and the two admirals on board the Franklin at the time she was hit.

Q: Was Bob Pirie with you?

Adm. R.: No. Bob had left, and had been replaced by a new chief of staff, Al Morehouse, a chap who was a couple of years senior to Bob, actually, a very fine fellow.

Well, Jerry Bogan, bless his heart - I was setting up a watch list, knowing how short-handed we were, he said, "I'm qualified to stand a watch." Well, here's a rear admiral, a former task group commander, and the one to take over the

the task group shortly, volunteering to take his turn on watch at the voice tactical and all the other things we had to do as staff officers to control the whole task group. Which I thought was really a wonderful thing. Jerry was a tremendous fighter, you know, a great guy.

Well, to go on with the story of the Franklin, and this would be better told by someone who was actually aboard her, because we had left after about an hour and a half. The boiler division officer organized a party of volunteers and went below early in the afternoon. And he got steam up in one of the boilers, and from there he got more boilers on the line, and she began to get power on her main propulsion. By noon the next day she was making 15 knots using two of her four screws. Meanwhile, Mitscher had sent additional ships to us and we organized a task unit 58.2.9, which we called the Salvage Unit, comprised of Franklin, 2 CBs (Guam and Alaska), 2 cruisers (Pittsburg and Santa Fe), and eleven destroyers, unit commander Rear Admiral Low.

Q: Were her fires out by that time?

Adm. R.: Smoldering and one thing and another. But the amazing thing was she never did get the other two screws in commission, I don't believe. You see, there are four propellers on an Essex class carrier, and she had two out of four, and she was making 25 knots with them. It was a pretty good show.

Perhaps the fellow who has the most thorough - there have been books written about Franklin, of course - but Steve Jurika, who was navigator and in a position to be on the bridge with the skipper, probably was the best informed of all the details as to what was going on. Well, I didn't see her again until we got down to Ulithi, when the new chief of staff, Morehouse, and I went aboard, and we found that the ship had the boat crane in commission. Using it we went aboard in a bosun's chair. Everyone who came aboard went before a reception committee. The skipper was determined he'd take nobody from his crew back aboard who'd gone over the side, which I thought was a little bit unnecessary.

Q: Enveloped in flames, should they stay aboard?

Adm. R.: And get burned to death? Should think they'd hit the sea! But he was intent on taking only those people who remained aboard. He knew he'd go back to a repair yard. Actually, the ship went all the way back to New York, to the Brooklyn Navy Yard. She never did get back in service, you know, in the war.

Well, that was the end of my fighting in the fast carriers

Russell #2 - 225

because Davison was detached at Ulithi, and went back to Pearl Harbor, where he was given the Distinguished Service Medal and what not by Admiral Towers, who was deputy CinCPac at the time. And I was relegated to the job of a staff man with Towers.

Q: You went back as far as Pearl with Davison?

Adm. R.: Yes. But here it was the end of April, May coming up, and it was very pleasant duty with Towers. He's a wonderful fellow, but, as you know, he had a disagreement with King a long time ago, which is rather an interesting story, and I think it's probably appropriate to recite it here as he told it to me.

He said there was a party at the Coronado Hotel, and King was, he thought, a little boisterous and unseemly in his conduct and talking too loudly. They met in the toilet and had words, and Towers called him a "penny whistle." And Towers said to me, "Jim, that was one great mistake in my career! The fellow went on to be Cominch, and here I am denied a combat command because of a personal dislike on the part of Cominch!"

But, came one night when a dispatch arrived in which Nimitz offered Towers the 5th Fleet, and of course he took it right now, but by this time he could see it was just about the end of the war. And John Henry Newton came in as deputy CinCPac, and he didn't have any use, really, for an aviation aide. Things were very quiet back there at the rear headquarters.

Q: What were your actual duties?

Adm. R.: Reading dispatches, briefing dispatches, arranging new schedules, and that sort of business - aviation plans.

Q: Did you meet carriers coming back?

Adm. R.: Oh, sure, yes. I tried to maintain contact with the operators as much as I could and learn their experience and how could we help out, and so forth. We went over the war plans for the landings on Kyushu and on the Kanto plain, and I have never seen anyone read so fast as Admiral Towers. I flew with him out to Guam one time, and he read the war plans and tossed them to me to read, and I spent at least four times as long as he did, and I thought, "Gee! Does this man really understand what's in this thing?" And I started asking him some questions, and he knew. He had read it fast and had the details in his mind.

Q: Was that his first contact with that plan?

Adm. R.: Well, I don't know, but it was the plan that was

Russell #2 - 227

to be executed.

Q: It had been in the process of being drawn up.

Adm. R.: I called on Le May in Guam, and we had a good conversation on the way he was running the B-29's. He'd brought them down, you know, from very high altitudes to reasonable levels, and they were doing a pretty commendable job. They certainly burned out Tokyo and Yokohama.

Q: Did you have any inkling of the forthcoming use of the atomic bomb?

Adm. R.: I was privileged to attend a debrief given by Parsons, who was the weaponeer on the first drop. He was on his way back from the - we knew something was up, and yes, we did know.

Q: You knew in advance.

Adm. R.: Yes. It was very, very closely held.

Q: You were one of the few.

Adm. R.: Yes, but Parsons debriefed rather thoroughly on the way back. And as you know, a naval officer was weaponeer in both the drops, in both the Hiroshima and the Nagasaki drops. Parsons, in the case of the Hiroshima drop, and Dick Ashworth in the case of the Nagasaki drop.

Interestingly enough, the Indianapolis, which had gone out at high speed with the nuclear interiors of the weapons, was released to steam independently to the Philippines and was routed directly over the known position of a Japanese submarine by error, and she was lost. They let her go at 25 knots.

Q: Captain McVey.

Adm. R.: Captain McVey, yes.

Well, when Towers went to the 5th Fleet and the war was almost over, Newton came in, oh, excuse me! Not Newton. It was Genial John Hoover. And Genial John Hoover lasted just twenty days. We were to entertain Julius Ochs Adler, of the New York Times, and we were all very carefully cautioned that the fellow was a little critical of the Navy, and unfortunately, Admiral Smith, who was logistics command at the time, said things that were very unfavorably received at dinner, and in not good taste. It was actually uncalled for, because we aides had carefully briefed all the dinner guests saying, "Now look. This is the situation." Admiral Smith just didn't take it in, and he made some remarks.

Q: Well, did Adler say some provocative things at the table?

Adm. R.: No, Smith.

Q: But had Adler said some provocative things?

Adm. R.: Well, a little bit. No, it was just a stupid sort of thing, a stupid sort of thing. The conversation ran to how can you support a big newspaper like the New York Times without having funny papers. Isn't that silly? Small things, you know, may have a big effect.

Well, this thing was built up to the point where when Adler arrived out in Guam, he said to his reporters, "You can say anything that damns the Navy." Well, Nimitz heard of this, and forthwith Genial John was assigned to other duty, and then came John Henry Newton.

Q: Well, Hoover was blamed for General Smith's remarks?

Adm. R.: For Admiral Smith's, yes. After all, he was in charge of the headquarters, you know, and it was his party. It occurred in his quarters, and that was that!

Q: He himself hadn't said provocative things then.

Adm. R.: No, no. We briefed him pretty carefully, too, you know! On the foibles of Mr. Julius Ochs Adler.

But then, John Henry Newton came in, and he really didn't

need me. I knew this. And the war was just about over. And it's rather amusing, though that while Genial John had deputy command, we had one false alarm on VJ day. And all hell started breaking loose. There were guns being fired down in Pearl Harbor and rockets going off and one thing and another, and we went out on the front lawn of 29 Makalapa Street to observe this phenomena. Genial John looked at this for a while, and finally he calmly turned to me and said, "Russell, have them stop it!" I said, "Aye, aye, sir!" It would be like standing in front of an onrushing locomotive when it's sixty feet away and saying, "Hey! Stop!" But the news got around, it was a false alarm, and it stopped eventually. But then John Henry Newton came and when VJ really came, the call went out for air technical intelligence work with General Carroll on MacArthur's staff, I volunteered, and, bless his heart, Admiral Newton let me go forthwith.

So I got over there in September, 1945 right after the surrender, and I landed at Kisarazu. And the fellow who met me had been my administrative officer in VP-42 in the Aleutians.

Q: Let me ask one question about Hoover and Nimitz, Nimitz dismissing him summarily. Was there bad blood between the two of them?

Adm. R.: No. Nimitz had confidence enough in John Hoover to

make him deputy commander to replace Towers who had gone out to take the 5th Fleet. And apparently on this episode that, well, you just can't allow that sort of thing. If you had a subordinate who didn't have the acumen to see that errors were not made like that, you'd obviously want to give him some other kind of duty. That's exactly what happened.

I left for Japan in early September. You will remember, the surrender was signed on the 1st of September. We landed at Kisarazu across the bay from Yokosuka and took a local flight over to Yokosuka.

Q: What kind of reception did you receive at that point? From the Japanese.

Adm. R.: I think perhaps the Japanese were relieved to have the war over. I met at Yokosuka one Commander Otsuki. Commander Otsuki was a graduate student at M.I.T., and it was he who showed us through the 1st Naval Air Technical Arsenal, a sort of the Langley Field of Japanese Naval Aviation. The Japanese had moved their flight test activities up to Misawa on the north end of Honshu to get further away from the war, but their wind tunnels and many of the experiments were done right there at Yokosuka.

It was very interesting to us, and the tour we took with Commander Otsuki sort of tugged a bit at your heart strings, because we'd go into a place, and he'd show us an experimental setup, for example, a test of a seaplane float or a test in the wind tunnel; and he'd say, "Well now, we are - we were going to do thus and so." He knew it was curtains as far as his activities were concerned there.

Q: That area had not been bombed?

Adm. R.: For some strange reason, that area had not been bombed, although there were very extensive underground facilities. There was a whole machine shop in the limestone caves in the little hills behind the town. There was a fighter hangar actually on the airfield that had gates with camouflage on them, heavy concrete affairs that rolled on railroad tracks. And they could open this hangar, they could go in from one side and out the other, but they could close off both the entrance and the exit with these tremendous, big, concrete gates that had camouflage on them, trees and this sort of thing.

Q: Very ingenious, aren't they?

Adm. R.: Well, we flew all over the empire, and all over the home islands, and where we saw things that we thought would be of interest to our aeronautical engineers in the States, we asked to have them manned and flown to Yokosuka. We'd put a U.S. fighter escort with them usually. We sent them down to Yokosuka and put them in escort carriers and took them back to the States.

Q: These are planes that were operational.

Adm. R.: Well, we found a plane we called the Patsy, which had a very high aspect ratio, a crew of three, and it had sufficient range to bomb Washington, D. C. flying from the home islands and making a landing in Mexico.

Q: And never been used, however.

Adm. R.: No. We saw another airplane that had a single main float and two wingtip floats, all of which could be released, from the cockpit. Their thought was to fly these off, drop the floats to increase range, then kamikaze the locks of the Panama Canal. We, of course, saw many of the baka bombs. The baka bomb translated was a "fools" bomb. You know, it was manned by a human and released from an airplane - a glide bomb manned by a human.

Q: Another suicidal thing.

Adm. R.: Yes.

Q: Did you run into those actually in combat?

Adm. R.: Some of them had been used over in the Okinawa area, but not very many of them. I remember intelligence before the war ended reported that they had such a device, and they'd been sighted and photographed, dropping away from an airplane.

Q: Well, I would think that with some of these, and especially those bigger planes that you talked about, that they couldn't implement, they couldn't manufacture such planes after all those heavy attacks.

Adm. R.: We estimated that there were 10,000 airplanes sufficiently put together to be used against our invasion of the home islands. They probably would have been used as kamikazes. Some of them were made of wood, of many cheap substitutes. And I remember that when we were at Yokosuka, a farmer from out in the hills, who had been making certain parts, aluminum parts, in sort of a home factory, came in with these things on a cart to deliver to the Japanese Navy to be assembled in an airplane. He just didn't realize that the war was over and this wasn't necessary any more, but here he was delivering the parts that he'd fabricated in his home shop.

Q: Well, would they have had the capability to assemble pilots for all these planes?

Adm. R.: That I doubt, no. But the idea was to train them just sufficiently so they could fly an airplane on a single mission.

We flew up to Misawa where there were experimental airplanes. They'd been moved up there to get away from the activities of the war. The commanding officer, when we landed and we were flying a Catalina amphibian, came out to meet us. He was attired in rather tired looking raw silk khaki fatigues, but he wore white gloves. He bowed from the waist in polite Japanese style, and asked what he could do for us. His airplanes were all lined up on the side of the field with the propellers off lying on the ground before them. It was a symbol of surrender.

The discipline was in great evidence everywhere. The Emperor had said, "We surrender." And the war was over for them. They were perfectly disciplined. I didn't see any untoward acts, save one way out in the country driving in a jeep. A little boy, perhaps ten years old, stood up very straight as I went by and said in Japanese, "I am a Japanese man." And he spit on my jeep.

I remember immediately after the war, English signs cropped up everywhere to direct traffic, road signs and things of that sort, and there was one village called Hayama down on Sagami Wan. And as one entered the village, there was a sign that said in English, "Please drive carefully. Our children may be disobeying us." The discipline was absolutely amazing.

I flew down to Hiroshima. I looked the place over and landed on the old parade ground at the barracks. There was utter desolation everywhere. The town was completely burned out. The only part of the town standing was in the lea of a hill in the shadow of the bomb burst. We landed on the parade ground and taxiied around looking for someone who could receive us and talk with us. And I noticed a raw lumber sentry box, obviously put up by the occupying forces. So I taxiied over there and got out of the airplane, and went in, and it turned out that there was a U. S. Army telephone set in there - you know, a field telephone with a leather carrying case. And I took the receiver out of the case and cranked the ringing magneto. Nothing happened. I then lifted the leather flap and looked into the carrying case. Someone had stolen the batteries!

So here we were in a strange area, utter desolation all around us, and nobody there! It wasn't very long before a U. S. Army jeep drove up, and a major who'd seen us coming to land came and joined us, and from then on we were supported. I then went on down to Kure. I have never seen such naval carnage as existed there. Ise and Hyuga, those two hermaphrodite battleships, which we had chased the year before, were sitting on the bottom with just their upper works awash. The Amagi, a great carrier, was lying on her side with her flight deck vertical, but her mooring lines were still out to the pier. Katsuragi, her flight deck looked like a gabled roof from the bombs which had burst in the hangar, but her machinery was intact enough for her to be used in the repatriation effort. She brought troops home from Manchuria.

Many ships were nestled up against the limestone cliffs with very cleverly placed netting over them, covered with camouflage - various branches of trees and things of this sort. But our pilots had discovered these and bombed or torpedoed them, and most of them were sunk right there at their berths.

The town of Hiroshima itself was utter desolation. Walking through, we could see shadows of people etched on the stone where their bodies had stopped the intense, hot rays of the bomb. We found several witnesses. There was a white Russian girl who was under ground zero, but she was in the basement of the building at the time and survived. There was a policeman who saw the bomb leave the airplane and dove into one of the canals and was saved.

Q: Protected by the water?

Adm. R.: He was under water when the thing went off, yes. Many strange instances occurred like that. We saw the old Foreign Trade Building which is still preserved as a monument. Do you know, I went back to this place nine years later, and you'd never know anything happened? The town of Hiroshima was completely rebuilt. There was the old firebreak, now a new boulevard down the center of town, a monument at ground zero, and the twisted skeleton of the old Foreign Trade Building, but no other evidence of the complete destruction we had seen in 1945.

I paid a visit to Kure with a little task group - an anti-submarine warfare task group in which I had my flag in an escort carrier. We went in to Kure harbor, and remembering all the World War II carnage, I looked for it but could find no evidence of it. I borrowed an airplane from the Marines over in Iwakuni and flew over the area, because I remembered so well those various areas where we spotted ships and recorded the damage to them. The only thing I found was a rusty hulk of a destroyer, obviously raised from deep water. It was in the drydock at Kure being cut up for scrap. Nine years later, completely tidied up, cleaned up. Amazing!

Well, I did a month of air technical intelligence and then shifted over and joined Admiral Ralph Ofstie in the naval analysis division of the U. S. Strategic Bombing Survey.


Q: Was your month's duty in preparation for this other service?


Adm. R.: Not at all. It wasn't related. That was air tactical intelligence. We wrote our reports and finished up in a month's time, and I could have gone home, but I volunteered to stay on with the bombing survey, and it was quite all right with Admiral Ofstie. So I joined up over there and stayed on for another three months.

Q: May I ask one question at this point about the attitude of the Japanese people? They received you, and they bowed in great politeness, and so forth, but it doesn't seem to be quite in keeping with human character to have had such intense feelings and patriotism and to have worked so terribly hard during the war and then to switch completely over night. There must have been some rancor.

Adm. R.: Well, I'm sure down inside, and I do believe that some of the Japanese men, when they found the girls going out with the American GI's, were very much angered by it. However, one of the features of the surrender was that the symbol of authority, the Emperor, was preserved, you see. So they still had an Emperor to look to, and his order was to surrender. I do know that a lot of the families, as the occupation troops came in, the wife and daughters took to the hills. And it wasn't very long after the troops came and when they found that we were really friendly, that they came down and joined their families.

It was quite an experience, but a very sobering one. After I joined the bombing survey, we were billeted in the University Club in Tokyo. At least two thirds of the town was just gone, burned out. Nothing was left but rusty tin-plate and various bits of iron and concrete, steel and rubble, burned out cars in the streets. Occasionally one would see a safe which had been in a building and just burned out and rusty sitting where the building had been.

The University Club had lost a great deal of the glass in the windows, and the steel in radiators had been used for warlike purposes. They'd all been taken out.

Q: Then it was a western style building?

Adm. R.: It was a western style building, and we lived there. The rooms were very comfortable. The electric elevators were still working. We dined in the diningroom on U. S. Army food prepared in the kitchen, but was served by the most delightful little Japanese waitress girls with very clean spick and span kimonos. They were extremely polite and attentive, but it tugged a bit at your heart strings to see them with a little bit of a basin and a silk towel go over and try to mop up the rain coming through the broken windows to keep the place tidy. Many people remarked that they would hate to spend the rest of the winter there, because people were actually dropping dead in the street. There was a squad going around picking up corpes.

Q: You mean from malnutrition?

Adm. R.: Malnutrition and exposure and so forth. But the recovery was just absolutely amazing.

Q: It began almost immediately, did it?

Adm. R.: Yes. They started immediately cleaning up, getting the debris piled up.

Q: Well, is this evidence of discipline or is this a -

Adm. R.: A national trait. They're industrious people. Discipline, of course, begins in the home. The children are well ordered. They respect their parents, they worship their parents, as a matter of fact. I remember Wally Higgins married a Japanese widow. There was one daughter by her former marriage, a beautiful young lady about nineteen years old, I guess. Visiting one time I found the daughter, whose name was Tae, I found Tae san in tears. And I said to Wally, "What has happened here? What's wrong with Tae?" And he said, "Obaesan came to visit. Baesan is grandmother, and Obaesan said to Tae san, 'You are a young lady now. You know the tea ceremony. You're quite eligible. Get married.' And to Tae san this was an order. She wasn't ready to get married, so she dissolved in tears." Amazing people. I'm happy to say that Tae san is happily married to a medical doctor. She was married in a Buddhist church. I haven't recent news of her family's present situation.

Well, we remained in Japan through Christmas. We came back by steamer in January.

Q: The survey having been completed by that time?

Adm. R.: The bombing survey was completed. We came back with records and a great sheaf of interrogations, which were lated printed up in two volumes as <u>Official Interrogations of Those in Japan at the End of the War</u>.

Q: Give me more background, will you, on this report? Some of the documents you located and where you found them, and that sort of thing.

Adm. R.: Well, we found there was a great dearth of written documentation. Before, and in anticipation of, the surrender, about the 15th of August, a general order had gone out to all the military to destroy their records. All the Japanese military. Many of them, such as Okumiya, had faithfully done this. I would have given a great deal to have had a photograph that Okumiya told me he had. It was one of my planes, possibly Stockdale's, burning in the water, taken by one of the planes from the <u>Ryujo</u>. He dutifully burned it, but within a day or two, the order was countermanded. But we still could find very little written material.

Q: How did that countermanded order coincide with the political events at that moment in Japan, do you remember?

Adm. R.: I really don't know. All I know is what they told us, that they had had an order to destroy and it had been countermanded about two days after it was issued.

Meanwhile, all the loyal ones had gone about destroying their records. Well, let me go on and say that one day we were telephoned from an infantry outfit up in the back country from Tokyo. They had discovered a cave, and in it were forty boxes of records, and their Nisei boy, looking at these records said, "These are naval records." And we were asked if we wanted them. So we said yes, of course, and we sent a truck train and picked up these forty boxes and brought them to Tokyo. And sure enough, these were the records of the Japanese Navy Board of Awards. Every unit which had been cited in action had its story in those records.

In the case of the Aleutian raids, and I was assigned the Aleutian campaign to cover in the naval analysis division, since I had fought there in the early days of the war, we found the record of Ryujo in the Aleutian action, because Ryujo's air group had gotten through to the target both days of raids. Junyo's air group turned back due to weather on the first day of raids, and her record wasn't in the books, because she hadn't been cited. Kimikawa Maru had the seaplanes which scouted, photographed, and made a reconnaissance of

Adak, and was in with the landing party on Kiska. It was from her written account that we obtained the photograph of the B-24 being downed over the pass at Kiska. Its record was there because it had been cited for its work. As a matter of fact, my former copilot, Leo Nuss, later on had conducted an attack against Kimikawa Maru, and the maneuvers of Kimikawa and Nuss's Catalina were recorded in one of the volumes. Rather interesting to see.

Q: I take it from what you say that the Japanese system of recognition and awards was not a great deal different from ours.

Adm. R.: Exactly. Well, these records were, of course, a great help, and as you saw in my photo album, I copied some of them taken from their side, like the discovery of our seaplane moorage and tender at Atka.

Q: Were these records brought back to the States?

Adm. R.: A great number of them were. However, we translated some of them then in Tokyo (we had quite a staff of translators) but many of the records were brought back. It is my understanding that they were later sent back to Japan. I think I would approve of that.

Now I have a history of the war in the northeast in

Japanese from General Okumiya, which describes the Aleutian campaign. It's here on my bookshelf. It has not been translated into English, but some historians have had a look at it, and I have had parts of it translated.

Q: What were some of your other experiences in outlying areas, finding documents. I understand that a part of the naval setup was preserved outside of Tokyo somewhere.

Adm. R.: Well, we found documents in odd places. I was very interested in the Komandorski action, which occurred after I left the Aleutians. I think it was in April of '43, or maybe earlier than that, possibly March, in which our Rear Admiral Sock McMorris had Salt Lake City, Richmond, and four destroyers cruising off Attu to intercept the supplies coming to Attu and Kiska. He saw some pips on his radar scope and decided that these must be supply ships running in to Attu, so he very carefully interposed his force between those ships and the home islands of Japan. But when the cold, cruel light of dawn came, he found there were four cruisers to his two, and four destroyers to his four, and what history had charitably recorded as a "retiring engagement" took place. McMorris running for his shirt, and the Japanese in hot pursuit.

Strange things happened. Nachi was the flagship of Admiral Hosogaya, a heavy cruiser. There were two heavies, two lights, and four destroyers. Nachi catapulted a float plane preparing to go into battle. There was some delay in launching the second plane. The captain got impatient, and fired the first salvo which wrecked the plane, so they jettisoned it. I think Samuel Eliot Morison claims that we shot one down, because the proof of it was the wreckage of the airplane found in the sea. Actually, the Japanese had ruined it with their own salvo from Nachi and thrown it over the side to get rid of it as a fire hazard! I wrote a letter on this subject, but the history was never corrected as far as I know.

But it was a very interesting action, and I was very anxious to get any written record if possible. I consulted with my new found friend, then Commander Okumiya, who had been Air Ops on Admiral Kakuda's staff during the raid on Dutch Harbor. He said, "Well, Captain, if you could get me to Hokkaido, I know the commanding officer of one of the light cruisers, I believe it was Kiso, in that action. And it's just possible that in his personal papers, he may have an account of the action." So I signed a little chit on our then Army Air Force, and got passage for my friend Okumiya in a C-47. He disappeared up to the island of Hokkaido, and I wasn't sure he would return. He'd been a great help up to that time. I thought well perhaps he knew some naval air station up there where he could claim a bit of land and plant some potatoes, thus survive in the winter. But in a week's time he came back. He came back with a rice paper volume, which was a personal account, the diary, of the commanding officer of Kiso; and in it was not only a complete account of the action, but a track chart of the action as they saw it. I could lay that track chart down against the track chart from our side, and piece out what went on.

Among other things McMorris was told that there were torpedoes passing them, and he said, "It can't be. They must be porpoises. We are out of range." This was not so. They had oxygen-charged torpedoes that did have the range. Very long range torpedoes.

Q: Actually, we had intelligence on those prior to the outbreak of the war, I believe.

Adm. R.: Is that right? I had not heard it.

Well, Nachi having fired her first salvo, the engineers excitedly were getting their generators, I think there were four of them, on the line together, and they lost the load. So whem it came time to fire the next salvo, they didn't have any electricity. And when they unscrambled the loss of the electrical load and got power back on the ship, they attempted to fire the next salvo from the master director, which was up on the foretop, and nothing happened. It was quite a number of minutes before they realized that one of

Salt Lake City's shells had gone through the island structure and severed the leads from the master director to the turrets. And then, of course, they went into secondary control and continued firing. But they made a very common mistake. The spotting officer would see the splashes grow, and he'd see the ship right in the middle of them, and he would spot, "No change." And they'd fire another salvo, and the same thing would happen, but what was really happening, the ships were steaming at high speed, and the shells would touch the water forward of the ship and clear of it, and by the time a sizeable splash had grown, the ship was right in the middle. So there was no change ordered in the alignment of the guns.

One Commander Miura, who was the communications officer on Admiral Hosogaya's staff, told me that - as a matter of fact, he complained - the dye of the shells from Salt Lake City, which I think were dyed dark blue, had stained his white cap cover, because these plumes of colored salt water going up from the shell splash were just descending on the ship as the ship steamed through them. Until the surrender we never could understand why the Japanese broke off that engagement when they did. It was for two reasons. One was they had a pretty well-kept rule that if they got down to their last third of ammunition, they would conserve and look for happier hunting grounds, unless there was an immediate chance for victory.

The other thing was, they were listening in on our airplane circuits from Adak, and they knew that the bombers had been ordered to arm up with armor piercing bombs instead of the common thin shelled high explosive bombs used against Kiska. They knew also when the airplanes had taken off. When they figured our airplanes were within fifty miles of the scene of action, they decided that it was time to break off. They didn't know they had <u>Salt Lake City</u> dead in the water at one time. Had it not been for a very gallant attack and smoke-screen laying by our four destroyers, the Japanese could certainly have polished off <u>Salt Lake City</u> and <u>Richmond</u>.

Q: In retrospect they could have.

Adm. R.: In retrospect, they could have and yet, they broke off at that particular time. We were told that the tactic of firing torpedoes and then laying a smokescreen by our destroyers was greatly admired, and it was adopted as a maneuver in their tactical schools. As a matter of fact, Commander Miura told me that if I ever met the officer who led that charge (he called the destroyer attack a "charge"), would I please shake him by the hand and tell him that he was a very brave man. And I had this opportunity considerably later when I was invited to speak before a Naval Academy alumni meeting at the Army-Navy Club in Washington, D. C.. I was invited by Ralph Riggs, who led the "charge" of the destroyers, and I told the story of Commander Miura's getting his cap cover dyed blue, and also his saying that if ever I met the officer who led that "charge," could I please shake him by the hand and tell him that he was a very brave man. At that point I turned around and shook Ralph Riggs by his hand. This made quite an impression on the audience there!

Q: Tell me. You said they had listened in on our radio, and so forth. Were these plain language messages, or did they have some kind of understanding of our code?

Adm. R.: No. This was chitchat over the airplane voice circuits mostly.

Q: And were we discussing the VT fuses, and so forth?

Adm. R.: No, no, we were discussing, "Don't take off with a common bomb." We are to return to base and arm up with armor-piercing bombs." This sort of thing. Chitchat between airplanes.

Q: Did the Japanese ever succeed with our code?

Adm. R.: A little bit. They, for example, knew exactly how far out we went in our searches, and they discreetly kept their evacuation force from Kiska Island just beyond the extreme range of our searches until Kiska reported a properly dense fog. Then they made the dash in. There was another mystery that we uncovered in our interrogation, and perhaps you would like to hear about that.

Q: Yes, I would.

Adm. R.: Well, you remember there was an action called the Battle of the Pips. This happened after I left the Aleutians. There was a Battle of the Pips in which there were old battleships and a pretty good sized U. S. force. This was after Attu and before the Kiska landing. The force fired in the fog at radar pips, which probably were due to a reflection from the mountains on Amchitka. As you know, the pulsing of a radar may give a near-in pip, or image, of an object which is actually at twice, three, four times the distance indicated by the pip. So it's suspected that the images fired at were actually reflected from mountain tops a considerable distance away.

This large U. S. force had retired to replenish at the time a Japanese evacuation force, comprised of two light cruisers and ten destroyers, made a dash for Kiska Harbor. The commanding officer at Kiska had said the weather was appropriate for covering an evacuation. There was a little dome in the fog over Kiska Bay, but it was very foggy over all the surrounding areas. So the Japanese evacuation force steamed in. They made a landfall in the fog on Cape St. Stephens, which is the southwest tip of Kiska. They navigated on soundings north around the island, and came into the harbor on radio bearings of their radio station. They told me as the lead cruiser broke out of the fog, she saw what she thought was the bow of an American cruiser, and she let fire two torpedoes at it. It turned out to be a head land, Little Kiska Island. But one of the torpedoes ran in to Kiska Harbor and blew up on the beach, which didn't add to the peace of mind of the 5400 troops that had gathered there to be evacuated. They thought they were discovered and being bombed through the overcast.

But the two light cruisers and eight of the ten destroyers went in, and they took aboard 5400 troops in fifty minutes.

Q: Fifty minutes!

Adm. R.: And sank the landing craft that were brought out from the beach. Two destroyers stayed out as guards at the entrance to the harbor. The evacuation force got away, steaming north around Kiska Island, but broke up into two groups. They were so unsure of their survival in this escapade that they selected different parallels of latitude on which to steam home. They hoped thereby that one half their group, at least, would get home. To their amazement, they had no engagement whatsoever with any American force. When I was interrogating Captain Arichika, who was chief of staff of the 1st Destroyer Squadron, an officer who had planned and been in on the execution of the evacuation of Kiska, I asked him, "You saw no American ship?" He thought for a moment, and then said, "Yes. We saw a submarine." And I said, "And where was the submarine?" He gave me a range and bearing from Pillar Rock. That's a tall rock which stands up out of the ocean on the westward side of Kiska Island. I said, "Well, what did you do?" He said, "Well, we made an emergency turn away. We thought of course we'd been discovered and it would lessen our chances of survival." I didn't remember any report by a submarine being made, and, in truth, we didn't know the troops had gone when we made our landing there, but I couldn't wait to look up our records when we got back to Washington to find out if, in fact, there was a submarine in the position he had given me.

And there was. There was an S-Boat there. The Japanese saw it first and turned away. Now, why a light cruiser and five destroyers wouldn't kick up enough fuss in the ocean for the submarine to hear them at least, I don't know. But it may have been masked by the breaking of the surf on the western side of Kiska, which was pretty heavy, but certainly that submarine was not on his toes! Strange things happen! But the evacuation force got back to Paramushiro and were amazed that they got through with no contact.

Q: Admiral, comment on that particular operation - the evacuation of Kiska. This in many ways doesn't seem in character with Japanese patterns of activities in the South Pacific. They usually stayed till the last.

Adm. R.: They explain this matter by saying those troops were needed for the defense of the Kuriles. They didn't admit they'd evacuated the place for any other reason than the use of those troops somewhere else.

Q: Interesting. Their policy's so flexible.

Adm. R.: Yes. Well, this occurred on the 28th of July, 1943, east longitude date. We made an amphibious landing on Kiska about the middle of August with 35,000 troops and were surprised to find no Japanese troops. They'd left slow burning fires, and the dog named "Explosion", which belonged to our weather station, was still there on the island.

Q: What other discoveries did you make during this survey tour?

Adm. R.: Well, we covered pretty thoroughly World War II history, and each one of us covered something in which we had had personal experience, like Tom Moorer's coverage of the Japanese invasion of the Philippines, East Indies, and

Southeast Asia. He had one assignment, and somebody else another and so forth.

Q: I suppose Moorer wanted to cover that flying boat episode in the south.

Adm. R.: He did, yes.

Well, we came back to Washington, and we wrote all this up, which was eventually released. It made quite a fuss, because General Orville Anderson was intent on proving that the Air Force had won the war, and we had a serious document which had the losses which were inflicted by the submarines, and I must say that the strangulation of Japan by submarines was one of the most important things that was done in World War II.

Q: This was an admission of the Japanese themselves?

Adm. R.: The effect of carrier raids, for example, as against bombing raids from fixed places and so on - these were all issues. And Orville Anderson came out with a report on bombing survey stationery something like many months after we'd closed out, and our analytical report was not allowed to be published. He came out with this thing, written on Bombing Survey stationery, that proved the Air Force had won the war. Sort of silly.

Q: Your report was written for the benefit of whom? If it was not published.

Adm. R.: All our interrogations and our analyses of the naval campaigns were published, and I have those here. I also have a copy of our unpublished analysis and you can understand why it was not released. It proves that naval aviation won the war, of course, which was not General Orville Anderson's idea. He headed the air analysis division.

Q: This perhaps causes me to ask you for some comments on the general policy of the Navy during World War II vis a vis publicity - the releases from Nimitz and his staff in the Pacific, as contrasted with those of the Air Force. Quite a different policy in action.

Adm. R.: Well, there are many very exaggerated claims, and believe me, the Navy was not innocent of these. The Patrol Wing 4 reports up in the Aleutians were among the most inaccurate things. They had reports of sunken ships and all sorts of things which didn't happen. They said that very few of the Japanese aviators who attacked Dutch Harbor had got home to their ships. There were all sorts of false reports.

Russell #2 - 257

Q: But I was thinking in terms of the Navy's reluctance to publicize its bona fide victories in contrast to the immediate publicity given by the Air Force people. Why was this?

Adm. R.: I cannot comment. As I said once before, I did call on Le May when he had the air force in Guam, and I was tremendously impressed with the efficiency that he instilled in his people. If a pilot taxiied out and had a mechanical that prevented his taking off, that pilot was sent to school for twelve hours a day for a week, and the next time he got to this point, he usually didn't have a mechanical. He had corrected it before he taxiied out to take off.

Q: You might say that Admiral Ofstie was somewhat disappointed because his report was not published.

Adm. R.: Yes, that's true. But, although it was based on fact, it was certainly one very favorable to the Navy and could be expected to generate a little antagonism in the Army Air Force.

Q: How did the Japanese react to the report, or were they privileged to know its contents?

Adm. R.: They had very little to say about it. The Japanese

Army Air Force was somewhat smaller and very much less in accomplishment than the Japanese Naval Air Force. And when the Air Self Defense Force was formed in years after the war, a great number of the Japanese naval aviators went in to it. For example, my friend Okumiya went into it. He retired as a lieutenant general a good number of years ago now. But naval aviation was certainly a very strong service in Japan.

Q: The bombing survey had been completed. You were back in Washington.

Adm. R.: And the records are contained in Volumes I, II, and III. Volumes I and II are interrogation of Japanese officials, Volume III is the staff analysis of the various naval actions. These books are out of print now. They were done by the Government Printing Office. I have copies here if you care to refer to them.

Well, we finished this up probably April of '46, and I was assigned then as one of twenty-three officers to serve with General Hoge to survey Alaska and to come up with a recommendation of how to dispose of the various real estate and other properties which had accumulated in Alaska during the war. This was very interesting to me to go back up to the country in which I had spent so much time just prior to and during the early days of the war. General Hoge was an Army

Engineer who arose to fame in the war; he actually had a division in France or in Europe in the latter phases of the war. A very find gentleman.

Of these twenty-three, I think there were about six naval officers perhaps. But I remember there was a Supply Corps officer, Captain Mellow. Notably, there were only two aviators, and one was Army and one was Navy. The Army aviator was General Dale Gaffney, who'd had the Alaskan Wing of ATC, the Air Transport Command, and yours truly was the naval aviator.

Q: And you say "notable." Why were there so few aviators on the staff?

Adm. R.: That I don't know. I thought there should have been more, because there was quite a bit of aerial activity up there. However, we joined in recommending to General Hoge that we start survey at Attu and work back toward the east from there. We were afraid that if this party started down the Aleutians from the east and encountered some of the weather which we knew so well down that way, that they would get faint-hearted and give up.

So we did that. We flew down to Attu. General Gaffney had two C-47's, winterized C-47's, and we staged at Umnak and on down to Attu, where we circled for twenty minutes while the snow plows went out (in April) and took about ten

Russell #2 - 260

or fifteen feet of snow off the runway so we could land.

Q: May I ask why you didn't wait until better weather had set in?

Adm. R.: The survey was to be completed at a certain time, and we just didn't have time for it.

What we saw was very revealing. On Attu there would be supply trucks that were driven so far the preceding fall, with perhaps a whole supply of canned goods or other material, they got stuck in the snow, and there they were. This was Spring now. I remember particularly that the sanitary drains in the camps on Attu were made of wooden piping. This, of course, was rotting through, and it was quite obvious that there was very little that could be salvaged other than perhaps the rolling stock and things that were more or less portable. The rest of the stuff had deteriorated so badly that it needed only to be cleaned up.

Q: Well, when you went out, did you know beforehand of what was to be dismantled and what was to be preserved?

Adm. R.: This is what we were to recommend.

So we worked back, and we overflew Kiska, and Kiska looked like Iron Bottom Bay. There were many, many wrecks in the harbor. We didn't land there. We landed at Adak, and there were literally acres of jeeps, for example; a tremendous amount of supplies and equipment, many quonsets. Some of the great storehouses had had roofs blown off, just lifted completely off the house. The airfield was very much in commission, of course. And, as you know, it still remains as a Naval Air Station. We stopped, of course, at Amchitka, which is a little farther down the chain than Adak and spent a day or two there. Those facilities are still usable. They're used by local airlines and by the Atomic Energy Commission for their underground tests up there. Shemya, of course, which is right next to Attu. I should start with Attu, we came to Shemya, to Amchitka, and then to Adak.

Shemya's a small island. It's about the only flat island up there, but it's close enough to Agattu, which is mountainous, and Attu, which is mountainous, to have a break in the weather, much more so than Amchitka. Amchitka projects down south and is constantly in the fog compared to Shemya. Adak, as I've explained, gets a break from the weather, because it's on the north or lee side of a mountainous island.

We got back to Umnak, and then to get from there into Dutch Harbor, (the field there was not in commission) we borrowed a Catalina amphibian from the Navy Command and flew over in relay. I was very pleased with an experience we had at Dutch Harbor. We had been used to rough lumber barracks, army cots with blankets and no sheets. And when we arrived at

Dutch Harbor, we were escorted to the commanding officer's house, which had been built under civilian contract at the beginning of World War II. Crutchfield Adair had been the skipper, and he was a very inventive man. It was rather a quiet place to be, so he had thought up all sorts of fancy things. We were served a cocktail by a very neat and tidy U. S. Navy steward of Filipino extraction, and in due time dinner was announced. We went into the diningroom and there was a tablecloth, a white Navy linen cloth, with Navy silverware and white china, and to our amazement, our names were projected onto the ceiling above us - our placecards. Crutchfield had thought this up. There was a sandblasting machine somewhere in the equipment which was left there in the war, and he would take a sizeable piece of glass, cover it with wax, and then scribe your name on the wax, and sandblast it, take the wax off, and here was your name etched on a reflecting piece of glass. He had boxed the center light in the dining room, so that the rays just covered the outline of the white linen tablecloth, but shining on the glass with your name engraved on it.

Of course, it brought back many memories to be back in Dutch Harbor, but the Army was tremendously impressed with the ingenuity of the Navy, and they said, "Look. The Navy touches the desert and it blooms!" We worked our way on back, and went, of course, to Fort Richardson, Elmendorf Air Force Base, up to Ladd Field at Fairbanks, to all the military airfields. We went to Nome. We spent quite a little time at Nome. There was a great deal of equipment left, and importantly, there was a warehouse full of canned beer and a great supply of cigars. So every GI going through the mess line was entitled to a can of beer and a cigar! Rather impressive!

Q: Were there many soldiers stationed there still?

Adm. R.: Practically none, you see.

Well, we returned to Washington, D. C., wrote up a report, and I was fortunate enough to be selected (ship commands were few and far between) to command Bairoko, CVE-115.

Q: One more question about the Alaska survey. Did you pay any attention to the Navy's oil lands while there?

Adm. R.: As a matter of fact, we missed going to Point Barrow. We were weathered out, and we didn't reinstate that trip, so we did not see the Navy oil reserves.

Well, I was assigned command of Bairoko, went to tactical school and to damage control school, and joined my ship. To my sorrow, she was tied up alongside the Coronado seawall along with two other CVE's. We got down to such a point in our shortage of personnel that the commanding officer of Rendova, I believe, or Siboney next to us, and I got a donkey boiler on a flat car and put it alongside the ships on the seawall. We had between us just enough firemen to fire that donkey boiler and provide steam to the two ships. That ship had had a complement of almost a thousand men in World War II, and I had something like one hundred.

Q: What can you do with such meager personnel?

Adm. R.: When it got to three hundred, I put to sea.

Now, my embarked squadron was a very interesting one. It was a squadron of Ryan Fireballs, the FR-1, I believe they were called. It was half jet and half propeller, the very first jets introduced in the Navy. The squadron was very kind to me. They let me check out and fly this contraption. You could fly either on your jet, your propeller, or both. You couldn't fly on your jet very long if you were using much electricity, because there was no generator on the turbine. You could feather your prop and fly the airplane on the turbine alone, but you had to be very careful to conserve your electrical energy to unfeather and start your reciprocating engine.

Q: How effective was a plane of this sort?

Adm. R.: It was of an experimental nature to see what could be done in the way of getting jets aboard ship.

Q: That was the complement on your carrier?

Adm. R.: That's right. And we operated with that type aircraft for a while, and then I was ordered to take a ship load of replacement F4U's to the Marines in China. So we set sail, and in Pearl Harbor I was the only carrier present. Towers was about to turn command of the Pacific over to Denfeld. Towers, being an aviator, wanted very much to have the change of command ceremony on a carrier. So it was my great honor and privilege to provide the scenery for my former boss' change of command.

We polished the ship up. She was alongside the "How" pier in Pearl Harbor, we borrowed CinCPac's band, we arranged in detail for the ceremony. We had, of course, many distinguished visitors. One impressed me very much, he was the Commanding General of the Army Forces in the Pacific, General John Hull. When these people came aboard, they each had a chalk-marked place to stand in the ceremony and were escorted there, but if they came a little early, I'd invite them up to have a cup of coffee or tea in my cabin as commanding officer of the ship. General Hull did come a little early, which gave me a chance to know him. I was tremendously impressed.

Q: Stationed in Hawaii?

Adm. R.: Yes. He was at Fort Shafter, of course.

The ceremony went off very well. As a matter of fact, we had a very nice congratulatory dispatch from Towers.

Q: Was he retiring at this point?

Adm. R.: No. He - I suppose he was retiring. I hadn't thought about it. I presume he was. He'd gotten command of the Pacific area, and I presume he retired from that. Of course, I saw him later at different times. After he retired, he became a member of the Board of Pan American Airways.

We loaded back aboard our F4U's, our fighters, which we'd put ashore for the ceremony, and carried them on out to China. I was intent on putting in at Tsingtao, because by this time my crew had in it many people who hadn't even served in World War II. And to get them ashore in a foreign port like Tsingtao in China would have been a great treat. But the naval commander over there would have no part of it. So we anchored. They sent a destroyer out to tend me as a plane guard when launching planes, but there was dense fog off the China coast, and we lay at anchor for a couple of days. When the fog lifted, we were so far offshore we could barely see the shoreline of China. That was the closest we got to China.

Q: Why was the CO so reluctant? Was it a sensitive political situation?

Adm. R.: The naval commander in the area had his hands full with Chinese Communists, who were on the outskirts of Tsingtao, and he just didn't want the responsibility of having my liberty parties ashore there.

But they sent out a destroyer, which anchored on radar bearings from me. We waited till the fog lifted, and then I got underway and launched my planes. They flew in and were delivered to the Marine Corps. The Marines weren't qualified to land aboard, so we had them fly their planes over to Okinawa, where we took them aboard later in Buckner Bay in Okinawa.

Going over we put in at Guam. On leaving Guam, we navigated the channel out of Apra Harbor with the assistance of a tug. My chief engineer reported that he thought one of our propellers touched bottom. I told him I thought it was the tug which had just bumped our side. However, as we steamed in the direction of China, I felt a little different vibration in the ship than I had felt before. I looked at my watch, and sure enough, it synchronized with the turns of the propellers. So when we got back to Buckner Bay to take aboard our Marine airplanes, I built a viewing bow - you know, a box with a glass face that you put under water so that you can see through the interface between the air and water, and looked at my propellers. Sure enough, on one of them there was the definite imprint of a wire line around the hub, and a tip of one blade was curled over a little bit. I'd obviously taken a steel cable through my prop in Apra Harbor.

I immediately sent this news off to the port captain and the commander of the Marianas in Guam, but I got no reply. After leaving Okinawa, we put in to Guam again. Immediately we took the pilot on board, I said, "What did you find in the way of something I might have taken through my screw?" It's very difficult to prove you haven't touched the beach, you know, when you're going down a channel, and I was, of course, concerned about this.

Q: Yes! Real concerned!

Adm. R.: Oh, he said, "You know we had a typhoon out here, and there was a lighter, which sank, but it was in a deep hole in the channel of eighty feet, so we paid no more attention to it. Apparently what happened was there was a line on the lighter, and it went from the sunken lighter up over the edge of the channel, and we had just taken the bight of line through one propeller as we went by. I said, "Well, it would have been a great news item aboard ship if you'd told us what you did have, because we were worried about it."

Well, before we arrived in Guam, I had dispatch orders

to a strange job. The job was to be number two in the military application division of the U. S. Atomic Energy Commission. And I think I owe that job to Admiral Ofstie plus Admiral Parsons, both of whom knew me.

Q: It was just being set up, was it?

Adm. R.: It was just being set up. It was to report in June of '47. So I left the ship in Guam and flew back to Washington, but for about two weeks, until I had an interim clearance, a check through the FBI, I couldn't work. Because everything was so highly classified we couldn't work without a security clearance. At the end of two weeks, General James McCormack, who was the director of the Division of Military Application, asked me to come in to his office. He said, "Jim we have very important weapon development tests to do. I would like to have you undertake this job for the Commission, find a place to make the tests and effect the arrangements." Well, this was a very challenging assignment indeed.

We looked worldwide for places where you could explode atomic weapons. I remember we looked at the Azores among other places. There were some rather barren islands out in the Atlantic. We looked at Amchitka. Bikini had been pretty well done in by the Bikini tests. There was still radioactivity rampant there, and it was not a good place to go. We looked at the north end of Kwajalein, and then we looked at Eniwetok atoll, a place I remembered from World War II. Eniwetok atoll is a near perfect ellipse - its major axis north and south, major access about twenty-two miles, minor axis about fifteen miles. All the major land masses are on the northeast side, so that you had, from the lagoon side, a nice calm beach for landing supplies. There was even a coral outcropping in the center of the lagoon which made a shoal useful to mount a camera tower and photograph things that were going on on the rim of the atoll.

It looked ideal to me, and I took it out to Norris Bradbury, who was the director of the Loss Alamos laboratory. We talked things over. Finally he said, "Why, this is ideal. How do we go about getting authority to use this place?" I said, "Oh, leave that to me. I'll fix it."

Q: Were there not some limitations on where you might make these tests? You were talking about the Azores, but did you have the right to do that?

Adm. R.: Well, a barren island or someplace that wouldn't matter, we'd have to make arrangements, of course. Amchitka belonged to the United States, Eniwetok was Trust Territory governed by the Navy at the time. But there were two tribes, one on Aomon (Aranit) Island, and one on Biijiri Island. The three major islands on Eniwetok Atoll were devastated in the war. Eniwetok Island itself, Parry, which was next to it, and Engebi, where the Japanese had a fighter field. So it was pretty well done in in World War II, but there were two native tribes there, one on the island of Aomon, and the other on the island of Biijiri on the perimeter of the atoll. I never will forget the two tribal chieftains names, one was Abraham and the other was Johannes. The Germans had been there before us, you know, and then the Japs.

We went out, visited with them and talked to the two chiefs. Colonel Starbird, who was on General Hull's staff, did a lot of conversing with the natives. General Hull had the two chieftains and a party of natives flown to Ujelang. There were fish in the lagoon, coconuts, pandanus for fiber, and breadfruit. The latter two were scarce on Eniwetok. They didn't mind moving.

Q: Well, that was moving them temporarily, was it not?

Adm. R.: They were moved to Ujelang, which was closer to the tropical front, a source of fresh water. The problem with the Bikini natives was they'd been moved away from the tropical front to an island which was almost a desert. And the Navy had all sorts of trouble with them. The Navy tried to stock them with livestock and that sort of thing, and the LST that brought the mamma and papa chickens, mamma and papa pigs, and so forth, was barely hull down on the horizon when the Bikini natives would declare a great feast and gobble up everything that had been brought and yell for more!

So we knew that the two Eniwetok tribes didn't mind moving to the atoll of Ujelang, which wasn't suitable for our purposes. The direction of the wind wasn't right. I was doing very well getting authority to go to Eniwetok until I got to the Navy, who were charged with caring for the Trust Territory, and Forrest Sherman, who was DCNO Ops, said, "Not on your tintype!" He said, "We've had trouble with the Bikini natives, and that's enough for us. Here the Navy's in charge of these Trust Territories, and you're not about to blow another atoll." So, the Atomic Energy Act of 1946 said when there was a serious disagreement between the Atomic Energy Commission and any other branch of the executive department, the matter would be settled in the White House.

So we made a date with President Truman. I prepared the charts, but knowing what the situation might well be, General McCormack, and Paul Preuss, a colonel in the Air Force, and yours truly borrowed a piece of White House stationery, and on it we typed a note such as we thought would be characteristic in expression and otherwise of President Truman to the then Secretary of the Navy, Mr. James Forrestal. Armed with this note on White House stationery, we went to the Oval Room to have forty-five minutes with President Truman. General Marshall, the Secretary of State, was over in England on some sort of an international deal, but he sent Mr. Lovitt, who was his number two. From the Commission we had David Lilienthal, the chairman of the Commission. We had Carol Wilson, the general manager, and then General Jim McCormack, Director of Division of Military Application, and Colonel Paul Preuss, who was my number two, and yours truly.

The President came in, I laid the charts out, and someone said, "Mr. President, Mr. Forrestal is not here yet." And the President snorted and said, "Jim is always late. Let's get on with the business." So I laid the charts out. First, a chart of the whole Pacific Ocean, showed the President where Eniwetok atoll was, and then narrowed it down to show him the comparative isolation of Eniwetok and then the details of the atoll, the beautiful ellipse with the major land masses on the windward side so you had calm water to work the beaches, the coral head where the camera tower could go, and that we had made arrangements to get the natives off. The President listened to this patiently, and then he looked up, and he said to me, "This looks all very fine to me. What's holding you up, son?" And I said, "Mr. President, the Navy." Well, he saw me standing there in a dark blue suit with four stripes on my sleeve, and he said, "Oh! Is that so!" By this time, Mr. Forrestal had come in. He was sitting across the room. So at this point, we pulled out our memo, and I said, laying the memo in front of him, "Mr. President, if you would sign this memo, perhaps we could get on with the job."

And he looked at the note, he read it, he laughed, and he reached for his pen, he signed it, and looked across the room, and he said, "Here, Jim," to Mr. Forrestal. "This is for you." And I thought, "Russell, you just blew it! You'll never amount to a damn in this man's Navy!" Forrestal took it. We selected a task force commander, which was very important. As a matter of fact, back in the office of the Atomic Energy Commission we were discussing whom we might have. There was an officer by the name of Dean over in Korea and some others that McCormack was thinking of, and I suddenly thought about General Hull. And I said, "Furthermore, General McCormack, if we get him, don't forget, he has all the resources of the United States Army in the Pacific." And McCormack snapped his fingers, he got on the phone, and called Laurie Norstad, who was on the General Staff over in the Pentagon, and Norstad said, "Well, why not?" And General Hull was sent a very private message telling him to report to Washington on an unusual assignment. He came to Washington not knowing what the problem was at all. And he was told by the Chief of Staff of the Army that he would be task force commander of Task Force 7. It was Task Force 1, I think, which Blandy had at Bikini in the Cross Roads tests, and it was the Army's turn. In normal rotation it had to be an Army officer, you see.

Well, he turned out to be a terrific leader, a wonderful fellow. You know, Groves had rubbed the scientific community the wrong way by his rather imperious methods, and Hull was such a relief, such a wonderful fellow who understood human nature. He did many things to smooth over the rough edges. He immediately called on our scientific director, Dr. Darol K. Froman, of the Los Alamos laboratory. Coming to Washington and not knowing what the assignment was, we had General Hull briefed very thoroughly over in the Atomic Energy Commission, which was then in the Public Health Building on Constitution Avenue.

He said, "Fine. I'd like to have people come back with me, and we'll go out and look at the atoll. He came in with a C-54 with bunks in it, and we flew out to Albuquerque and got Darol Froman and Al Graves, and headed for Hickham Field, and Fort Shafter, his regular headquarters. Well, it was very nice traveling with a general. Here was a plush C-54 with bunks in it. We flew night and day. And when we arrived in Honolulu, General Hull said to me, "You know, since this thing is so highly classified, it would be rather compromising for me to appear at Fort Shafter with two atomic scientists in tow." He said, "Do you suppose, Captain Russell, that you could make these two gentlemen disappear for about three days while I straighten out my business at Fort Shafter, and then we'll go on out to Eniwetok." And I said, "Yes, indeed, General. Will you loan me your airplane?"

Q: Ask and ye shall receive, I guess!

Adm. R.: He took it very well, and he said, "Why yes, of course." So we freshened up at Hickham and took right off and went down to Hilo and up to the Kilauea rest camp where I hid out for three days with Dr. Froman and Dr. Graves. We had a wonderful time. We'd sit around in the evening and hike during the day. In the evening we'd sit around the ohia log fire in the cabin, and the two scientists would try to instill some atomic knowledge into my rather thick skull.

Q: That prompts me to ask you sir, what was your background in atomic energy when selected for this job? And what did you do to prepare for it?

Adm. R.: Well, it was nil, but Rear Admiral Parsons took me in hand forthwith and gave me not only a lecture, but things to read, and so forth. I had no original grounding in atomic or nuclear physics.

Q: So you boned up during the period when you were being investigated by the FBI?

Adm. R.: Yes. I had a lot of time with Admiral Parsons, who was very bright in this field. Of course, the moment I was cleared, I spent a lot of time at Los Alamos and got into all sorts of different conversations, briefings, and that sort of thing.

Well, at the end of three days we went back over to Hickham and gathered up General Hull and Dodd Starbird and some other staff members, and flew out to Eniwetok, and pursued further the matter of moving the natives and all that sort of business.

Q: Where were you moving them to?

Adm. R.: To Ujelang. It's about one hundred and fifty miles to the southwest.

Q: And how many involved in this move?

Adm. R.: There were one hundred and forty-five. So on Christmas Day of 1947, we went into Eniwetok with two LST's, and we loaded mamma and papa and all the children and all the canoes, all the fishnets, all the pigs, all the chickens, and other worldly belongings of two tribes of Polynesians and sailed them down to Ujelang, where the U. S. Army Engineers had built a model village for them. They moved in and lived happily ever after, until some ecologists got next to them and said, "You want to go back to Eniwetok, don't you?" And this stirred the old urge, and I think they're going back to Eniwetok. Whether they've gone back or not, I don't know.

Q: But it was uninhabited until now.

Adm. R.: Right. Well, things progressed, and many preparations were made, and we went out, and in the Spring of 1948 we blew three atomic devices on the three sites, and it was the first time that I had witnessed an atomic explosion. And believe me, it was very, very impressive. In the first place, you can't look at this thing unless you look through dark glasses that you can see nothing through till the actual brilliant light of the burst appears.

We detonated just before dawn for various reasons of measurements, and so forth. We had many interesting experiences. There were various elements which became radioactive under various intensities of neutron bombardment, and these were strung out on radial strings to gauge the energy which was actually in the neutron flux which was present at the explosion. When the bursts actually go off, there's this tremendous piercing, bright, brilliant light first. It makes everything much lighter than day. Then you see the pressure wave build, and it comes across the atoll at you, or across the sea at you, like a very intense, but very narrow wind squall.

Q: What kind of speed?

Adm. R.: The speed of sound. You see the fireball grow,

and then you see a mushroom form and go up and up and up. And what I hadn't realized is that there's a wind sheer at very high altitude, and even though the trade wind on the surface was from the northeast, this cloud went up and eventually it turned in the other direction.

The surface of the sea in the vicinity of the burst had this ghostly, greenish glare as a result of, I believe, the radioactivity induced in the sodium of the sea. The isotope of sodium which is generated has a very short half life, so the sea's radioactivity cools off very quickly.

The coral is just melted into a dark gray powder. It's completely pulverized all around the crater where the thing went off. The steel tower in which the weapon was mounted is just completely vaporized and disappears - nothing there at all.

But the records, which were taken by coaxial cable at various reinforced concrete dugouts and bunkers, were perfectly preserved. There was even an auxiliary power diesel that kept chugging away after the blast had gone off, I remember. It was inhaling this intensely radioactive dust into its intake system. We had to destroy the diesel to get rid of the radioactivity.

Q: How far did you stand off the other side?

Adm. R.: We went to sea, but we had a control booth on

Parry Island at which our scientific director, Darol Froman - I'm sorry, his number two, Dr. Graves, and my number two, Colonel Preuss, closed circuits beginning at the weapon on down the tower to the ground and on into the control dugout which was in a completely different part of the atoll. It was they who pressed a trigger from this concrete dugout in a different part of the atoll to actually ignite and set the weapon off.

Q: But you had gone to sea.

Adm. R.: We were at sea observing.

Q: How far distant from the blast?

Adm. R.: Oh, I would think about fifteen miles, maybe - something like that. The whole thing was visible to us. I knew the distance to the horizon and I was gauging the size of the fireball by comparing it against the horizon and various other things.

Q: That was the minimum, safe distance, was it?

Adm. R.: You could probably have been a little closer, I would think.

Q: What was the overriding intention in these experiments?

Adm. R.: The intention was the development of the weapon itself. There were several new principles which were being tried and tried successfully, I might say. And it was a beginning, although we didn't have a thermonuclear reaction. It was the beginning of the thermonuclear era.

Q: And there were three blasts.

Adm. R.: There were three.

Q: Was there a different intention for each blast?

Adm. R.: Yes, there was. Each one had its own purpose. And, of course, there was tremendous security. I was charged with the custody of the nuclear material, and we had a trusted Army officer sitting with the stuff the whole darn time we were underway. We even went so far as to put a great vault up ashore and put Marines around it, and transported, not the "real McCoy", but a lead dummy of it, to this storage place. We kept the real McCoy on board ship - all sorts of precautions were taken like that. And you know, within a year of that time, I learned that Claus Fuchs had betrayed us, and all these things that we were very carefully concealing were already known to the Russians.

As a matter of fact, I went up with Dean Rusk to the United Nations when we made the announcement of a safety area, declaring a safety area around Eniwetok atoll. And I watched the Russian delegate, the foreign minister, Gromyko, the expression on his face, and it didn't change a damn bit when we announced this thing.

Q: He never changes!

Adm. R.: I'm not so sure that he didn't already know all about it and also about Mr. Claus Fuchs. And you know when we discovered that Mr. Claus Fuchs was the traitor, I knew of it and couldn't talk about it for quite some time, but finally, I could talk to Parsons about it. Parsons had worked with this chap, you know, at Los Alamos during the war, and he wouldn't believe. He wouldn't believe it.

Q: What provision did you make, sir, for possible failure of a given bomb. Was there an alternate explosion contemplated in case one didn't work?

Adm. R.: If it didn't go off? We were pretty sure they would go off. No, we didn't. We would have had to go back, and there probably would have been an open firing circuit, an electrical failure somewhere. But we were pretty well backed up with alternatives - as far as that was concerned.

Q: How big a staff did you have to assemble?

Adm. R.: I had about two hundred and fifty in my task group, which was 7.1, the Atomic Energy task group, but there were Army, Navy, Air Force, and radiological task groups in addition to mine.

Q: And how many ships were involved?

Adm. R.: Oh, I would think fifteen - something like that. My old ship, the Bairoko, was the headquarters for the radiological safety task group, and they had all their laboratories aboard for geiger counters, film badges, and so forth. We all wore film badges.

We went in to some of the sites pretty soon after the explosions, and you had to be very careful and not go over your allowed radiation dosage. Froman was determined that we wouldn't have a radiological incident. Unfortunately, we did. There were two men who were removing filters. We had a drone B-17 that flew through the cloud and collected in a filter the atomic debris. Removing these filters, instead of having their safety gloves on, two of them used their bare hands. They had burns, radiation burns, within days of the time they were exposed.

Q: That's a permanent defect, isn't it?

Adm. R.: No. They recovered. Now Dr. Graves, who was the

deputy scientific director of the '48 tests, had had a nuclear accident at Los Alamos in which a man was killed. It was known as the Slotin incident. Al Graves was standing just behind Slotin, and Slotin had built up a mass of urna 235, of uranium enriched in 235 to a certain concentration, and he was bringing the last cubic centimeter of uranium close to this mass. This cubic centimeter would have made it a critical mass. The cube fell off the blade of the screwdriver he had it on, and it made a critical mass. This meant it would blow up, you see.

Realizing what he'd done, he hit the mass with the heel of his hand and spread the little cubes all over the bench, you see. But he died. They gave Al Graves a blood transfusion, the gold fillings in his teeth became intensely radioactive, and until they could bore them out, they put a lead shield over them to keep from burning his cheeks. He lost all his hair. He was senile for seven years after this.

Q: And then recovered from this?

Adm. R.: He recovered yes. His wife was a nuclear physicist. They had one little girl, and when this accident happened, he figured well, no more children.

Q: Well, you said senile. You mean impotent.

Adm. R.: Sterile. I'm sorry, I meant sterile. He was sterile for seven years. But at the end of seven years, he regained his potency, and they had another child, which pleased them very much. He's dead now. He died of a heart attack, nothing connected with his radiation injuries. But all his hair came out, and his hair grew again - it was a very fine, baby-like hair. And every time he came to Washington, there were all sorts of doctors who descended on him and wanted to see him and talk about this incident. Particularly Colonel Jim Cooney, who was our radiological safety officer - a wonderful fellow who knew quite a little about these things. There were all sorts of tests they did on Graves. He recovered to be a very normal man.

He was our number two, and a very wonderful fellow. And he was one of the two scientists who tried to teach me nuclear physics at the Kilauea Rest Camp on the island of Hawaii.

Q: I know that with the Bikini tests, various livestock and what have you were planted in various places to see what effect the explosion would have on them and certain ship hulls were there to see what effect. Was anything like this done for these Eniwetok tests?

Adm. R.: Dr. Darol Froman tried to keep experiments of that sort at a minimum. The object of the exercise, of course, was the development of the weapon, not its effect. Bikini was for effects. So, we did have effects experiments, but Froman was determined not to let them interfere with the main thrust. We had very few biological experiments, as I remember.

Q: But having so few opportunities to test some of these things, you have to take advantage.

Adm. R.: That's right. He was very selective, however, and those that he thought would make a real contribution to our learning, he would let go through. And we had a lot of engineers' structures to see how they would withstand the blast and so on. It was a well-run exercise.

Q: Were there any international repercussions to the fact that he -

Adm. R.: Not to that one, but you remember later on, in some of the later tests, some Japanese fishermen had atomic debris settle on the decks. It would have had no effect if they had washed down their decks, but they didn't do that. They just tracked the dust around and got it in the fish and on their bodies and everywhere else. And over that one, which was, I've forgotten whether that was 1950 - let's see, we were '48, there was a test in '50, and then there was a later one. The Japanese started raising all sorts of hell, and there's still a great aversion in Japan to the fact that Hiroshima and Nagasaki were wiped out by atomic weapons. And then their fishermen got in trouble.

Q: But at the time of these explosions, was there not some concern about these clouds wandering to other parts of the globe and dropping debris?

Adm. R.: Oh, yes. We traced debris from those explosions around the world about three times.

Q: Was the fallout in various parts dangerous?

Adm. R.: No. There was some concern lest a tropical storm would concentrate - the rain would pull the atomic debris out of the air and deposit it with sufficient intensity to be harmful, but there were no such effects. As a matter of fact, this radiation danger is greatly overdrawn. You're bombarded, you and I right now are being bombarded by cosmic rays, which have a helluva lot more energy than X-ray. It's greatly overrated.

Jim Cooney was a very sensible fellow. He knew all about radiation injuries, and so forth, and how they should be treated and what not, and he tried to calm people and keep them on an even keel. Many, many times it's just an emotional issue, you know. It's like the present-day ecologist who goes all out for reverting to aboriginal nature.

But this tour of duty with the Atomic Energy Commission was an extremely interesting employment for me. It put me in the forefront of knowledge in nuclear affairs. Of course, we had our brushes with the Congress. Senator Hickenlooper of Iowa accused Lilienthal of incredible mismanagement, and there were congressional investigations, and all sorts of nonsense.

Q: Were the congressional people invited to be witnesses to these experiments? Was there any special committee?

Adm. R.: Yes, there was a joint committee of the Congress on atomic matters made up of members from the House and the Senate.

Q: That existed at that point.

Adm. R.: Yes. And we had a good number of those people out to witness the '48 tests.

Q: Was your friend Paul Foster there?

Adm. R.: No. To the best of my knowledge, he was not. Usually, if he was around, we'd get together, because he had

had that experience in the Aleutians with me. But my tenure with the Atomic Energy Commission extended on through 1950 when I finally left. I was slated to go to the War College in June of '50, but General McCormack got ill, and because I was his number two, they asked me to stay on. I missed that opportunity.

And it wasn't all bad, because when I was finally released about December time, Trapnell had made the grade of admiral, and he was in command of Coral Sea, and somebody needed to relieve him, and all my friends were in school. I was available, and I got command of the Coral Sea a little ahead of my time.

Q: Kind of a reward. But can you at this moment talk about anything else that you did at the AEC during that time?

Adm. R.: I can talk about defending government housing before the Congress, getting money, budgets, and so forth, but it's not very exciting.

From the peak of activity connected with the atomic tests at Eniwetok, this duty tapered off until I was engaged in the mundane business of getting money to do government housing at Los Alamos. You know, at Hanford, it was a government town for a while, but later was opened up. It was very interesting employment. We did many things, such as setting up manufacturing concerns, better means of fabricating in-

Russell #2 - 290

gredients like plutonium, which is a deadly poison. It's a metal. And the manufacture of the mechanical and electrical components of the bombs. We developed ways of getting industry into that - to change/industrial methods from laboratory methods.

But I think first and foremost I enjoyed the meeting, and becoming familiar with and getting to know the atomic scientists at work at Los Alamos. That was a great treat for me. And visiting places such as Los Alamos, and the bit accelerator in Livermore. And the very inspiring operation in the chemistry of radioactive materials at a place like Hanford. This was a great experience really, a very broadening experience.

Q: It was not too long after that when Eisenhower came to the presidency, that he began to talk about the use of atomic energy for peaceful purposes.

Adm. R.: That was talked about from the very early days.

Q: Well, this is precisely what I want to ask you. Was there much of this while you were serving there?

Adm. R.: Well, you remember when the war ended, the United States offered to share the knowledge for peaceful purposes of nuclear fission, nuclear fusion. It was the Baruch Plan for worldwide use for the good of mankind. And we couldn't move the Soviets in that direction at all. There were such things as inspection of production facilities and all this sort of thing, and they'd have no part of it. And the whole thing fell flat.

Now, we also wondered in the early days, beginning in '47 when I joined, what do you do when some other country explodes an atom bomb? What do you do? Some radicals said, well immediately you attack it and eliminate it. Well, you remember in 1949 the Russians exploded one. And there you were. I'm sure they were helped along the way by Claus Fuchs' defection and his traitorous action. But here we were now faced with competition.

In the present day, there is not only the Soviet Union and the United States, but there is India and China recently. There's England, there's France, and Japan certainly has the knowledge to make nuclear explosives.

Q: And according to newspaper reports, Israel also.

Adm. R.: And Israel, and also Egypt has talked about it. Well, let me go on and say it was a tremendous experience for me to be on the staff of the Atomic Energy Commission, meeting all these famous people.

Q: Who were some that stand out in your mind - some of

these scientists?

Adm. R.:  Well, Bob Bacher of Cal Tech.  Urey, E. O. Lawrence, Edward Teller, Johnny von Neumann, Niels Bohr, Enrico Fermi, Rabi, Hans Bethe, Alvarez, Oppenheimer, and at the laboratory itself, of course, there was Norris Bradbury, John Manley, and Harold Agnew.  Meeting people of this character was, of course, a great privilege.  There are truly great minds in the world of nuclear physics.

Now, from the Atomic Energy Commission I was privileged to go to sea as commanding officer of Coral Sea.  And of course, as you know, the highlight of any naval officer's career is ship command.  I had had command of Bairoko.  We had a wonderful ship, but here was a much larger ship with very much more power, and really a delightful ship to handle. She handled like a motor boat.

Q:  I take it this was your great command.

Adm. R.:  It was, indeed.  And I took it in February, 1951, from Trapnell, and as soon as we could check out an air group, we went right back to the Mediterranean, and we were there for six and a half months.  And embarked on the ship was our division commander, Rear Admiral Dan Gallery.  You remember, Dan Gallery was writing for the Saturday Evening Post and Collier's at the time, so it was a great treat to be with him, because he was always out for a story, for an adventure, and so forth. As a matter of fact, one had to be careful going ashore with him lest you got into more trouble than you'd bargained for!

Q: In what sense?

Adm. R.: I remember one time going ashore in Cannes. There was some sort of entertainment going on, and there was a beautiful lady sitting at a table almost alone, and the good admiral went over and introduced himself and sat and talked with her, asked for a dance, and one thing and another. And it turned out to be the sister of the king of Egypt, who had been divorced from the Shah of Persia! And there were people with dark looks.

Q: Fawzieh was her name.

Adm. R.: These people were haunting the grape arbor behind where this table was. And I wasn't sure about the wisdom of courting this beautiful lady in the presence of all the body guards that went along with her.

Q: Did he know her identity?

Adm. R.: No. That didn't matter to him. He introduced

himself as Daniel Gallery, probably with a slight Irish accent. As a matter of fact, we went ashore one time at Taranto to Admiral Lubrano's very delightful party ashore. Admiral Lubrano corresponded to a district commandant in America. And he gave a very stately party. Present was an Italian rear admiral, Bigliardi, whom we had known earlier on in the cruise, when he was superintendent at the Naval Academy at Livorno - Leghorn in English. He had now been transferred to the ministry in Rome and had come down to be at that party. He may have been visiting in the neighborhood. But he collared Admiral Gallery in the course of the evening, and said, "Now this is a very nice party, but it's rather staid and it will end fairly early in the evening. I would like to invite you to go to Bari. There at the Air Force Club in Bari is a party that's really an excellent party in progress. Won't you come with me to Bari this evening when this party ends?"

Gallery came over to me and asked me what I thought about it, and I said, "Well, perhaps, Admiral. But I think I would have my Navy car and my Marine driver follow us over, so that if you want to come home from the party in Bari, you can." "That's a good idea, and you'll come with me." So, we embarked in the official Italian Navy car with Admiral Bigliardi and an enlisted driver, and went screeching across the heel of the Italian boot at 120 kilometers per hora, swinging around curves on mountainous roads with great high-wheeled donkey carts in the roadway every once in a while, which the driver narrowly missed.

We arrived in Bari, and indeed there was a party going on. There was a flotilla of British corvettes in the harbor, and it was commanded by one Captain Graham. And Captain Graham said he'd like us to meet some of his captains. And we went around meeting this one and that one, and he then introduced us to a tall, handsome fellow. You know, when you meet a movie character in person, you say, "Where have I met that fellow before?" Well, this tall, handsome chap did look very familiar to me. Captain Graham said, "Here I would like to have you meet the commanding officer of Her Majesty's Ship, Magpie, the Duke of Edinburgh." I did a double-take and, sure enough. Here was Prince Philip! And he was in fact commanding Her Majesty's Ship, Magpie, doing his bit of active duty with the Navy.

We became quite talkative, and vied for pretty ladies' hands for dancing, and one thing and another. As the evening wore on - it was a beautiful party - a marble courtyard encased by an office building, which was an Air Force headquarters in the city of Bari. There was an orchestra at either end, and when one tired out, the other would start playing. All the offices on the level of the terrace had been converted in to bars or entertainment places of one sort of another, wine and sweetcakes and all that sort of thing; vermouth, (the Italians, of course, are great for drinking Negroni and Vermouth of various sorts), but as the evening wore along, Gallery came to me, and he admitted that he'd had quite enough of wine and sweetcakes, and couldn't we find some place where we could get a good scotch and soda!

So I said, "Let's organize an expedition here. Perhaps we can." And over in the corner of the courtyard, we did, in fact, find one of the offices which had been converted to a bar, and there was scotch and soda. And guess who was at the bar - the scotch and soda place - the Duke of Edinburgh! Well, Gallery, putting on a slight Irish brogue, looked up at this tall, handsome fellow, and said, "The Duke of Edinburgh, eh?" said he. "You know, Duke, I was on duty in Scotland once." And the Duke said, "Is that so!" And Gallery said, "Yes. And the place is mentioned in the opening stanzas of Annie Laurie. How does Annie Laurie go, Duke?" Well, I began to feel smaller and smaller as this thing was going on, and the good Duke looked at me and said, "Captain Russell, I don't rightly remember how Annie Laurie goes. Do you?" And I said the only line I could remember was "her neck was like a swan." "Oh, yes, yes," said the Duke, "I remember that line, too, but how does it begin?" Well, suddenly we thought, "Maxwelton's braes are bonny."

"Maxwelton," says Gallery, "that's where I was on duty in Scotland!" So we drank a scotch and soda to Maxwelton!

Well, that's the sort of occasion that you could get involved in if you went ashore with Dan Gallery.

Q: Actually, you didn't have any home base in the Mediterranean, did you?

Adm. R.: No. We made twenty different ports in my six-and-one-half months, with a lot of time at sea. We did a lot of flying. I had two banshee jet squadrons and two conventional fighters, prop fighters, and a sky raider squadron. We developed some tactics that were rather ingenious, I thought. We could get an extremely small launching interval with the AD's by launching diagonally across the deck, and having the pilot hold the nose down so that his wheels were firmly on deck as he went through the wing wash of the fellow who had just taken off on the opposite diagonal. So you'd have one go toward the port side - the port corner of the forward ramp - and the other one, just as soon as number one was well underway, would start diagonally across toward the starboard corner of the forward ramp, you see.

Q: How much of a time span?

Adm. R.: Oh, perhaps ten seconds between airplanes. It just looked like a bursting bomb. I could get all my sky raiders in the air in no time at all. Of course, the banshees had to be catapulted, and we had many adventures there.

One day, Admiral Gallery appeared on the navigating bridge, and he said, "Jim, I'd like your permission to fly a sky raider in the next launch." I looked at him and I said, "Admiral, who the hell am I to give you permission to fly a Sky Raider!" I said, "You're strictly on your own! But there will be a Sky Raider available for you." Well, I knew that he'd been checking out in the cockpit. He was quite an aviator, very much interested in flying. He had a very thorough cockpit checkout and, sure enough, he got in a sky raider, and we launched him with the rest of the Air Group for that particular flight. When he came back to the ship, the landing signal officer put him off to the side, and made him make several passes, so that he was sure that the admiral would respond to his signal, and then he brought him aboard, and Admiral Gallery made a beautiful landing. And all the rest of that cruise, every once in a while, he would get one of the sky raider squadrons to loan him an airplane, and away he'd go, flying with the regular air group.

Q: This must have given him tremendous standing with the groups.

Adm. R.: It did. Well, he had a chief of staff, Eddy Renfro, who, seeing his boss cavort off the end of the deck and land back aboard, decided that he really shouldn't be outdone under the circumstances, and he appeared on the navigating bridge one time, and he said, "Jim, could you let me fly one of your SNJ's?" We had two training planes with hooks on them which we used as utility planes, to fly in to the beach, carry the mail, and all that sort of business. Those were our ship airplanes, and the officers attached to the ship flew them.

I said, "Why, of course, Eddy." So he went down and took off with an SNJ in a regular launch. He was barely off the deck when Admiral Gallery appeared on the navigating bridge. And he had rather a sly smile on his face. I thought, "Gee! what's up?" He said, "Jim you haven't had a fire drill recently, have you?" And I said, "Admiral, that's correct. I have not had a fire drill recently, and I haven't had a fire drill on an airplane burning in the arresting gear on landing." "That's right!" he said, and he went off down to his own bridge. When Captain Renfro came in the little training plane with the hook down and so forth, he landed nicely in the arresting gear and was ready to taxi up the deck, but the yellow shirt plane director jumped up and down, and gave him a frantic "Cut! Cut! Cut!" Cut your engine, you know. Whereupon the man with the asbestos suit came out along with men with fog nozzles, the foam, the fire hose, and Captain Renfro was lifted out of the cockpit by the fellow with the asbestos suit. So we had a fire drill, you see!

Well, this was the sort of thing that was going on with Dan Gallery all the time. It was just one thing after another. I remember one time we were in a battle against the <u>Roosevelt</u>, and one of her sky raiders dived on us, but when he pulled up, he found he had a rough engine, so he requested a deferred forced landing and we took him aboard. Admiral Gallery was ready with a squad of Marines, and when he landed, he was made prisoner of war, and his head was shaved! So that's the way cruising with Dan Gallery was! It was a lot of fun. We had a wonderful time. I think the most difficult circumstance as far as ship-handling was concerned, was when we were in the roadstead of Istanbul.

You know, the Bosporus runs usually with a 4 to 5 knot current. There were three cruisers and the <u>Coral Sea</u> at anchor pretty well in the center of the Bosporus, and there were four Turkish destroyers in shore of us towards the town of Istanbul. They were lying with their sterns upstream, because the current, which was running at about 5 knots, comes down the center of the waterway and bifurcates on a stony, rocky point. Half of it goes up the Golden Horn and reverses and goes close in shore back up to an eddy at the bend in the Bosporus above Istanbul. The other half goes on into the Sea of Marmara.

Well, I thought about getting underway. In the first place, I'd had bad luck with a pilot, French pilot, at Mers-el-Kebir, the military harbor at Oran, when I had had to take the conn away from him. He just didn't understand the power we had and how the ship would maneuver. So, I was discussing getting underway with Freddie Warder who had one of the cruisers upstream of me. I said I wasn't going to take a pilot, and he said he wouldn't think of taking a pilot. One of the skippers did take a pilot and had a tug. He had a terrible time in turning around and getting out.

But here I was the last ship downstream, the next one just above this rocky point, and I saw myself impaled on that point if I in any way failed to get turned around in time to steam out to the Sea of Marmara. I read up the Coast Pilot, and I found a caution that there were old cables on the bottom where previous ships had slipped their anchors and gotten underway. And I thought, gee! Supposing my anchor comes up fouled with something - say an old cable leading down to the bottom - and that would prevent me from turning around, and yet I'd be drifting down on the point.

Q: Remembering Guam!

Adm. R.: Yes! So I got a party of ship fitters up on the fo'csle, equipped with an oxy-acetylene cutting torch, with orders to go over the side and cut loose any old cable which might be afoul the anchor. I steamed to my anchor, holding the ship up against the current, steaming at 5 knots, you see, until the anchor came up. It came up clear. This is the only time I used airplanes to help me turn around. I had four sky raiders in each of the four corners of the flight deck with their tails outboard. And once the anchor was announced as clear, I fired up the opposite corners of the flight deck to help me turn around. I backed full on the starboard propellers and I went ahead standard on the port. And we started turning with a very high rate of turn. And, of course, once we started turning, we were creatures of the current. We were drifting down on this point.

Well, when I got within 30 degrees of the heading out to the Sea of Marmara, I gave all ahead standard. That's quite a bit of power. It should give you 15 knots, you know. She swung on around through the rest of the 30 degrees, and we went shooting out through the entrance.

Well, my friend, Freddie Warder with his cruiser - once I got out in the Sea of Marmara I had to wait for the rest of the ships to join up. And I couldn't see the roadstead, because it was obscured by the headland on the Asiatic side of the Bosporus. But I did see Freddie Warder's cruiser appear stern first and then disappear upstream, and then the next time I saw him, he was headed out and came out and joined me. Well, over a beer at Canea in Suda Bay, many days later, I was with Freddie Warder, and I said, rather casually, "Freddie, how did you make out getting out of Istanbul the other day?" "Oh," said Freddie, "there was nothing to it." Freddie's an oldtime submariner and quite a character, you know. "Well," he said, "no trouble at all." And I said, "Well, from where I was out on the Sea of Marmara, it appeared to me that you came downstream stern first and then disappeared. And the next time I saw you, you came out bow first." "Oh, yes," he said. I said, "What did you do?" He said, "You remember that whirlpool up at the bend in the Bosporus above Istanbul?" I said, "yes." And he said, "Well, I went up there and I put my bow on one side and my stern on the other and it turned me around, and I came out!"

Q: Like a turnstile! Tell me that technique of using four planes to help you turn around. That was not an unusual technique, was it?

Adm. R.: Not at all. That's called pinwheel, but I always thought that it was a disgrace to admit that with all the horsepower we had in our ship's engines, that we couldn't handle a ship and we had to have airplanes to help us turn around. And I regarded it as a sort of a sacrilege to waste the power of an engine that wasn't doing the airplane any good, you know, sitting there turning up at full power.

Q: How does that work with a jet?

Adm. R.: Just as well. A jet doesn't develop quite as much thrust when it's standing still as does a propeller, but it still works.

Q: And it's in the book of rules. You can do it.

Adm. R.: Yes. It's permitted.

I had a wonderful, wonderful one year and two days in command of Coral Sea.

Q: You spoke about twenty-one ports where you visited at this time. These must have been a lot of diplomatic niceties that you had to attend to.

Adm. R.: Oh, yes. We were in Bizerte, many ports in Italy, ports in Greece, Istanbul in Turkey.

Q: You were welcome in North Africa then.

Adm. R.: We were indeed. We did Tunis, and Oran, Mers el Kebir. And remember, the French Foreign Legion was then at Sidi-bel-Abbes. I flew one of our little airplanes down, landed in a local field there and had lunch with the colonel, then picked him up on another day and brought him back up to the ship where he had lunch with me. A very interesting experience.

Q: Were you able to use Wheelus at that point?

Adm. R.: I never used Wheelus. It was not near a harbor which we used. We didn't go into Libya. But we used to great advantage Suda Bay. We went in there many times. Augusta Bay in Sicily, for example. Oh, I'm trying to think of the name of the roadstead. You know, there's a strait between Sardinia to the south and the French island to the north, Corsica, and they are the Straits of Bonifacio, I think, through there, and there is a harbor just on the eastern side, and we went into that place, which was rather an out-of-the-way place (Golfo Aranci). We went at least twice into Phaleron Bay where we anchored to visit in Athens.

Q: What about Malta?

Adm. R.: We didn't go in to Malta, because of the size of my ship. Going into Valetta Harbor is not too healthy for a big carrier. We went to the French Riviera, of course.

Q: What did you do if you needed repairing?

Adm. R.: We didn't need repairs.

Q: Well, I know, but in case this happened.

Adm. R.: If it was a matter of dry dock, we could have gone into Toulon at the French Naval Base. As a matter of fact, we did go in to Toulon, and Rene Bloch, who was my liaison officer there, is now a rear admiral. He's an aero-engineer, and the chap who was instrumental in the design of the Atlantique, the NATO patrol plane. We went in to Golfe Juan, to Cannes in France, and to Gibraltar, of course. It was really a delightful, wonderful cruise. And I had a great air group. I did lose a couple of people, unfortunately. I never will forget, and it's really something to remember in handling a carrier. A banshee towing a sleeve for gunnery, intent on climbing rapidly, he got on the reverse side of the proper curve, stalled and fell into the sea directly ahead of me. He was very close aboard, and I had thought this thing through. I knew if I put my rudder over either way, I would take him under the keel, because the ship doesn't turn right now when you put the rudder over. It develops its turn by first twisting sidewise. And if the fellow in the water is close aboard, all you do is put him under the keel of the ship.

The only thing I could do was to order emergency back, which would begin to stop the power to the screws with their tremendous indraft. So I couldn't turn. The squadron pilots thought I had run the guy down. They said, "You should have turned." I said, "Well, look, if I had put the rudder over either way, I would have taken him under the keel." And they said, "But he was far enough ahead so you could turn." And I said, "Take a look at the movie." He had a 600-foot towline, and his sleeve was still on deck when he splashed in the sea, so he was less than 600 feet ahead of me. And my ship, you know, is 900 feet long.

After that what I did was to put an off-duty pilot down in the secondary control station, which is right under the forward ramp of the flight deck, and I had a sight mounted which showed the center line of the ship extended forward, and this pilot's only duty was to tell me on the bridge down which side the fellow in the water was going to go. And if he was going to pass on my starboard side, if he's a little bit even to the starboard side, the moment this lookout gave me "he's here", I would put the rudder over toward him (right rudder), and that would swing the stern away from him. But if he was going down the port side, I'd give left rudder, and it would swing the stern away from him. But that is something to remember, if there's a fellow in the water dead ahead of you and you put your rudder over and start your ship turning before he passes the stem you'll take him under the keel.

Q: So this fellow was lost.

Adm. R.: Oh, yes, he was lost. I talked to Gallery about it, and he said, "Jim, don't give it a second thought. He was dead when he hit," - because he hit with tremendous force, you know. I watched another fellow. Strangely, he rolled on his back and bailed out, and we found his chute and not his body. He was in a corsair. I don't know what happened to him, whether he had a heart attack after he got in the water or what. He could have tangled in his chute and panicked, but we recovered the chute and the empty harness and no man.

One time I was the only one who saw an airplane go in the water at night. This chap was in a night Sky Raider. He was watching his running lights. All of a sudden they went out. I ran to the pelorus, took a bearing of him and plotted his position, and then gave the alarm that we had a plane in the water. Nobody else, although I had visual lookouts, saw that plane go in the water. I raised a lot of cain about that. The only reason I knew it went in the water was that it's light disappeared - just suddenly, like that. And sure enough, shortly thereafter, we saw a red flare shoot up. The crew had gone into the water, and were firing a red flare. Of course, our accompanying destroyer went over and picked them up.

We had rescue helicopter on the ship. It was a fairly early model, a Boeing Vertol Hup, a tantem rotor affair. And those, of course, were worth their weight in gold for rescuing people. You could get there in a hurry, and pull people out of the water quickly.

Q: Was the Royal Navy at that time very much in evidence in

the Mediterranean?

Adm. R.: Quite a little bit. Also we had a French carrier visit with us somewhere once. I've forgotten whether it was the Clemenceau or another of their carriers. We had maneuvers with the Greeks, for example, and Turks, and Italians. All in all it was a very wonderful cruise.

Q: You didn't go through the canal.

Adm. R.: Suez? I couldn't get through. We drew too much. It we were fully loaded, and we had about a two or three foot drag, I believe, our draft was about thirty-eight and a half feet aft, and the canal is at most forty feet. I don't know that it's forty, in fact, I don't think it's that much. Essex class could get through, but I couldn't. I couldn't get through the Panama Canal either.

Q: Were the Russians at all in evidence?

Adm. R.: Not at that time, no. Well, so much for the Coral Sea.

I came back and took, in effect, the job I had left in 1944.

Q: Your tour of duty was over when you came back to Norfolk?

Adm. R.: I came back, and took the ship in to the shipyard. We went through our three-months overhaul, and I took the ship to sea for her post-repair trial with Robert Burns Pirie along with me, and when we got back in, I turned it over to him, and he took the ship.

Coral Sea we called the admiral maker, because the first ten skippers all made flag rank. Very interesting.

I came back to the air warfare division in the office of the CNO under Op-05, the head of aviation in the United States Navy. And this was essentially my old division of military requirements in the Bureau of Aeronautics.

Q: Grown up now.

Adm. R.: Grown up now and over on the big staff. I was there for a regular tour of two years, I believe. And while there, I was selected to flag rank. As a matter of fact that Spring of '52 I was selected. And my first job as a flag officer was with an escort carrier, a CVE division. I flew to San Diego to join it, and we exercised from that port. We had one CVE and usually a squadron of destroyers, with three tame submarines along. Submarines were very, very valuable. Submarine time for anti-submarine forces was hard to come by. We took that task group over to Japan, where I based at Yokosuka largely, but we would go out on a two-week exercise and go in to some other port - either in Japan or over in Okinawa, one time we went in to Hong Kong. I had finished my tour over there and was about to come home when Bud Ruble became ill. He had command of Carrier Division 5, and somebody was needed to replace him. I was ordered from a CVE division to a CVA division which rarely happens in this navy. I was extremely lucky to get a big carrier division.

Right away we were in serious business, although I took it over a little before Christmas. That February we were directed to give air cover to the evacuation of the Chinese Nationalists from the Tai Shan Islands off Shanghai. Mel Pride was the 7th Fleet commander. And there was some question, some argument with Chiang kai-shek about taking his troops out of there. The beaches on the Tai Shan Islands were zeroed in by the Communist artillery. We had a task group and Stan Ring came over and joined up with another task group. Together we kept very heavily armed strikes airborne over the Communist area. If they had opened up with their artillery, we were going to take out their artillery. It was a very strenuous operation, and the amphibious force evacuated something like 18,000 troops and 13,000 natives of the islands and brought them back to Taiwan.

As that thing finished, I was ordered to be Chief of the Bureau of Aeronautics.

Q: You came back to shore duty from the Coral Sea and took

over this division in the Navy. There were some new developments that you were involved with?

Adm. R.: Yes. One of the more interesting airplanes, for example, was the RA-5, which was built by North American Columbus - one of our reconnaissance planes. A beautiful looking thing. It was not the best carrier plane, but it developed into the RA-5-C with a tremendous photo-reconnaissance capability. It was a real step forward in reconnaissance.

Q: Was this the first real advance since World War II?

Adm. R.: I think so. We had reconnaissance fighters, you know. They'd adapt a fighter to reconnaissance, and call them RF's. The RA-5-C's are just going out of service now. But in the carriers, there was a tremendous advance, really. The angled deck came in. The steam catapult, and the mirror landing sight, which provided an optical glide path. The fact that the deck was angled, allowed you to do away with the barriers, which used to be the cause of many airplanes' demise, because if you overshot the arresting gear, you could crash into the barrier.

Q: Who was responsible for this development?

Adm. R.: The British. A very good friend of mine, Rear Admiral Dennis Campbell, R.N., was a leader in this. He was talking in the Admiralty about the mirror landing sight, and he told his secretary, a female secretary, to put her lipstick on the left side, the port side, of a table, and to put a pencil beyond it. Then he told her to make a circuit around the room, and when he was lined up with the major axis of the table, to keep the top of her lipstick container in line with the lead of the pencil lying on the table. This the girl did and she wound up with her chin on the edge of the table. Whereupon Dennis Campbell said, "See. This is the mirror landing sight. It brings you down very accurately to the deck."

Well, in fact it did. And then we got Fresnel lenses as a development of the mirror landing sight. Primarily from the pilots' viewpoint, you see a bar of white lights with a space at the center, and then you see a yellow light in the center. The yellow light is called the 'meatball'. It's a simple device. If it's on a field, it's very simple, but aboard ship, because of the pitch of the ship, you have to have it gyro-stabilized. But this yellow light, if you're high, is above your broken line of white lights; and if you're low, it's below. So when you comeaboard, you keep this yellow light between the ends of the two white bars, and this means you are on a glide slope, which is usually about three degrees to the horizontal, and you don't even flare, you fly into the deck. Carrier-based airplanes have a stronger landing gear than land-based planes, and they can stand the impact of the $3°$ descent when they touch the deck. This system was particularly needed for jets, because, with your flaps, your wheels, and your hook down in a jet, you are fairly aerodynamically dirty, and you're drawing about 80 percent of your jet thrust just to keep flying at a steady speed, around 120 knots. So, coming down on the optical glide path, you touch down, and even though you catch a wire in your arresting hook, you immediately apply full throttle. If you don't have a wire, that full throttle will carry you around and you can take off and come around and try again. That's called bolting if you miss the arresting gear. Simple, but when the angled deck came, I wasn't completely sold on it, until I realized its great virtue in handling jets, with which we'd had all sorts of trouble, because a jet was so structurally smooth that when it hit the barrier, sometimes it went right on through it and crashed into the airplanes up ahead. So here was a way of solving that problem.

Now, the catapult was another matter. We had gone from torpedo air to gunpowder as a launching source of energy. But in carriers, if you had a powder charge to expend every time you launched an airplane, you'd soon sink the ship carrying powder charges. So, something had to be done, and it was done in this fashion. We had a accumulator with compressed air, which was used only as a spring on top of a liquid -

an hydraulic fluid. And the hydraulic fluid under pressure was admitted through a quick-opening valve behind a piston, which overhauled wires and towed the airplane into the air. The business side of the catapult was a shuttle in a slot in the deck. Power was applied by the hydraulic fluid pushing a plunger out which overhauled the cables which drew the cable and shuttle forward to launch the airplane.

This meant that instead of wasting energy by exhausting the launching pressure by blowing down to atmosphere at the end of every catapult stroke, as you would with a powder charge or with torpedo air, you conserved the elastic medium, the compressed air, because when you reached the end of the stroke (incidentally, the piston was stopped by hydraulic dash pots with plungers) you could cut off the pressure by closing the launching valve. Then retracting the piston, you just drain an incompressible fluid into a sump from which it can be pumped back up into the accumulator against the pressure. So you saved all that energy, and thus made catapulting a very common, practical thing for a ship.

So we went along with the hydraulic catapult from the days of Yorktown, CV-5. Historically, we had an inertia catapult on the Lexington, CV-Z, at one time. It didn't work out too well.

But with the ever-increasing size of the airplane, the ever-increasing velocity at which you had to launch it in order to make it fly, the sheaves and the wires, got bigger and bigger and bigger, and finally too much energy was going in to starting and stopping, sheaves spinning, wires translating. So you needed to do something to get away from all the wasted energy in starting and stopping.

Again the British came to the rescue. They developed the steam catapult in which a piston bearing the shuttle was driven down the deck by steam. Thus, the launching force was more directly applied to the airplane. Well, how did they do this? They did it by having a closed cylinder behind the piston and an open cylinder ahead of it. There was a steel ribbon, actually two steel ribbons, that lay on the bottom of the tube, so you had an open cylinder forward of the shuttle; but the shuttle picked these two steel ribbons up and sealed them, so that you had behind the piston a closed cylinder. And furthermore, you controlled the acceleration by injecting steam through a series of ports as the piston moved along the deck. The object, of course, was to give a stead acceleration to the airplane, to avoid peaks which would give impact loads to the airplane structure. Here was a piston, directly hooked to the airplane, so there was practically no inertia to stop at the end of the catapult stroke, except the mass of the piston itself, and the shuttle, of course.

Q: Isn't it interesting that the British had these two ideas, which we took over, and yet our naval aviation was much more advanced than theirs.

Adm. R.: We just didn't think of them. Sometimes when you're in austere circumstances and you think a lot, you come up with an idea that the fellow who has a lot doesn't. These are our British cousins. It certainly created a revolution in carriers.

Q: Does this mean that they had a constant liaison and communication between the two?

Adm. R.: Oh, yes. Yes. Dennis Campbell had been on duty here, and I went to England with him in March of '44 on a standardization meeting, when we flew all over England. We went up to Crail, where they trained torpedo pilots, and East Haven, where they trained their landing signal officers, and so on. With Dennis Campbell, the chap who was behind a lot of these developments.

Q: Now you mentioned something else, too, which I didn't catch.

Adm. R.: I was going to say that after this time, but certainly contemplated at the time, and something we developed ourselves, was in the air refueling. When I had command of Coral Sea, we were asked to participate in the Paris Air Show in 1951. We cooked up an idea. I launched fourteen banshees. At first I was going to fly the whole air group up but the embassy said that was overwhelming, to cut it down. So we flew off fourteen banshees from our deck in the Mediterranean. They flew up, let down, and made two very low passes in formation across the field at Le Bourget, climbed to altitude, came back and landed on my deck. But the low man on the totem pole, the fellow who had turned most fuel, had seven minutes of fuel left. And that was just enough for one more pass, possibly, before he ran out of fuel if he'd missed the arresting gear. And that's too close. I got caught once with a chap who had to come back aboard with a mechanical difficulty, and I spent too much time steaming into the wind. Finally, I wound up taking the last banshee jet of a scheduled recovery aboard in a turn in a cove in the island of Sicily.

Now, the old sailing ship captain used to abhor a lee shore, because you could get blown down on it. A carrier skipper abhors a windward shore, because he runs out of sea room running into the wind to take his airplanes aboard. This is rather an interesting feature of carrier operations. But now, with in the air fueling, if you get in a jam, you say, "Go up, rendezvous with a tanker over head, take a drink, get more fuel." And it makes all the difference in the world. No longer are you pressed, knowing that that fellow is going to run out of fuel in a certain length of time. You just tell him to go up and get some more fuel.

Q: Now, where was this first experimented with?

Adm. R.: Well, it's been tried many times, and, of course, SAC had used aerial refueling to lengthen the legs of their bombers for some time. The Navy uses a probe and drogue. It is called the buddy system. They have a refueling drop tank on an airplane of the same type. A buddy has a tank that he carries along just for refueling with a drogue that sails out behind. The airplane to be refueled flies so that his probe comes in and mates with the drogue; that establishes a connection, and the fuel flows from the tank into the airplane.

Q: Now, this came into being as a technique?

Adm. R.: This came into practical use in the fleet after I had Coral Sea and after actually, I was director of Op-55, the division of military requirements in OpNav.

Q: Had you experimented with it before you came in as director?

Adm. R.: Well, it had been experimented with.

Q: But had you in particular?

Adm. R.: Not particularly, no. We recognized it as a possibility, but it didn't come into vogue until after I left the OpNav desk. It came into vogue really, later on when I was with the Bureau of Aeronautics.

Q: Well, those were three tremendous improvements. Were there others perhaps minor or less?

Adm. R.: Actually four - angled deck, steam catapult, optical glide path, and aerial refuelling. The arresting gear is still hydraulic, but the valve through which the hydraulic fluid is forced in the arresting process, is now programmed so that you get a constant retarding force on the airplane, throughout a constant length runout down the deck. You set the arresting gear to apply a steady deceleration, the setting is determined by the type of airplane, to bring the airplane to a stop in, normally, 220 feet.

There are other improvements, but they're minor ones.

Well, let me see. We got to Carrier Division 5, the evacuation of the Tai Shan Islands.

Q: While you were on the desk for military requirements and new developments, were there any new planes that were being designed and which now are in evidence and use. Was there anything of that sort that might be of interest for the historian?

Adm. R.: Yes. The Vought F-8, and the McConnell F-4. The P3, an anti-submarine plane, was adapted from a turbo prop transport of Lockheed, the Lockheed ELECTRA.

But it wasn't actually until 1956 when I was at the Bureau of Aeronautics that we got the Collier Trophy for the first ship based airplane which flew faster than 1,000 miles an hour, the F-8. The F-8 took about four and one-half years to come design inception to first service use.

Q: Did you personally have any input for that?

Adm. R.: Not particularly.

Q: What was the status of the flying boat at that time? Had Martin begun to experiment with a jet-propelled one?

Adm. R.: Yes, the SEAMASTER, but that again was developed and flew first after I had been to sea and back again as Chief of the Bureau of Aeronautics.

Q: Well, then, shall we go to the Air Warfare Division?

Adm. R.: I'd left that and been to sea on Carrier Division 17 and Carrier Division 5, and as we finished the Tai Shan Islands, I received dispatch orders from James L. Holloway, Jr., the Chief of Naval Personnel, saying that my employment on shore duty had been determined in the governments' interest by the Secretary of the Navy, and I would be Chief of the Bureau of Aeronautics.

I had arranged to have my wife come and join me, because I would have been in the western Pacific over thirteen months with the two assignments. She got eighteen shots, a passport, and got as far as Honolulu, and I was ordered to the Bureau of Aeronautics. I stopped her there, joined her, we married our oldest son off in the Makalapa Chapel, and I proceeded on back and reported in to the Bureau of Aeronautics in February of 1955 in time to defend a budget before the Congress which I had not seen before, a rather difficult job.

This all came about because Apollo Soucek, then Chief of the Bureau of Aeronautics, had a heart attack, and had to leave his post. This left the chief of bureau position vacant, which I filled.

Q: What sort of a budget was this in terms of millions of dollars?

Adm. R.: It was billions, actually. It was the Navy Procurement Budget for airplanes for the year, the fiscal year '56, as I remember - probably on the order of three billion dollars.

Q: Was it difficult to shepherd this through the Congress? You had contacts on the hill, did you not?

Adm. R.: Quite difficult. We, of course, had many hearings on the regular budget, but we were also beset with investigations. We had a number of aircraft designed to take what was to be known as the J-40 engine. The Westinghouse Company had done very well with an axial flow engine called the J-34, but the J-40 was to be of similar design but greatly increased in power. It was a very compact engine in its design. Westinghouse fell down badly on the job. The engine came out greatly reduced in power. It was the only engine which would fit into the F3H-1, a McDonnell fighter.

When we started losing airplanes because of the engine, I, as Chief of the Bureau of Aeronautics, gave the order to ground the aircraft. This was done, and my staff informed me that there were twenty-six F3H gliders at the McDonnell plant, and what did I choose to do with them. I said, "Well, we have a mechanics school at Memphis. Let's put these airplanes on a lighter and take them down to Memphis and let the mechanics assemble and disassemble them and find out how a modern airplane is built." We were towing these aircraft through the streets of St. Louis down to the waterfront to put them on a lighter in the dark of night, when we were discovered by the press, and headlines broke out across the country of the Navy's abysmal lack of appreciation for good business, that we had invested in an airplane which couldn't fly or didn't have an engine to make it fly. It was immediately, of course, made a subject of congressional investigation.

Russell #2 - 324

The airplanes were, in fact, loaded on the lighter and taken down to Memphis and served a purpose, certainly not the intended purpose. But to add insult to injury, the reporter who discovered our towing act won the Pulitzer Prize for his reporting for the year.

Q: Based somewhat on this incident?

Adm. R.: Quite. Thinking of how to defend this before a committee of the Congress, I decided that the best thing to do was to confess our error and quite honestly face the problem that one has when he designs a high-performance fighter. I explained to the gentlemen of the Congress that a second-rate fighter was no fighter at all.

Q: What committee was that?

Adm. R.: This committee was, I think, chaired by Mr. Holifield. It was a sub-committee of the House Armed Services Committee.

I explained to the gentlemen on the committee that a second-rate fighter was no fighter at all, and a fighter really had to embody the very latest in technology. And, in doing that, one, of course, had to run certain risks, and occasionally, these risks turned out to be very real; and in this case, the Navy made a mistake in putting their faith in the J-40 engine. The chairman couldn't adapt himself to the fact that I was admitting a mistake. He rose in his chair and glared down at me like the bull in the pit. You know, they sit in an elevated circular arrangement, and you're down below in the pit. He rose from his chair and pointed his finger at me, and he said, "Admiral, do you mean to say that you admit that you made a mistake?" I said, "Yes, sir. We made a mistake." And that sort of took the wind out of the sails of the investigation. We produced all the figures they asked for, how much money had been spent in the development of the engine, which had not panned out, and the fact that other manufacturers such as Douglas with the F4D had left a big enough hole in the fuselage to put an alternate engine in, the Pratt and Whitney J-57, but McDonnell had economized in space to the point where no other engine would fit this particular fuselage. He did come out with an F3H-2, a succeeding model, and they were flown reasonably successfully, but the only engine that would go into that was the Allison J-71. And we had some trouble with the turbo jet flaming out if it was flown through a driving rain storm.

So, not only did I have to defend a budget, which I had no hand in preparing, but I had two rather serious investigations to testify before. One was the J-40 engine itself, and one on the F3H-1, which was an airplane that would take no other engine than the J-40.

Of course, time went along and I had other congressional

investigations. I remember very well when Senator Symington decided that there was an airplane gap - that the Air Force was not receiving the attention it should with better airplanes, and the U. S. was falling behind. He'd very carefully planned this, but President Eisenhower insisted that if the good Senator was going to investigate airplanes that there was a naval air force, and Senator Symington must, of course, include that in the investigation. So, we came to that particular investigation with two strikes against us, because we'd been thrust upon the Committee unwantedly. I'm sure that we didn't care to appear, but because of the rather one-sidedness of Senator Symington's investigation, the President had told him that he must include the Navy in his investigation.

Q: But as I understand it, the Navy was adequately prepared to defend itself in this.

Adm. R.: As Chief of the Bureau of Aeronautics I attended many, many long days with stacks of statistics on airplanes, including prices and weights, and times to develop, and so on. I remember one day Senator Symington was investigating the unit price of aircraft, and I was reciting figures on - oh, say the A3D which cost so much - and I came to the A4D. That airplane, strangely enough, cost only $450,000 at that time, which was well below anything like the F-104's or other contemporary aircraft. And, when Senator Symington heard this, he said, "Say. That's a very economical airplane." And I said, "Yes, Mr. Chairman, that's the poor man's airplane. It was designed to be economical." And he said, "The poor man's airplane?" And I said, "Yes, sir, the Navy, you know." And Mr. Symington had to pause for a moment and engage in a moment of levity!

But congressional investigations, I must say, were rather numerous in those days. An investigation was generated by the least excuse, and Congressmen tried to make headlines by their investigations. I remember the past chairman of the Armed Services Committee, Mr. Hebert, started an investigation on the exorbitant profits of the aircraft industry. He conducted a good number of hearings, and he'd made a number of headlines. He, I think, accused Chance-Vought of spending money unnecessarily in their advertising. He accused Grumman of spending money unnecessarily in conducting school and so on. And each time there was enough to get a headline for him.

Well, it finally came to the Navy Department itself, and dear old Mr. Fogler, who was the Assistant Secretary of the Navy (Materiel) and I appeared upon that particular day. Mr. Fogler had a prepared statement and I had a prepared statement. And when it came my turn, I read my statement putting as much emphasis as I could in it, and when I finished, the chairman of this subcommittee investigating the "exorbitant profits of the aircraft industry", Mr. Hebert, said, "Admiral, I find your statement very unsatisfactory." I smiled and said, "Thank you, Mr. Chairman." Then he said, "You say practically nothing." And all the while, he was looking out of the corner of his eye at the press box. He knew that at 11 o'clock the reporters would have to leave to make the afternoon edition and generate some more headlines. He said, shaking his finger at me, "Admiral, I suppose it's a good old Navy custom to pass the buck." I smiled at him, and he said, "But, Admiral, in this case you forget. You have no place to pass the buck. Do you realize that, Admiral?" And I said, "Yes, Mr. Chairman, I realize that." And so on it went, and I'm afraid Mr. Hebert could see headlines in the paper the next morning about "Mr. Hebert castigates the brass". However, the pressmen apparently thought it was so raw that they published nothing on it! And this was the sort of thing that one gets in in the day to day conduct of the government business.

Q: Well, it's quite a handicap, isn't it, to conduct the business of the Navy under such circumstances?

Adm. R.: It certainly is. But you should see how detailed involvement the committees of the Congress get into in the present day. It's much worse than this.

Q: But there are on these committees some very knowledgeable men, are there not?

Adm. R.: And some very decent ones, and by and large, they mean to get the government's business done on time, but occasionally you run into these rather far-out situations.

Q: Well, now, this takes an awful lot of time for the head of the Bureau of Aeronautics to prepare for these hearings, does it not? You can get people to give you the statistics, but you still have to do some preparation.

Adm. R.: Of course. Of course. Well, let me see.

Q: What percent of your time was taken up with budgetary matters?

Adm. R.: It would be hard to say. I had time to do other things, of course. I would say that we had in our preliminary design two models of each type of aircraft coming along all the time, which we never do any more. And there were really some forward-looking designs.

One very interesting thing came up while I was there. That was the matter of guided missiles, and ballistic missiles. The combination of a nuclear-powered submarine and a ballistic missile was a very intriguing thing. The Bureau of Ordnance I tried to push to look into ballistic missiles, but they had an air breather that was their favorite at the moment - a super sonic air breather missile. I think they were really fearful that that project might be damaged by a truly ballistic missile. It so often happens, particularly if the Congress gets wind of something that might be better than what you have aboard and what you're asking for, they will postpone that in the name of economy to get something better. It's the old story of the dog and the bone. You know, the dog saw the reflection of his bone in the water, went for it, and lost the bone.

We, in the Bureau of Aeronautics, were very intrigued with the idea of putting ballistic missiles in submarines, but we had a couple of handicaps. One was that the Bureau of Ordnance was very backward about ballistic missiles. We had difficulty, because Arleigh Burke was now the CNO, and he tended to support his old Bureau, and beyond that, Mr. Charles Wilson, who was Secretary of Defense, said, yes, we could have a ballistic missile on a submarine, but we'd have to use the Army's Jupiter rocket. Well, the Jupiter rocket was a liquid fueled rocket, and you can imagine nothing nastier than having liquid fuel loose in a submarine.

Q: Also, it was an impossible size, was it not?

Adm. R.: And it was also too large, yes. That's true. But I got sort of fed up with this, and I made - in those days we Chiefs of Bureau reported directly to the Secretary of the Navy, you know - three study contracts with three aircraft companies to study the problem of putting ballistic missiles in submarines. That sort of forced the hand and really bought attention to bear on the subject. This, of course, became a practicality when the solid fuel ballistic missile turned out as well as it did. Polaris became a project. Then, it was a matter of who would take this project. The Bureau of Ordnance - we'd tried to push in that direction. The Bureau of Aeronautics, which had been pushing, and yet the rocket, one might say, should belong to Ordnance as being a piece of ordnance rather than an airplane.

And this case came before Mr. Gates, who was Secretary of the Navy. Mr. Gates joined in a conference among us to pass judgment on whether it would be put in Ordnance, whether it would be put in Aeronautics, or where it would be put. He led off with, "I believe in giving projects to the people who work at them." I thought to myself, "Well, he's going to give it to the Bureau of Aeronautics." Then he said, "One might think that this is in the province of the Bureau of Ordnance." But he said, "A curse on both your houses!" I'll have it directly under me. However, because Aeronautics has pushed it, we'll put an aviator in charge of it, but the Polaris project will report directly to me." This was the genesis of the SPECIAL PROJECT. The first SPECIAL PROJECT in the Navy.

Red Raborn, an aviator, was taken from the guided missile

division of OpNav and put in charge of it. A very astute ordnance engineer by the name of Levering Smith was his number two, and the master technician on the job. They set up special offices. They had carte blanche to take any of our people in the technical bureaus that they desired to man the project. This was used with great effect. A lot of our very good people were shifted over to the Polaris project.

The PERT system was invented, and I can give you the name of the civilian, Gordon Pehrson, who developed the PERT system. Polaris was off and running. As you know, it became a great success.

Q: Other than personnel, what did the Bureau of Aeronautics do to contribute to this SPECIAL PROJECT?

Adm. R.: We had had the three studies made. And, of course, those were turned over. Aside from that, Ordnance was given the housekeeping chores, and that was it. They set up shop in a wing in the munitions building, and Aeronautics, of course was pleased that this project could be brought to fruition, as it was adroitly and compentently done by the team which was assigned to it.

Q: How was Secretary Wilson handled - his insistence that it should be the Jupiter, and very shortly thereafter the

Navy cut loose from the Jupiter. How was this handled?

Adm. R.: He was convinced, finally, when the ballistic missile with solid fuel became a reality. Of course, the solid fuel rocket, the Polaris rocket, put the Air Force on notice that they would have to do better than their big liquid fuel rockets, and they, too, then, went into a program which was known as the Minuteman program, but it was really kicked off by the fact that Polaris turned out to be such a success.

Q: Do you want to say something at this point about the flying boat, the Seamaster, which Martin was developing?

Adm. R.: It was developed when I was Chief of the Bureau of Aeronautics. It was a beautiful airplane. The tips of the wings drooped downward and acted as wing tip floats. The hull itself was very sleek looking. It had a bomb bay which rotated, so that when the aircraft was performing as a flying boat, there was a continuous surface underneath the airplane sealed by inflated gaskets so that it was water tight; but when it was airborne, the bomb bay, which was in cylindrical form, just turned around, so an open side of the cylinder was down, and you could drop your bombs through the bottom of the seaplane.

It controlled nicely in the water. It had a water rudder which was quite effective. Of course, in the old days when you could reverse propellers, you could do quite a bit of maneuvering a flying boat. You could actually back up in them, but with the Seamaster there were no jet reversing buckets, so taxiing was a matter of controlling the direction. I remember that Admiral Mountbatten visited. Arleigh Burke, Mountbatten, and I went to Baltimore and looked at the aircraft. We went out in a boat while the aircraft was flown overhead, demonstrating its various features, like rotating the bomb bay, and so forth.

Much to our sorrow, an aircraft was lost under rather peculiar circumstances. It was in the higher part of the speed envelope approaching the speed of sound, and the airplane pitched up violently enough so that a structural failure occurred, and everyone in it was killed. We, of course, started an investigation to find out what the trouble might be. A second Seamaster was being tested at Patuxent River when another failure in flight took place. This time, instead of pitching up, it did what we say "tucked", it pitched down. It pitched down with such violence, it was evident that the wings had come off and the two tips touched underneath the body of the flying boat.

Q: Just folded up!

Adm. R.: Now, I may be wrong, and perhaps it was the "tuck" that occurred first in which we lost people, and the pitch up second when people actually ejected. I think the pitch up was near the Martin plant, as I remember, and the people safely ejected. I'm wrong. The sequence was a "tuck" first, and then a pitch-up; and after the people ejected in the pitch-up, the aircraft slowed, of course, and actually recovered and almost flew itself down to the ground. But of course it crashed, because there was no one in it.

Well, it was discovered that there was a rather simple arithmetical error in scaling up the control forces. And what was happening was in the hydraulic control. If the nose of the airplane started up, of course the pilot would push his yoke forward, and what he was doing was opening an hydraulic valve intending to put pressure on the control surface to make it counteract the rising of the nose; but actually the force on the control surface overcame the pressure of the hydraulic fluid and actually forced it back through the system. So all you were doing in trying to control the airplane's altitude was opening a valve that allowed the control surface at the tail to go to an extreme position under aerodynamic loads in a direction opposite to that desired. Thus a violent tuck, or pitch-up resulted.

Q: Was there any basic incompatibility between concepts, I mean the jet-propelled plane and the flying boat as such?

Adm. R.: No, except perhaps the concentration of mass. We

were a little suspicious as to whether the mass distribution of the airplane was suitable for a high-speed airplane. It was not a supersonic airplane. It flew very close to the supersonic speed. But the difficulty encountered just really made it impossible to continue with the design. Mr. Gates wanted to continue. He thought that it was a good concept, but the project was canceled.

Q: What were the merits of a plane of this sort? What were the real advantages of a jet-propelled flying boat?

Adm. R.: Extension of the art of jet propulsion to a large seaplane, and a very fast, very high-speed airplane. As a matter of fact, the Strategic Air Command got interested in it. It had the great virtue of being able to operate off water when you had no runways, which, of course, is one of the primary virtues of having a seaplane in the first place, that you can operate from the surface of the water. But that project, unfortunately, was canceled. It was canceled after I left the Bureau of Aeronautics.

Q: What was the fate of lighter-than-air in your time as the Bureau head? Was this to the fore at all?

Adm. R.: It was completely secured. There were blimps. The rigids, of course, went out with the Macon and Akron. Akron, of course, was lost in a thunderstorm off the Jersey coast with Admiral Moffett, who'd been Chief of the Bureau of Aeronautics for so long. The Macon was lost in fairly calm weather, quite calm weather, off the California coast. They put the rudder over and just the rudder forces started a structural failure, and she broke up very slowly and settled in the water, and I think there was no one lost at all.

We had some heavier-than-air pilots on board in what was called the belly bumpers' club. Airplanes hooked on to a trapeze and were hoisted into the hangar of the dirigible, but, except for the Goodyear blimp, which was a commercial endeavor, there was practically no activity in the lighter-than-air.

Q: And no foreseeable use for such airships in the Navy?

Adm. R.: No. The blimps had done fairly well at patrolling off the coast. One place that they were used was across the Straits of Gibraltar where a magnetic anomaly device was carried at low altitude searching for submarines. No, there was no lighter-than-air activity to speak of when I was Chief of the Bureau of Aeronautics.

Q: You might want to comment on the recent resurgence of interest, and I think there was a meeting up here in this part of the world recently, dealing with lighter-than-air craft and the possibility of using them once again for lifting heavy objects.

Adm. R.: Essentially, it's a very awkward device, a lighter-than-air ship - big and bulky. I have flown in blimps, and it's very much, as I would imagine, like riding an elephant. Its motions are very slow, its response is slow, and one has to be trained as a free balloon pilot, really, to understand everything that's going on.

Q: It's kind of dangerous, too, isn't it?

Adm. R.: Well, the safety record was quite good. But if you had a strong headwind, you just didn't get there. They're slow.

Why don't I go on and tell you, then, that various people got interested enough in my career as Chief of the Bureau of Aeronautics to suggest that I should go to sea and get groomed for higher things. And I was in fact assigned as Jerauld Wright's deputy commander for the Atlantic Fleet. A very wonderful job for a wonderful gentleman. It was the first time my wife and I ever lived in government quarters. We lived in Delaware House at the Norfolk Naval Operating Base. It took three stars in my day to get in to government quarters, and I had just that. I became a vice admiral.

Russell #2 - 339

It was a very interesting time, because of - not particularly the fleet operations, but the fact that we had the NATO activity, the SAC Lant command, which was not in my purview. That was across the way. But we were close enough to be fairly familiar with what was going on. We got in the NATO exercises and so on.

I was there only a year when I was appointed Vice Chief, and I went back to Washington, D. C..

Q: Incidentally, what exercises were you involved in? That famous one off the Norwegian coast?

Adm. R.: No. We didn't have a big one. That occurred about every two years. They didn't have one of those. We had what is known as SPRING BOARD, which is a series of training-up exercises down in southern waters, off Roosevelt Roads and Vieques and Culebra Island down in the Caribbean area. We did have the problem of getting the President to Europe and back. We had a chain of destroyers across the ocean, when a great storm came up, and it looked almost as if a couple of our destroyers would run out of fuel before we could get an oiler to them. And when the oiler did arrive, the sea was very rough, and it was very problematical whether we could get the fuel to them. A destroyer which runs out of fuel at sea, of course, is in considerable danger, particularly in a storm. But fortunately, things worked out all right. We got the oiler there, and the destroyer which was low in fuel was properly refueled. A matter of planning and so on.

We trained the ships up and sent them over to the 6th Fleet.

Q: Was the Strike Force in being as a concept?

Adm. R.: Oh, yes. The 6th Fleet is called the Striking Force by the NATO planning group. Strike Force South is the NATO name for the U. S. 6th Fleet. The 2nd Fleet on the U. S. east coast, engaged every so often in a northern exercise with NATO Navies. Of course, we had the Amphibious Force, and many exercises, but none of tremendous note.

Well, from the deputy commander of the Atlantic Fleet I went back to Washington and became Vice Chief to Admiral Arleigh Burke. As you know, Arleigh Burke is a man of tremendous energy, and working for him was truly a great pleasure. It was something like hanging on to the tail of a rampant bull, I would say! Many, many things to do.

My first experience, however, was being cut out of normal activities largely each day to serve on the Franke Board, which was studying the organization of the Department of the Navy. And that is a sport which has been going on before and more or less constantly ever since - how to reorganize the Navy.

Q: Well, anything tangible came out of it?

Adm. R.: A lot of words, and the idea of the bilinear system was upheld, which kept the materiel bureaus directly under the Secretary as the suppliers of materiel, and the CNO as a generator of requirements off to the side. As a matter of fact, it wasn't until McDonald, I think, was the CNO that we put the entire Navy family under the CNO - the Chief of Navy Materiel with the functions of the old materiel bureaus, as well as the CNO staff. Unified commands, of course, were in vogue at the time and still are, in which unified commanders report directly to the Joint Chiefs of Staff, and the service Chiefs merely train and supply the forces to the unified commanders.

Q: Was this a part of the amendments to the National Defense Act of 1958?

Adm. R.: There were things done, particularly the concentration of power in the office of the Secretary of Defense, which were done under the system in which a reorganization could be - a planned reorganization - reported to the Congress, and if nothing was done in a certain period of time - I believe it was something like sixty days - it was presumed to have had permission and the endorsement of Congress and it could proceed.

Russell #2 - 342

There were some notable changes in the makeup of the unified commands. We had a Navy commander who was known as CinCNelm. As a matter of fact, when we went into Lebanon in 1958, CinCNelm was sent down from London to take charge of the operation. The 6th Fleet, of course, were the performers in it, but it was an operation under CinCNelm. At the time, it was Admiral Holloway who had left the Bureau of Naval Personnel and become CinCNelm. He went down from London and took charge of the operation.

Q: When you became deputy to Arleigh Burke, what was the understanding? By this I mean, he told me that when he chose Don Felt to be his deputy, he chose him expressly because he was not a "yes man." He was a "no man", and he wanted somebody who would say "no" rather than "yes sir". Was this your role as well?

Adm. R.: Well, Arleigh gave me a tremendous charter, which said, "You can do everything required in my name when I'm absent." And it was truly a broad delegation of authority to me, one which I appreciated very much. We got along very well together. There were many amusing incidents.

The decision to go into Lebanon, of course, was one of the crucial times. We finally got the okay to do that, and Burke, of course, moved very fast. He got the 6th Fleet in there in a hurry, and then, after the operation was actually started, CinCNelm came on down to take charge of it. It was done with rapidity and a degree of efficiency that was very pleasing.

I remember one of the trips I made was out to be speaker at the recommissioning of my old ship, the Coral Sea. She'd been overhauled in Bremerton Navy Yard - modernized, if you please. She'd been placed out of commission and modernized and was being placed back in commission. The chap, Jim Gray, who'd been my operations officer, when I was commanding officer, was to take command of her. Jim was a Scotchman. I flew out in a C-118, invited Senator Jackson to come along, and he did - very good company, I might say. And when we went to the ship in the Bremerton Navy Yard, naval procedure, you know, is to pipe the senior officer aboard. As I approached the brow to go aboard ship, I was amazed to hear not the bosun's pipe but a set of bagpipes. I went up to the quarterdeck and there was a bagpiper who marched me down to where I was to go. I explained when this bit of ceremony was over that I had played the bagpipes in a bagpipe band when I was a youth in Tacoma. So the pipe major took the pipes off his shoulder and handed them to me, and I said, "I'm sorry. I play left handed," which is a fact. I learned from a lefthanded bagpiper to play left-handed, not that I am lefthanded. Andrew Lowe, who lived across the prairie from us here at American Lake.

The pipe major disappeared, and it wasn't very long

until he came back with a set of bagpipes rigged for a left-hand bagpiper! So there was nothing I could do except put these on my right shoulder, which is the wrong shoulder to an ordinary piper, and the only tune I could remember was Highland Laddie. I played through that and then passed the pipes back to him. But meanwhile, the press were there, and the Associated Press took a photograph, and they put it on their wire. And it spread across the country, a photograph of Russell playing the bagpipes on the quarterdeck of the USS Coral Sea.

Q: In full uniform.

Adm. R.: In uniform, with broad stripes and three little narrow ones. And after speeches and so forth, and winging on my way back to Washington, D. C., I went in to see Arleigh Burke to say, "I am back, boss, and ready to go to work." He was sitting all hunched up at his desk, with a scowl on his face, and he had a newspaper clipping in front of him. And it was from a Dallas newspaper, and it was a picture of Russell playing the bagpipes left-handed on the quarter deck of the USS Coral Sea. And what did he say? He said, "Oh, jeez, I wish I could play the bagpipes!"

Q: You were there during the Suez crisis, were you?

Adm. R.: Not the Suez crisis. We were there at Lebanon in 1958.

Now, I left the Vice Chief's job after Burke had retired, and, incidentally, we had a great retirement ceremony, a great shenanigan down in the Washington Navy Yard, and again I played the bagpipes. This time borrowed from the pipe band of the Air Force - their Highland band. I had one of their pipers, and the two of us played. And we did a skit, which was a takeoff on Holy Loch. There were a bunch of irate Scotchmen in kilts who complained against the United States Navy, that the USN was interfering with the Loch Ness monster concession with their big, black submarine beasts that they were bringing in to Holy Loch. The Air Force piper and I piped to actors to the stage, marched them through the audience up to the stage, where we stood by while they performed. And then we inflated our pipes and marched them back down through the audience and out the back door.

You've asked, Jack, if I was the Vice Chief when the Bay of Pigs fiasco took place, and the answer is an emphatic "Yes!" And believe me, it was a heart-breaker. We were informed on what was going on, but we had no authority over it, no power to do otherwise. You see, I served in the Joint Chiefs of Staff when Burke was not present. I would be there with the Joint Chiefs in all their sessions.

We watched the development of the Bay of Pigs, and the first thing that went wrong in my opinion was when the last of the carefully planned raids of B-26's, which were supposed to destroy all airplanes available to Castro, was not allowed, because of, as I understand it, intercession by the State Department. That Department said that we were making bad character with our Latin-American neighbors by the air raids. This amounted to a fatal mistake, because there were a few old British fighters that survived, and they actually took charge of the air over the Bay of Pigs and put a rocket, as I remember, into the rudder of one of the principal supply ships, one that had radio gear in it and other important cargo. But it was really a heart-breaker to watch this thing develop and yet have no control over it. You could see it was heading for a great fiasco.

Of course, Burke, who was a very aggressive type, was all for stepping in, and finally, he just went ahead and ordered the destroyers to pick up refugees all along the beaches. He was very disappointed when Rear Admiral John E. Clark - and I'm not sure whether Clark was then commanding officer of the carrier or whether he was embarked on it as a flag officer. I think he was commander, as I remember. With a bunch of A-4's, I think Burke more or less expected him, when things were not going right, to step in, and yet he was under rather stringent orders to not show himself in sight of land, and under all sorts of other restrictions. It was truly an artificial situation as far as getting any fighting done was concerned.

Russell #2 - 347

And after the fiasco, the President's brother, Bobby, had a small committee to look into the why's and wherefore's of the operation and what to avoid in the future. And Burke was privileged to serve with that group.

Q: What lessons did they learn?

Adm. R.: Well, I think the primary lesson was don't let the CIA run a war! As you remember, there was a chap by the name of Dick Bissel with CIA at that time. He'd done truly a great job in the development of the U-2's and the over-flights which produced very valuable intelligence from high altitude photographs. Dick Bissell had come to me, actually, when I was Chief of the Bureau of Aeronautics, with again a blank check to draft any equipment that we had available. We were very glad to help him, and we did help him in the matter of cameras and some other things.

You remember, the U-2 was the brainchild of one Kelly Johnson, the aero-dynamicist and airplane designer with Lockheed.

Thinking back on those days, one of the events that was also a snafu of the first order was a flight when the U-2 with Powers in control was shot down, and Powers survived and was made a prisoner by the Russians. I remember the flight had a window, you might say, of time, that if it was not conducted by a certain date, it was not to go. If a flight could not be conducted before a certain date, the flight was not to go, because it was too close to a visit which was planned by President Eisenhower.

Q: That was a summit.

Adm. R.: A summit conference, yes. And it went about the last day, and lo and behold!, it was shot down, and, of course, the summit conference was canceled because of it.

The other event of very considerable interest which happened - of course, Sputnik had put us in a position of looking as if we were lagging the Soviet Union in modern technology, and in fact, we were in a way, at the time. Everyone was casting about for ideas on how to regain some of the world attention and do something to counteract the terrific impact which Sputnik had had on the world in general. Captain Marmaduke Bayne, USN, known as Duke Bayne, was our project officer, and the scheme we offered was to sail the Nautilus across the north pole under the ice. After one false start, this was accomplished, and after her passage under the pole we had Nautilus steam close to Keflavik. A helicopter was sent out from there, picked up Commander Anderson, who was the skipper. At Keflavik he was put in a Navy airplane. Meanwhile, we asked Mrs. Anderson to come to the White House, and we had a number of dignitaries like the Secretary of the Navy (it was Mr. Gates at the time), and others at the White House. There we produced Anderson and broke to the world the news that we had a submarine cross the north pole under the ice.

Burke was out of town at the time, Mr. Gates squawked my squawk box, when I was quite new in the job. He said, "Jim, do you think we should invite Rickover to the White House?" We had been asked by the White House to cut down the number of people we were having as much as we possibly could, and I had already asked the Fleet Commander, Admiral Wright if he would want to come, hoping that he would say no, but he did come, and it looked to me as if we were going to invoke the displeasure of the White House by having too many people there. And I also knew that Rickover was violently opposed to this stunt, for hazarding one of his nuclear-powered submarines by the foolishness of sending it under the ice across the north pole. So my response to Mr. Gates over the squawk box was, "Well, I don't think so, Mr. Secretary. This is an operational matter, and I think it won't be necessary." Well, of course, when we had our ceremony at the White House, and the press noticed the absence of Rickover, which they did immediately, they went to Rickover's office and said, "Why weren't you at the White House on this auspicious occasion when one of your nuclear-powered submarines, of which you were the father, transitted the pole under the ice?" And Rickover, in his usual helpful style, said simply, "I wasn't asked." Then all hell broke loose.

Russell #2 - 350

Q: With the Congress, I suppose.

Adm. R.: The President looked to the Secretary of the Navy, and Mr. Gates stepped forward and took all responsibility for the absence of Rickover. Eventually that storm died down, and I paid penance for my lack of good judgment by riding in the tickertape parade in New York with Anderson on one side and Rickover on the other, and introducing the speaker at the gathering in New York City, and starting out with a great harangue as to what a wonderful fellow Rickover was. One has these rather sharp memories, but mine is the voice of Mr. Gates over the squawk box, "Jim, do you think we should invite Rickover to the White House!" It was a question I shall remember for a long, long time!

Q: Do you want to say anything about your relations with Admiral Rickover?

Adm. R.: Well, Rickover is a dedicated man. I first met him when I was assistant flight deck officer on <u>Yorktown</u> fitting her out at Newport News. I think I've related this before, but perhaps not on tape.

Well, in those days we had 24-volt circuits in airplanes and the engine was started with an electric starter, on current which came from a storage battery. Often the pilot would over prime, underprime, and in attempting to start on the flight deck would run his battery down. He'd then become a dud, and we'd have to cut him out of the pattern and pull him off to the side. And I had the thought, well, let's get a 28-volt circuit around the flight deck and run a jumper to the airplane, so that even though his battery is dead, we can get him started and get him launched, and, of course, once his engine is turning up and his generator is working, the battery will recharge, and he will be in good shape.

So, I was commissioned by the air officer and the skipper to fly one of our ship's airplanes up to Anacostia and go see if we could get a low-voltage direct current loop around the flight deck. I flew to Anacostia and took the boat across to Haines Point and a car up to the Navy Department. In the Bureau, I think it was in the Bureau of Steam Engineering, I was directed around, and finally I wound up in the office of the electrical division officer. This individual was one Lieutenant Rickover, who listened to my story, rather impatiently, of our difficulty with airplanes which ran their batteries down and the need for a jumper to provide electricity to get them started. He said in a haughty tone, "Do you know how much copper wire this would take?" And I told him I had calculated in to be a rather large copper wire, but with four motor generators spaced around the deck, the IR drop wouldn't be too great. He then proceeded to read me off in no uncertain terms as being extravagant, unrealistic, and that he wasn't about to give me any copper wire to do this.

Well, he was so obnoxious, I left, cursing under my breath, thinking if I ever meet this fellow in a dark alley, I would really let him have it. I went back to the ship and confessed the failure of my mission.

Years later, when I was with the Atomic Energy Commission, and General Jim McCormack, Director of the Division of Military Application, was invited down to make a Fourth of July speech at Oak Ridge in 1947, I volunteered a Navy Beechcraft airplane and flew him down. In honor of the distinguished visitor, the Post Commander - it was still a military post under Groves at the time - gave a reception at his quarters, and it was a very gay affair. At it I was amazed to find that a Captain Rickover was one of the more popular people at the party. And I set about to try to find out why this phenomena - why he was so popular. I discovered that he was standing at the top of his class in the reactor school, and he was absolutely obsessed with the idea of putting nuclear power in submarines. For this, the scientific personnel there respected him very much, and he was very popular.

Of course, everyone knows that he did in fact make a great success of nuclear power in submarines. He did it with great skill and much of the success is due to his conservatism, to really working things out. If a high pressure water pump was to be used, it was tested for thousands of hours and tested very, very thoroughly.

Q: He didn't want to have a failure ever.

Adm. R.: Never have a failure, and as a matter of fact, we had no failure until we lost Thresher and then Scorpion. These failures, I think, were largely due to the fact that the submarine with high speed under water can, in any failure of the control system, or even inattention to controls, get to great depths in such a short time that she's in great peril. Of course, Thresher's loss is, I believe, attributed to a failure of plumbing or flooding which resulted from the failure of internal piping.

Q: Silver soldering, or something.

Adm. R.: But a nuclear powered submarine with all its power, depended too much, perhaps, on using that power to drive up to the surface rather than increasing buoyancy.

Of course, we had a very involved program called sub-safe after that in which all sorts of things were done. Among other things, means of a rapid deballasting for buoyancy.

Q: I understand also that Rickover has always feared a disaster which would result in great unfavorable publicity, and that one major disaster would kill the whole program.

Russell #2 - 354

Adm. R.: Exactly. And that's one reason for his conservatism.

Q: Why is this necessarily so? In any program, it seems to me, the possibility of failure in one instance or two is always great and can be overcome.

Adm. R.: The emotion which goes with something new, something different, something that's not easily understood, such as the radiation hazard; the atmosphere under which these things are considered is different, really, and people don't reason, they emote. They fear the unknown. They don't know much about it. Much of the atomic information is limited to a few people, not generally known across the board, and anything that is new and unusual, and considered dangerous, becomes an emotional issue with people. And you could very well kill a lot of things.

Look at the difficulty we've had with the Japanese since their fishermen were burned after one of the tests in the Pacific. And, of course, the damage that was done at Hiroshima and Nagasaki has become an emotional issue. So, I think the risk is very real, and there would be serious damage done if we had a nuclear accident in a submarine.

Well, on the next assignment. When Arleigh Burke retired, George Anderson came, and I stayed on through to some time in November, as a sort of link in continuity between Burke's administration and the one which George Anderson was setting up. George and I had been shipmates on the Yorktown. He was landing signal officer, and I used to spell him in that job. I had flown with him. He was in one of the patrol squadrons at one time, and I had known him from the days at the Naval Academy right on through. He and I had been on duty in the Bureau of Aeronautics in the old days together. And I admired him very much. But he was one who believed in the chain of command, the prerogatives of command, and he objected very strenuously when the Secretary of Defense, Mr. McNamara, started dealing directly with individual ships, and such, instead of through the normal chain of command. This was very foreign to George's makeup.

But I did stay on with him for a length of time, and then was ordered as Commander-in-Chief Allied Forces Southern Europe, reported to Naples, and did about a two-week stint with Cat Brown, when I discovered he was determined to stay on until his retirement date, which was the 1st of January. So, my wife and I took leave and went off up to Florence and came back down in time for a relieving ceremony on the 2nd of January. We couldn't very well relieve on the 1st of January.

So I took over command of Allied Forces Southern Europe on the 2nd of January in 1962. And, believe me, that was the most delightful assignment that anyone could ask for.

Q: Why?

Adm. R.: The defense of Italy, Greece, and Turkey - three very, very different people - was a tremendous challenge. It was a whole new world, really, to learn to know these people. The components of the command - there was the Italian general in the north of Italy with a command called Land South, the air component commander was a U. S. officer, first General Swafford, and then General Webster. There was a Land Southeast, which was a combined Greek and Turkish command, and because it was not politic to place a Greek over Turks and vice versa, this job had to be an American general. I had General Brown first, and then about mid-span of my term, General Michaelis took over that job.

There were two allied tactical air forces, the 5th in the north of Italy at Vicenza, and the 6th at Izmir in Turkey. Every admiral has a boat which is known as a barge, and the boat which was available when I got to Naples was in such poor condition that it had to be replaced, and the Bureau of Ships, in its kind wisdom, sent me over a smaller boat, but one which was acquired open purchase. It just happened to be a yacht off the production line of Chris Craft at Pompano Beach. Admiral Rivero, my amphibious commander friend, put a crew aboard and sailed it up to Norfolk, put it in one of his LSD's, and brought it over to me, and it was a wonderful asset, because one way to get cooperation among my officers was to take them out on the boat! And it was such a delightful cruise, nice atmosphere, and so forth, that they would enjoy themselves thoroughly, and it added to the ability to make peace, let's say, between the Greeks and the Turks and create a greater appreciation for the Italians.

It was amusing at times, too. General Frontistis was the chief of staff, chief of defense staff, in Greece, and I was visiting with him the defenses along the northern border of Greece. We came to the headquarters of B Corps. I had asked General Frontistis if it would be satisfactory with him if I brought along my deputy chief of staff Plans, who was an Italian general by the name of Pistotti, and General Frontistis, of course, said, "Why, we're all allies, and by all means, bring him." So when we were being lectured at Kozani, I believe it was the headquarters of B Corps at the time, in the north of Greece, General Frontistis in his opening remarks quite obviously said some things to make my good General Pistotti feel that he was welcome and at home in the atmosphere there. However, after the meeting, General Frontistis and I were driving away alone in his Mercedes with his driver and Colonel Vidalis as interpreter. We were silent for quite a while, and he finally said, "Do you know Admiral, we dislike the Italians intensely. They invaded our country in World War II. Also, we dislike the Germans intensely. They invaded our country in World War II. But we respect the Germans, because they won their battles, and we despise the Italians, because they lost theirs." And you can imagine the deep down feeling in my Greek Chief of Defense staff about the NATO nations on the southern flank whose defense I was to coordinate!

Q: And not to say anything about Turkey and the Turks.

Adm. R.: Well, the Turks, on the other hand, I learned to admire very much. They're a simple people. They're very direct. The Turk makes a wonderful soldier, because he's absolutely uncompromising when it comes to doing his duty. It was the Turkish officer always who asked the most obvious, but the most embarrassing, let us say, questions at our conferences. But truly a simple, straight-forward people.

The Greeks are wonderful. They're a little devious sometimes, far better educated than the Turk. The Italian is a happy-go-lucky fellow ordinarily, intense in what he has to say, but very forgiving in what he has to say. He's seen so much history pass by in his country that he's rather prone to smile at the world and figure everything's going to come out all right in the end anyway.

But you can't imagine any three more different people in temperament, in the manner in which they think, and even their religions, of course, were different; the Roman Catholics in Italy, the Greek Orthodox in Greece, and the Moslems in Turkey.

I had some wonderful trips, wonderful experiences. We had maneuvers. I would always try to, if the maneuver was over in the Greek-Turkish area, mix the Turks and Greeks usually with the Marines from the 6th Fleet. We had visiting NATO troops from Central Europe. We had a parachute brigade come down from Germany, for example, when we were having maneuvers in Turkish Thrace. We had the Marines land from the 6th Fleet and establish a perimeter, and then we landed a follow-up force to extend the perimeter, a force made up of a mixed group of Greeks and Turks, in command of a Greek, if it was on Turkish territory. Conversely, if we had our maneuvers over in Grecian Thrace, we would have the follow-up force a combination of Greeks and Turks and put it in command of a Turkish colonel.

I did this under rather amusing circumstances one time. We had gotten the Marines ashore. It was rather rough, and there were some delays, and in the viewing tent, which was a lean-to on a hill facing the beach, was none other than King Paul of Greece. We had arranged to have the LST that bore the Turkish battalion land first, and the King was going to greet the Turkish troops as they came ashore. The operation, you remember, was in charge of a Turkish colonel. And in the other LST was a Greek battalion. These were Greek LST's, and the group commanding officer of the landing ships was a Greek officer.

Well, the Marine Corps were delayed in their landing, because of the rough sea, and as they established their perimeter, it came time, rather belatedly, for the mixed force to land. By this time, the King had already left. He had a date up in Kavalla and had to leave, so there was no King on the beach. To my great surprise, instead of the LST, which I knew bore the Turkish troops heading in, the LST that had the Greek troops headed for the beach. So I had the Fleet Commander called, and the Fleet Commander said that the landing ships were in charge of Captain so-and-so with a Greek name, and then I began to realize what was happening. In the ships they knew that the King couldn't stay very long, and if any troops reached the beach after the delays involved in the amphibious landing, this Greek officer was going to be damn sure that they would be Greek troops. So the Greeks came ashore first.

But the Turks came in right after them in good order, and they formed their lines and went on up through the established perimeter of the Marines. The Marines, then, withdrew and reembarked on their craft and went back to the Fleet. The next morning I flew up by helicopter to visit Colonel Alpogan of the Turkish Army, who was in charge. I found his headquarters beautifully concealed behind the reverse slope of a little hill. I landed in a cow pasture, and he was there to meet me with great military precision. He escorted me over to his command and gave me a lecture which only a Turk can give. It's very military, it's very precise, beautifully done, and he said, "Admiral, early this morning

I had a command decision to make. My orders are to hold the Angitus River valley and strike Serrai Serrai." And I said, "And, Colonel, how did you distribute your troops for this?" He said, "Sir. My Greek battalion is holding the Angitus River valley, and my Turkish battalion is striking Serrai." So, he turned the tables on the Greek captain of the day before, and he was now occupying the spotlight with his own Turkish troops!

Well, there were all sorts of amusing and interesting incidents like this which happened. I had a wonderful tour.

Q: So much of it is diplomatic in nature, is it not?

Adm. R.: Yes. One time we had maneuvers over in Turkish Thrace. We were doing a similar thing. This time with a Greek colonel in charge of the mixed troops. But this time instead of King Paul, we had a Prime Minister who had been a past president of Turkey, Mr. Inonu. Mr. Inonu had been the military brain with Ataturk. It was his planning which defeated the Greeks and turned them back in 1922. He practically threw them into the sea at Smyrna, which is now called Izmir.

Well, Inonu was sitting in the viewing stand with us, and I put Admiral McDonald, who was the commander of the 6th Fleet between Inonu and myself. There was an interpreter behind us. Inonu could see that the Marine landing was just about completed, and he leaned over and addressed me saying, "Admiral, when this phase is over, where are you going?" And I said, "Well, your Excellency, I am going to go in a helicopter and land on yonder hill where the Marines dropped a parachute reconnaissance team early this morning, and have a look at them. Then I shall fly on up to Uzunkopru, where the main maneuver is taking place - where General Ewell with his paratroop brigade down from Germany is performing. And I'll have lunch with General Ewell." "Fine!" said Mr. Inonu, the Prime Minister of Turkey, "I'll go with you!" Well, I thought, gee, Russell, that dilapidated old Navy helicopter you're flying in - supposing something happens to this gentleman, then you're really in hot water! But go he would. And he wanted to bring his chief of defense staff, General Sunay, for whom we made room. He wanted to bring his Chief of the Land Forces, and we made room for him. And then there was Admiral Uran, who was chief of the Turkish Navy, and I thought, well, the Prime Minister won't mind if we don't take him, he's not interested in a land battle. So I suggested he be left behind, but Inonu let me know that he'd like to have him go too. By this time I was in the brigadier general passenger portion of my party. We made room, however, for Uran.

It was very interesting. We landed on the hill top. The Marines were properly camouflaged with black faces and bits of verdure on their helmets. The Prime Minister talked to every Marine in that team, had him demonstrate his weapon, and was very thorough in what he had to say to the troops.

While this was going on, there was a school in the neighborhood down in the valley that heard that their Prime Minister was there, and all these little school children in their uniforms came parading up to the hilltop. They grabbed their Prime Minister by the hand, kissed his hand, and then put his hand to their foreheads. It was very impressive.

Well, we finished our inspection there, got in the helicopter, and flew up to have lunch with General Ewell, who had arranged some mess tables out in the shade of a tree on the maneuvering plain. Everything we ate came out of a tin can, save some watermelon and some that the commissary had acquired from a local Turkish village. Well, Mr. Inonu was very interested in everything we were eating, even bread came out of a tin can. He came upon some little tins, and he said to General Ewell, "What's this?" General Ewell said, "Well, that is peanut butter." "Oh," said the Prime Minister, "what's it used for?" And he said, "Well, you spread it on your bread." So Inonu spread it on his bread and ate the piece of bread. General Ewell said, "Peanuts are a very fine crop. They're very nourishing. You should grow peanuts in Turkey, Mr. Prime Minister." After a pause, Mr. Inonu said, "Yes. We will, if we can sell them to the Americans!"

Russell #2 - 364

Q: Grow them in place of poppies!

Adm. R.: It was a great treat to go out to places that I'd never seen before. I saw Sarikamis Pass to the west of Erzurum. I visited the Soviet border. I visited the Bulgarian border, the Yugoslav border, the Albanian border, and of course, the borders in the north of Italy. I was charged by General Lemnitzer to coordinate the ground battle plan between the Turkish 3rd Army, which was deployed in eastern Turkey, and the 1st Imperial Army of Iran, which was deployed in northwestern Iran, and General Batmanglidj, from the CENTO Permanent Military Deputies Group in Ankara, said that he would escort me. It was really a trip to remember.

I flew him in my plane, a C-131, to Teheran, and we took an Iranian airplane, a C-47, which could get into the smaller fields. We went up to Lake Rezaiyeh and up to the Turkish border at a place called Jolfa on the Aras River where there was team of Iranian and Soviet engineers - a joint team - who were designing dams to harness the energy of the Aras River and to provide irrigation for the local people. To go to Jolfa, we set out first from Rezaiyeh in a sedan, but we soon found the road was in such condition we'd never make it through, so we went back and got jeeps. And we drove up to the border in jeeps.

I was amazed to find at this out-of-the-way place, Jolfa, that across the river on the Soviet side were all the contraptions that one found between East and West Germany, between Czechoslovakia and West Germany - plowed ground, minefields, barbed wire entanglements, dog teams, lookout towers, searchlights - all the paraphernalia necessary to keep the happy workers inside the happy workers' paradise, way up there in the middle of nowhere.

Well, we went on down to the Caspain Sea, and I had always wanted to swim in the Caspian Sea, because I thought perhaps the quality of the caviar from sturgeon in the Caspian Sea was due to the difference in salt content. Well, there were flags up, the beaches were unsafe, because of the heavy surf, but fortunately, the hotel where we stayed had bronze plumbing, which piped the salt water from the Caspain Sea into the swimming tank and right out again. So I swam in the water of the Caspian Sea, despite the fact that the surf was too heavy to go into the Sea itself. But when General Batmanglidj put on his swimming trunks and we went swimming together, I noticed there were rather extensive scars on his body. I said to him, "General, you have been wounded?" And he said, "Well, not quite that. I was run over by a tank!" And sure enough, you could see the tread marks across his body, diagonally up and off to the side, and I said, "My God, man, how did you ever survive?" He said, "Well, the ground was soft!" He was actually run over by a tank!

He told me, at the time Mossadegh was in power in Iran,

how it felt to sit in a prison in Teheran, wondering, he was to be hung the next morning, how it would feel to have the hangman's noose under the corner of his chin. And at 4 o'clock that afternoon, Mossadegh had been overthrown, and General Batmanglidj was being borne on the shoulders of the crowd through the streets of Teheran. He had been rescued from jail. He had occupied the post of Chief of Defense Staff, and Mossadegh had been told that if he really wanted to control the country, he would have to do away with my friend Batmanglidj. Messadegh was about to do that, but was overthrown just in time to save General Batmanglidj from the gallows.

Q: You retired now.

Adm. R.: I retired on the 1st of April, 1965. I left my command, turned my command over to Admiral Griffin on the 31st of March, 1965. My wife by this time had become quite ill. I had to bring her home - terminal cancer, unfortunately, and she died on the 18th of April, Easter Sunday, after I retired.

I came home a widower and rattled around Puget Sound country for over a year as a widower, then proposed to the loveliest of all the Seattle widows. She is the lady you met, Gerry, who is now my wife, a very delightful character.

I have been recalled twice since retiring, once in 1967,

when I was asked by Admiral Moorer to return to active duty and chair a panel to review carrier operations with the idea of coming up with recommendations to enhance safety. We'd had two very bad fires, one on Oriskany, and one on Forrestal. The Oriskany fire was due to the premature ignition of a magnesium flare. The fire on the Forrestal was due to the premature discharge of a rocket, which went across the deck and not only penetrated the drop tank, but also knocked the ordnance off an A-4 which was manned by John Sydney McCain III. He is the grandson of the dear old man who had checked us out as officers-of-the-deck on the Ranger so many years before. But these two very difficult-to-control fires had caused a very considerable amount of concern, so I had two months of rather intense work coming up with things to do to enhance safety.

I rode four of the carriers in the Guld of Tonkin at the height of the early raids against Hanoi and Haiphong. It was sort of heart-breaking to see our pilots take off with a pad on the knee which listed things they could not do. I saw them also taking off with a not full bomb load, because there was, in fact, a shortage of bombs.

But we recommended a great number of things which I have seen accomplished on a number of our carriers. For example, a sprinkling system which sprays up through one of several subdivisions of the flight deck when a corresponding button is pressed on a flight deck diagram in the primary fly control station, or the navigating bridge. This serves to keep the ordnance cool under the wings of the airplanes in an area of the flight deck where there might be fires. This is just one example of what we recommended and what has been installed on our carriers.

Then I was recalled to duty again in 196 , this time to serve the Director of Defense for Research and Engineering, Mr. John Foster, and the chairman of the Joint Chiefs of Staff, General "Bus" Wheeler. I had a team of four scientists and four general officers. I took those who had not recently been to Vietnam, and again, went to the Southeast Asia theatre. We spent some time going all over Vietnam itself, and also, in Thailand, to the various bases which were used by our Air Force. I got up to Kontien on the DMZ. I couldn't get into Que Sanh, although I tried. There was a very heavy tropical rain storm on at the time, and the helicopter pilot thought it was unsafe to try to bull the weather to get into the place.

I got up to the Parrot's Beak and visited with the 1st Infantry Division. I called on General Keith Wade, that wonderful two-time Medal of Honor winner - very much a fighting man, who later lost his life in Vietnam. Before I got there, he had seen a fire fight from his helicopter involving one of his battalions. The Battalion Commander was killed, and things looked as though they weren't going well, so he landed his helicopter and took charge of the of the battalion himself until matters were straightened out.

It was very interesting duty for me. We looked at a lot of things, including Mr. McNamara's fence! Seeing the Vietnam affair from ashore was something which I treasure very highly. It was my great pleasure to know General Jack Lavelle of our Air Force. He later on came a cropper when his aggressiveness led him to overstep a little the various restrictive instructions. He told me that he just couldn't stand to see enemy supplies building up, knowing full well that they were going to be used against our men later on. He used any excuse at all to let his Air Force chaps destroy them. But he got in hot water over it.

Well, generally, Jack, that's my story. I'll be happy to enlarge on or tell you anything that I can further if you can think of something about which you'd like to have me talk.

Q: Thank you very much, sir. I guess that about covers it.

*A Profile: "Too Many Things to do to Retire."*

# Admiral James S. Russell, USN

Photo shows Admiral James S. Russell in 1962 when he was Commander U.S. Naval Support Activity, Naples, Italy. (USN photo by PH-1 E. B. Cantral)

## THEN

If a boy can successfully pass a high school entrance examination when he is only ten years old, it is a safe prediction that a rather stellar career awaits him! Such a one was James Russell who upon graduation at the age of fifteen, attempted to join the Navy. The recruiting officer promptly turned the lad away, not realizing he was rejecting a future 4-star Admiral.

Russell did manage eventually to ship out and served three and a half years as a seaman in the Merchant Marine. He entered Annapolis in 1922, graduated in 1926, and won his wings in 1929. He became the first aviator to fly from the decks of all six of the Navy's first aircraft carriers. He later earned a Master of Science degree in Aero Engineering from Cal Tech in 1935.

He commanded ships and forces of all kinds, led the action against the Japanese in the Aleutian Islands, and engaged in the campaigns of Palau, the Philippines, Iwo Jima, and Okinawa. He also commanded both the attack carrier BAIROKE and the carrier CORAL SEA.

It was Russell, then head of the Atomic Energy Commission Test Group, who suggested that the hydrogen bomb tests be conducted at Eniwetok, a Pacific atoll. There was concern that trouble might occur among the Bikini natives. However, after a personal visit there, Russell learned that the natives would accept the idea of moving. His charts and reports convinced President Truman who signed the order.

While Russell was Chief of the Bureau of Aeronautics, he was awarded the Collier Trophy for 1956, along with C.J. McCarthy of Chance Vought Aircraft, for the development of the supersonic Crusader navy fighter, the first ship-based aircraft to fly faster than 1000 miles per hour.

He became Vice Admiral, then Vice Chief of Naval Operations as Admiral (4 stars) and then was appointed commander-in-chief of NATO forces in southern Europe, committed to the defense of NATO's southern flank and the nations of Italy, Greece and Turkey. After 43 years of service, he retired in 1965. His decorations include: two Distinguished Service Medals, three Legion of Merit, Distinguished Flying Cross, Air Medal, and various foreign honors.

Retired Admiral James S. Russell in a recent photo taken at his home near Tacoma, Washington.

## NOW

Admiral Russell's home is on American Lake, Tacoma, Washington. His combination den and office resembles a museum room with all the accumulation of his lifetime. There is the flag presented to him on retirement, the model of his old carrier plane, the 5-B-11, presentations and plaques from many foreign countries, maps, magazines and books, scrapbooks and albums, paintings by his father, ship models, guns and swords, and stacks of papers.

Actually, the Admiral does not seem to have retired at all. The activities and interests that he briskly describes would fill a long list. In July of 1965, he accepted an invitation to be a part-time consultant to The Boeing Company of Seattle. He joins in work on Navy airplane design, on the hydrofoils, on subcontracting for the Trident submarine, on a long range patrol aircraft, and on lasers. He is a director of Airtronics Corp. in Virginia. As a trustee of the Washington State Oceanographic Institute, he participates in their study of oil tankers in Puget Sound and methods of transferring oil.

He serves on various Navy boards. The latest of these is NMARC (Navy Materiel Acquisition Review Commission). For the next ninety days, he and other specialists will be considering the testing and evaluation of equipment, etc.

In August of 1967, he was recalled to active duty to serve for two months as the director of a panel to review safety in aircraft carrier operations in the Navy. This panel was formed after fire and explosion rocked the carrier FORRESTAL, resulting in much loss of life and damage to the ship.

The following year, he was again recalled for another two months when, as chairman of a study committee for the Secretary of Defense, he made a second visit to the Southeast Asia theater.

He travels to the Navy Post-Graduate School in Monterey, California once or twice a year to advise on curriculum and facilities. About six times a year, he meets with an advisory board to Navy Laboratories which are involved with air warfare and ships.

For five years, the Admiral was a director on the board of Alaska Airlines. He is also president of the Puget Sound U.S.O. which provides a special serviceman's lounge at Sea-Tac Airport between Seattle and Tacoma.

His wife, Geraldine, shares his interests and many of his travels. He has two sons, Donald and Kenneth, from his first marriage to Dorothy Johnson who died in 1965. In 1966, he married Mrs. Geraldine Haus Rahn, a widow, who had two children, Fred and Barbara.

Some days, the Admiral takes out his Thunderbird, a 26-foot sailboat, into the waters of Puget Sound. But, flying is still his great love, and if he repeated his life, he would become a flyer all over again, "there is nothing quite like it...."

Perhaps some day, James Russell will really retire, but, not for a long time, "there are too many things that need to be done!"

by B. L. Schoen

FB2-2/A12-1/
A16-3

UNITED STATES PACIFIC FLEET
AIR FORCE, PACIFIC FLEET
CARRIER DIVISION TWO

Serial: 0045

S-E-C-R-E-T

27 March 1945.

From:   Commander Task Group FIFTY-EIGHT Point TWO (Commander Carrier Division TWO).
To  :   Commander-in-Chief, United States Fleet.
Via :   (1) Commander Task Force FIFTY-EIGHT.
        (2) Commander FIFTH Fleet.
        (3) Commander-in-Chief, United States Pacific Fleet and Pacific Ocean Areas.

Subject:    Operations of Task Group FIFTY-EIGHT Point TWO during the period from 14 to 24 March 1945 - Action Report of.

Reference:  (a) ComFIFTH Fleet Operation Plan No. 1-45, dated 3 Jan. 1945, serial 0003.
            (b) ComFIRSTCarTaskForPac Operation Order No. 2-45, dated 1 March 1945, serial 00029.
            (c) CTG 58.2 Op Order D2-45, dated 12 March 1945, serial 00011.
            (d) CTG 58.2 Op Order D3-45, dated 20 March 1945, Speed-letter serial 0001A.
            (e) CTF 58 Despatch 202055 (March), dated 20 March 1945.

Enclosure:  (A) Selected Photographs.
            (B) Track Chart of Task Group 58.2 and Task Unit 58.2.9 from 14 to 24 March 1945.
            (C) Weather report 14 to 24 March 1945.
            (D) Copy of reference (d).
            (E) Copy of reference (e).

1.      This Action Report is submitted prior to receipt of ship and unit Action Reports of the Task Group in view of the separation which now exists between these units. Some sacrifice in completeness is made, therefore, in the interest of timeliness.

2.      All times are ITEM (Zone minus 9); all dates are East Longitude dates.

- 1 -

## CONTENTS

PART I — BRIEF SUMMARY

PART II — PRELIMINARIES

    A — TASK GROUP ORGANIZATION

    B — OPERATIONS PRIOR TO ACTION

    C — MISSION, DOCTRINE PLANS

    D — OWN FORCES AT OUTSET OF ACTION

PART III — CHRONOLOGICAL ACCOUNT

PART IV — ORDNANCE

PART V — DAMAGE

PART VI — SPECIAL COMMENTS AND INFORMATION

    A — STATISTICAL INFORMATION

    B — COMMUNICATIONS — RADAR

PART VII — PERSONNEL PERFORMANCE

PART VIII — LESSONS LEARNED, CONCLUSIONS AND RECOMMENDATIONS.

FB2-2/A12-1/
A16-3

Serial: 0045

27 March 1945

~~S-E-C-R-E-T~~

## PART I - BRIEF SUMMARY

### OFFENSIVE ACTION

1. Task Group 58.2 sortied from ULITHI on 14 March as one of the four Task Groups of Task Force 58. After cruising on northwesterly courses, and refueling at sea on 16 March, the Task Force arrived at a point southeast of the island of KYUSHU early on 18 March. Sweeps and strikes were launched against KYUSHU airfields; Task Group 58.2 striking airfields at IZUMI, KAGOSHIMA and MIYAKONOJO. Considerable damage was done to ground installations at these airfields and small numbers of aircraft were destroyed in the air and on the ground. No attacks were made on this task group by enemy aircraft although the presence of many planes in the vicinity and attacks on adjacent groups indicated the Japanese were aware of the position of the task force. On 19 March this group damaged at least one CV, one CVE and many merchant vessels in KOBE Harbor.

2. At 0707, 19 March, while FRANKLIN was launching the second strike, an enemy plane approached her through the broken overcast, undetected from ahead and in a high speed glide. Two bombs were dropped. Both penetrated the flight deck on the center line, one just forward of Number 2 elevator and one abreast the after elevator. The bombs apparently exploded as they penetrated the hangar deck causing blast damage down to the third deck and setting fire to fully fueled and armed planes both in the hangar and on the flight deck. F4U planes armed with twelve inch rockets were parked at the after end of the flight deck spot and five were in the hangar. The discharge of these rockets as well as the detonation of bombs added to the damage incurred on FRANKLIN.

3. Tactical command of the group was turned over to Commander Task Unit 58.2.2, Rear Admiral L. J. WILTSE, Commander Cruiser Division TEN, as soon as possible after FRANKLIN was struck. This was done by flag hoist since all radio communications were lost. The eventuality of the flagship being put out of commission had been discussed with the staff of Commander Cruiser Division TEN prior to sortie. PITTSBURGH, SANTA FE, MILLER, HICKOX, HUNT, TINGEY and MARSHALL stood by damaged FRANKLIN. Commander Carrier Division TWO, Commander Carrier Division FOUR (Rear Admiral Gerald F. BOGAN, U. S. Navy), eight staff officers, and eight enlisted men of the flag complements were transferred to MILLER between 0835 and 0900, and delivered to HANCOCK (CV19). Commander Carrier Division TWO hoisted his flag in the

PART I

FB2-2/A12-1
A16-3

Serial: 0045

27 March 1945

S-E-C-R-E-T

## PART I - BRIEF SUMMARY

### OFFENSIVE ACTION

latter ship at 1120. Meanwhile Commander Task Force 58 had ordered Commander Task Group 58.5, Rear Admiral M. B. GARDNER, Commander Carrier Division 7, in ENTERPRISE to join the group and assume command of Task Group 58.2. Commander Task Force 58 had also directed Commander Cruiser Division 16 with Cruiser Division 16, the destroyers of Task Group 58.8, ASTORIA and FLINT to join Task Group 58.2. Upon reporting, Commander Cruiser Division 16 with Cruiser Division 16 and Commander Destroyer Division 96 with Destroyer Division 96 were ordered to join FRANKLIN group. At 1800 Commander Carrier Division 2 assumed command of Task Group 58.2; but Rear Admiral GARDNER was ordered to retain tactical command of group because of his complete staff and better facilities on ENTERPRISE. Additional enemy aircraft were reported during the remainder of the day and night, but no close attacks against our ships were effected.

4. FRANKLIN had been taken in tow by PITTSBURGH about 1400 on the 19th and proceeded on a southeasterly course toward GUAM. During the night she regained her own power. At 1153 on 20 March her speed was 12 knots. At about 1220 the PITTSBURGH cast off tow line. During the day the enemy launched a series of attacks on both Task Unit 58.2.0 and the FRANKLIN group which had been designated as Task Unit 58.2.9 with Commander Cruiser Division 16 as Commander Task Unit 58.2.9. A suicide bomber was shot down out of control at about 1500 above HANCOCK and crashed into the stern of HALSEY POWELL as the latter pulled away from fueling alongside HANCOCK. Alert handling of HANCOCK averted a serious collision with HALSEY POWELL. Another plane also attacked HANCOCK with a bomb which resulted in near miss on the port bow. Later ENTERPRISE was attacked, resulting in two near misses and a fire on her flight deck. At the present time it is believed this was caused by friendly anti-aircraft fire striking ready service ammunition with the fire spreading to planes on the flight deck. This fire was controlled within 31 minutes, but reduced ENTERPRISE's capacity for operations and made night operations impossible. At this time Commander Carrier Division 2 took over tactical command of Task Unit 58.2.0.

5. During the night of 20-21 March an attack on Task Unit 58.2.0 was made by four enemy planes which dropped flares. No damage was done to the ships of this unit, but neither gunfire nor nightfighters succeeded in destroying any enemy aircraft. As this task unit continued southward on 21 March air attacks continued on a diminished scale. About noon a single engine and a twin engine plane were shot down by the Task Unit's combat air patrol. A twin-engine plane, which dropped a bomb near SAN JACINTO, was destroyed by ships' gunfire.

PART I

FB2-2/A12-1
A16-3

Serial: 0045	27 March 1945

~~SECRET~~ Air

PART I - BRIEF SUMMARY
------------------------------------------------------------

6.	Task Unit 58.2.9 closed Task Unit 58.2.0 and both joined the other tasks groups of Task Force 58 at dusk on 21 March. Task Force 58 proceeded southwest to the fueling area during the night. During fueling on 22 March Task Force 58 was reorganized in accordance with reference (e). Task Group 58.2 of new organization was ordered to ULITHI. Passage to ULITHI was completed on 24 March.

PART I

FB2-2/A12-1
A16-3

Serial: 0045

27 March 1945

S-E-C-R-E-T

## PART II - PRELIMINARIES

A. ORGANIZATION

    1. The organization of Task Group 58.2 on 14 March was as follows:
TASK GROUP 58.2 - Fast Carrier Group 2 - Rear Admiral Ralph DAVISON, U. S. Navy.

(a) Task Unit 58.2.1 - Carrier Unit - Rear Admiral Ralph DAVISON, U. S. Navy.
    FRANKLIN (CV13)(F)
    HANCOCK (CV19)               2 CV
    SAN JACINTO (CVL30)
    BATAAN (CVL29)              2 CVL

(b) Task Unit 58.2.2 - Support Unit - Rear Admiral L. J. WILTSE, U. S. Navy.

    Task Unit 58.2.21 - Battleships - Rear Admiral T. R. COOLEY, jr., U. S. Navy.

    Bat Div 6
    WASHINGTON (BB56)(F)
    NORTH CAROLINA (BB55)      2 BB

    Task Unit 58.2.22 - Cruisers - Rear Admiral L. J. WILTSE, U. S. Navy.
    BALTIMORE (CA68)(F)
    PITTSBURGH (CA72)          2 CA
    SANTA FE (CL60)            1 CL

(c) Task Unit 58.2.3 - Screening Unit - Captain J. P. WOMBLE, jr., U. S. Navy.

    DesRon 52 - Captain J. P. WOMBLE, jr., U. S. Navy.

| Des Div 103 | | Des Div 104 - Commander P. L. HIGH, U. S. Navy. | |
|---|---|---|---|
| OWEN | (DD536)(F) | HICKOX | (DD673)(F) |
| MILLER | (DD535) | HUNT | (DD674) |
| THE SULLIVANS | (DD537) | LEWIS HANCOCK | (DD675) |
| STEPHEN POTTER | (DD538) | MARSHALL | (DD676) |
| TINGEY | (DD539) | | |

    DesRon 53 - Captain H. B. JARRETT, U. S. Navy.

| DesDiv 105 | | DesDiv 106 - Commander J. H. HOGG, U. S. Navy. | |
|---|---|---|---|
| CUSHING | (DD797)(F) | WEDDERBURN | (DD684)(F) |
| HALSEY POWELL | (DD686) | TWINING | (DD540) |
| COLAHAN | (DD658) | STOCKHAM | (DD683) |
| UHLMANN | (DD687) | | |
| BENHAM | (DD796) | | |

FB2-2/A12-1
A16-3

PART III
CHRONOLOGICAL ACCOUNT OF THE ACTION

Serial: 0045

~~S-E-C-R-E-T~~

---

north of KAGOSHIMA. SAN JACINTO group rocketed assembly and hangar area at KAGOSHIMA, and in addition destroyed 2 twin-engine, strafed 5 twin-engine and 3 single engine planes at IZUMI. BATAAN VF rocketed KAGOSHIMA assembly plant west of field and strafed 7 twin engine, 8 single engine planes at IZUMI. One was definitely destroyed. HANCOCK sweep shot down 1 Tojo, lost 1 Hellcat when attacked by 6-8 Tojos.

At 1500 six TBM's from HANCOCK were launched to make a local search for downed pilots in the task force operating area, but results were negative.

By 1815 all scheduled flight operations were completed.

At 1858 Commander Task Force 58 set course 135°T, speed 20 knots, axis 045°T.

At 2330 Task Force 58 changed course to 345°T, commenced approach to KOBE-OSAKA target area.

19 March 1945

At 0000 Task Group 58.2 was on force course 345°T, speed 18 knots and in station 3 of force disposition 5W, during approach to KOBE-OSAKA target area.

From 0000 to first launching a large number of bogies were reported. General Quarters was sounded at 0330 when bogies closed to 25 miles. Task Force course was changed to 325°T.

At 0445 condition One Easy was set.

At 0545 task force Point Option was latitude 32°-09'N; longitude 134°-05'E; course 045°T; speed 3 knots. Task Group 58.2 launched sweep 2A, consisting of 42 VF from HANCOCK and FRANKLIN with airfields in the KOBE-OSAKA area as primary targets. The sweep reported covering NORTH KOBE area, striking 112 NISHINOMIYA and 113 ITAMI with undetermined results. In addition an unidentified industry at KAINAN was strafed, a small merchant vessel (SC) was strafed and left burning, an FTC and three SD's were strafed with unobserved results. Weather was clear over target area.

At 0630, four Zekes were reported 320°T, at a distance of 45 miles, closing. Zig-zagging was commenced at 0634 and terminated at 0648.

At 0657 a bogey was reported bearing 280°T, distance 22 miles, closing; this was identified five minutes later by Combat Air Patrol as a friendly aircraft.

- 13 -    PART III

FB2-2/A12-1
A16-3

27 March 1945

Serial: 0045

~~S-E-C-R-E-T~~

PART III
CHRONOLOGICAL ACCOUNT OF THE ACTION

At 0700 task group commenced launching strike 2B, consisting of 72 VF and all available VB and VT with 22 VF from FRANKLIN loaded with 12 inch rockets.

At 0705 a twin engine plane was sighted visually by HANCOCK bearing 035°T, distance 10 miles, and Anti-Aircraft Batteries were alerted.

At 0707, while FRANKLIN was launching strike planes, an enemy single engine plane, dropped 2 bombs on FRANKLIN amidships; one abreast the forward part of the island structure and the other abreast the after end of the island structure. The resultant damage was severe, FRANKLIN's hangar, flight and lower decks were swept by fires and explosions. The ship continued underway but was unable to maneuver or to defend herself. The attacking plane came through a broken cloud layer dead ahead of FRANKLIN, holding the advantage not only of cloud cover but also of the confusion created by FRANKLIN planes taking off in the same area at the same time. When the bombs hit, 5 VB, 12 VT and 17 VF were on the flight deck armed and warming up for take off; 5 VF armed with 12 inch rockets for the strike plus other planes were on the hangar deck. The enemy plane which made the attack was reported shot down a few minutes later by the Combat Air Patrol.

About 0715 Rear Admiral WILTSE (Commander Cruiser Division 10) in BALTIMORE assumed tactical command of Task Group 58.2 as the flagship, FRANKLIN, was out of action. At this time the following ships were standing by FRANKLIN: PITTSBURGH, SANTA FE, MARSHALL, MILLER, TINGEY, HUNT, and HICKOX. Captain FITZ in SANTA FE was in tactical command of this group. At 0830 Rear Admirals DAVISON (Commander Carrier Division TWO) and BOGAN (Commander Carrier Division FOUR) with members of staff transferred to MILLER.

About 1010 FLINT joined Task Group 58.2 on orders from Commander Task Force 58.

About 1045 Rear Admiral DAVISON (Commander Carrier Division 2) and Rear Admiral BOGAN (Commander Carrier Division 4) with staff members completed transfer to HANCOCK via MILLER. Rear Admiral DAVISON hoisted his flag in HANCOCK.

At 1152 Rear Admiral GARDNER (Commander Carrier Division 7) in ENTERPRISE joined Task Group 58.2 and assumed command under orders of Commander Task Force 58.

Strike 2B seriously damaged 1 CV, 1 CVE, 1 small AO, and 1 Submarine in KOBE HARBOR; plus shooting down 2 Tojos, 1 Nick, 1 Myrt, 1 Judy and 2 Jills. Two SB2C's were shot down by Anti-Aircraft fire at the target.

About 1200, sweep 2C was launched from HANCOCK. The sweep strafed and burned 20-30 single engine planes at 204 HIMEJI, and burned or damaged 20 more single engine planes at 116 TOKUSHIMA.

- 14 -    PART III

FB2-2/A12-1
A16-3

Serial: 0045

S-E-C-R-E-T

PART III
CHRONOLOGICAL ACCOUNT OF THE ACTION

At 1350 Commander Task Force 58 ordered Rear Admiral LOW (Commander Cruiser Division 16) in GUAM with ALASKA to join Task Group 58.2. Task Group 58.8 was also ordered to join Task Group 58.2.

About 1300 FRANKLIN was taken in tow by PITTSBURGH.

At 1444 ASTORIA reported for duty.

At 1800 Rear Admiral DAVISON (Commander Carrier Division 2) resumed command Task Group 58.2 and directed Rear Admiral GARDNER (Commander Carrier Division 7) to retain tactical command of Task Unit 58.2.0. At this time Task Group 58.2 was reorganized as indicated below:

Task Group 58.2 - Rear Admiral DAVISON

Task Unit 58.2.0 - Support Unit - Rear Admiral GARDNER

Task Unit 58.2.01 - Carriers

    HANCOCK (CV19)(F)(Rear Admirals DAVISON and BOGAN)
    ENTERPRISE (CV6) Rear Admiral GARDNER
    SAN JACINTO (CVL30)
    BATAAN (CVL29)

Task Unit 58.2.02 - Heavy Ships - Rear Admiral WILTSE

    WASHINGTON (F) (Rear Admiral COOLEY) (BB56)
    NORTH CAROLINA (BB55)
    BALTIMORE (F) (Rear Admiral WILTSE) (CA68)
    ASTORIA (CL90)
    FLINT (CL97)

Task Unit 58.2.03 - Screen - Captain WOMBLE

Destroyer Squadron 52

Destroyer Division 103 - less MILLER, TINGEY

    OWEN (DD536)
    THE SULLIVANS (DD537)
    STEPHAN POTTER (DD538)

Destroyer Division 104 - less HICKOX, HUNT, MARSHALL

    LEWIS HANCOCK (DD675)

Destroyer Squadron 53

FB2-2/A12-1
A16-3

27 March 1945

Serial: 0045

PART III
CHRONOLOGICAL ACCOUNT OF THE ACTION

S-E-C-R-E-T

Destroyer Division 105

    CUSHING (DD797)
    COLAHAN (DD658)
    HALSEY POWELL (DD686)
    UHLMANN (DD687)
    BENHAM (DD796)

Destroyer Division 106 - less TWINING, STOCKHAM

    WEDDERBURN (DD684)

Destroyer Division 50 - less RINGOLD, SCHROEDER, plus MURRAY

    SIGSBEE (DD502)
    DASHIELL (DD659)
    MURRAY (DD576)

Destroyer Division 107 - less WADLEIGH

    REMEY (DD688)
    NORMAN SCOTT (DD690)
    MERTZ (DD691)
    MONSSEN (DD798)

Task Unit 58.2.9 - Salvage Unit - Rear Admiral LOW

    FRANKLIN (CV13)
    GUAM (CB-2)(F)(Rear Admiral LOW)
    ALASKA (CB-1)
    PITTSBURGH (CA72)
    SANTA FE (CL60)

Destroyer Division 104 - less LEWIS HANCOCK

    HICKOX (DD673)
    HUNT (DD674)
    MARSHALL (DD676)

Destroyer Division 96

    BLACK (DD666)
    BULLARD (DD660)
    KIDD (DD661)
    CHAUNCEY (DD667)

FB2-2/A12-1  
A16-3  

Serial: 0045

27 March 1945

PART III
CHRONOLOGICAL ACCOUNT OF THE ACTION

~~SECRET~~

TWINING (DD540) Destroyer Division 106
STOCKHAM (DD683) Destroyer Division 106
MILLER (DD535) Destroyer Division 103
TINGEY (DD539) Destroyer Division 103

At 2030 Commander Cruiser Division 16, Rear Admiral LOW in GUAM assumed tactical command of Task Unit 58.2.9. This unit was directed to proceed to at best speed toward GUAM, covered by Task Unit 58.2.0.

20 March 1945

At 0000 Task Group 58.2 was on base course 260°T, speed 15 knots, operating independently while conducting night operations on ENTERPRISE, and covering Task Unit 58.2.9. At 0835 FRANKLIN was reported making 8.5 knots.

About 1000 numerous unidentified aircraft began approaching the task group, and at 1028 the task group Combat Air Patrol shot down one Kate 20 miles from the formation.

1156 FRANKLIN reported making 15 knots under her own power.

Commenced topping off destroyers about 1035, but at 1155 fueling exercises were discontinued upon the approach of bogies to within 10 miles of the formation. No attacks developed at that time, so fueling was resumed at 1341.

1213 PITTSBURGH cast off tow from FRANKLIN.

About 1440, two Jills were shot down by task group Combat Air Patrol about 75 miles from group, and about 1450, a bogey was reported approaching the formation; fueling was discontinued, destroyers were cast off, and Anti-Aircraft Batteries alerted. At 1454 the task group opened on an enemy plane diving on the HANCOCK; the plane approached from about 120°T in a 60 degree angle of dive. It was hit by gunfire at an altitude of approximately 1500 feet, rolled and missed the HANCOCK, but hit HALSEY POWELL, which had just cast off from HANCOCK. Both the bomb and parts of the plane hit HALSEY POWELL, the bomb passing through the hull without exploding, and the plane hit just abaft the after 5 inch mount, causing the ship to lose steering control and commence flooding aft. HANCOCK narrowly averted collision with HALSEY POWELL which had lost steering and was crossing HANCOCK bow close aboard. At 1518 THE SULLIVANS was instructed to escort HALSEY POWELL at the best speed the latter could make.

At 1532 FRANKLIN reported making 20 knots.

Index

to

Series of Interviews

with

Admiral James S. Russell

U. S. Navy (Retired)

ADAK: p. 89; p. 111; U. S. occupation in 1942, p. 139-40; weather conditions make for a good airfield, p. 141; p. 142-3; p. 145-9; p. 260.

ADLER, Gen. Julius Ochs: his visit to Pearl Harbor, p. 228-9.

AIRCRAFT CARRIERS - Safety measures: Russell recalled to active duty to chair panel for recommendations to enhance safety on carriers, p. 367-8.

AKUTAN ISLAND: site where Japanese ZERO was found and used to develop tactics against the ZERO in combat, p. 120-1.

ALASKA POST WAR SURVEY: under direction of Army General Hoge, p. 258; Russell was the naval aviator on the team, p. 259.

ALEUTIAN CAMPAIGN: Russell (post war) covers this campaign as member of the U. S. Strategic Bombing Survey in Tokyo (1945-6), p. 243 ff; see entries under DUTCH HARBOR: ADAK: KISKA: KOMANDORSKI ACTION:

ALEUTIAN ISLANDS: see entries under KISKA, ADAK, DUTCH HARBOR, VP-12

ALLIED FORCES, SOUTHERN EUROPE: Russell becomes Cinc, Jan. 2, 1962, p. 355 ff; his account of three different nations in his command - Italy, Greece and Turkey, p. 356-8; an account of some of his trips as Cinc South, p. 359 ff.

AMCHITKA: U. S. establishes a base there (1942), p. 147-8. p. 261

ANDERSON, Commander Charles E. (Squeaky): beachmaster at Attu, p. 149-150.

ANDERSON, Admiral George: becomes CNO and Russell stays on, p. 354-5;

ANDERSON, General Orville: his report as supplement to the U. S. Strategic Bombing Survey, p. 255-6.

ARRESTING GEAR: see entry under LANGLEY.

ATKA (ADAK ISLAND): p. 90; p. 143.

U. S. ATOMIC ENERGY COMMISSION: Russell takes job as #2 in Military Application Division (June, 1947); p. 269; charged with making arrangements for weapon development tests, p. 269 ff; selects Einewetok Atoll, p. 270-1; p. 276-7; p. 289; Russell works on money for government housing at Los Alamos, p. 289-90; "atoms for peace", p. 290-1; list of scientists involved in atomic work, p. 292;

ATTU:  p. 89; p. 108; p. 141-2; p. 147-9; p. 201-2; post war survey of Alaskan properties begins at Attu, p. 259.

USS BAIROKO (CVE 115):  p. Russell takes command, p. 263 ff; voyage to the Far East, p. 265-7; brush with a cable in Apra Harbor, p. 267-8; ship participates in Einewetok Tests, p. 283.

BATMANGLIDJ, General (Iranian):  on CENTO staff - p. 364-6.

BAY OF PIGS:  Russell's account, p. 345 ff.

USS BELLEAU WOOD:  hit in fantail by a kamikaze in Philippines, p. 189-90.

BISSELL, Richard M. Jr.:  p. 347.

BOGAN, Vice Admiral Gerald F.:  p. 172; p. 179; p. 181-3; takes over T.F. from Adm. Davison, p. 222-223.

SS BOTTINEAU:  p. 10-12.

BUCKNER, General Simon Bolivar:  Commander, Alaska Defense Command (1942), p. 108 ff; p. 111-13; p. 155-7.

BUREAU OF AERONAUTICS:  p. 39; p. 71 ff; Russell leaves in June, 1941 for VP-42 (Seattle), p. 83. Russell goes to job (1943) in Aircraft and Equipment Section, p. 153-4; p. 160; sets up new division of MIlitary Requirements, p. 160-5; the Naval Aircraft Factory and the PBN's - for the Russians, p. 165 ff; p. 168-9.
Russell becomes Chief, Feb. 1955 - p. 322; defends Navy Procurement Budget for 1956, p. 322; Russell faces Congressional Investigation on the F3H1 (McDonald Fighter, p. 323-4; other investigations, p. 326-9; the SEAMASTER, p. 321; p. 333-4; Lighter-than-air, p. 336-8; departs from BuAir to become Deputy CincLant, p. 338;

BURKE, Admiral Arleigh:  p. 180; p. 207-8; p. 330; brief description of Burke when Russell becomes his Vice CNO, p. 340; p. 342; his retirement ceremony, p. 345-6.

USS CASCO:  Theta Combs skipper - puts in at Kiska Harbor, p. 109-110; p. 129.

CAMPBELL, Rear Admiral Dennis:  (R.N.) instrumental in developing the mirror landing sight, p. 313-314;

CAR DIV 5 (CVA), evacuation of the Tai Shan Islands, p. 311

CAR DIV 17 (CVEs), p. 310-11;

CASTNER'S SCOUTS: advance scouting party on Adak Island, p. 139-140.

CINC LANT: Russell becomes Deputy to Admiral Wright, p. 338-9.

SS CITY OF SEATTLE: passenger freighter - Russell serves in her on Alaskan run, p. 9-10.

CLARK, Rear Admiral John E.: p. 346.

COLD BAY, Alaska: p. 118-119; p. 128-9; p. 131; p. 136.

COONEY, Col. Jim: radiological safety officer, AEC, p. 285; p. 287.

USS CORAL SEA: Russell takes command in Feb. 1951, p. 289; p. 292. p. 297; problems of navigation in roadstead of Istanbul, p. 300-1; loss of several pilots, p. 306-8; Russell turns command over to Robert B. Pirie, p. 310; p. 319; recommissioning ceremony, p. 343-4.

CROMMELIN, Rear Admiral John G. Jr.: Chief of Staff to Adm. Davison, p. 167-9;

DAMAGE CONTROL: measure taken on U. S. carriers in Pacific, p. 208-212;

Davison, Vice Admiral Ralph E.: Commander, Division of CVE's - asks Russell to be Chief of Staff, p. 167-9; p. 172; p. 175; p. 179; a description of Davison's traits and method of command, p. 193-5; p. 204; p. 206; p. 217; p. 220; p. 222.

DOOLITTLE RAID: p. 144-6.

DUTCH HARBOR: p. 89-91; p. 103-4; story of the Catalina accident at Dutch Harbor, p.103- 7; p. 108; Japanese attack on Dutch Harbor, (June 3, 1942), p. 113-4; p. 119; story of the 2nd attack on June 4, p. 124 ff; destructive nature of an Aleutians winter storm, p. 138-9; p. 146; Squeaky Anderson as Port Captain, p. 149; visit of post-war survey team, p. 261-2.

EARECKSON, 'Wild' Bill: p. 158-9.

ENIWETOK ATOLL: p. 270; selected for site of atomic tests, p. 271 ff; natives moved to Ujelang, p. 271-2; decision is made by President Truman to use Eniwetok - over Navy objection, p. 272 ff; p. 277.

EINEWETOK TESTS: p. 278-281; Rusk announces safety area around Einewetok to United Nations, p. 281-2; p. 283; p. 285-6.

USS ENTERPRISE: knocks off a large aircraft park in Luzon - p. 187-8; p. 204; p.220.

EISENHOWER, The Hon. Dwight D.:  p. 326; p. 348; p. 350.

ESSEX Class Carriers:  BuAir imput into first of ESSEX class carriers, p. 77 ff; the rectangular flight deck, p. 79-80.

FLOAT PLANES:  Russell joins squadron in 1929, p. 41-3; a forced landing in the Chesapeake Bay, p. 48-53.

FORRESTAL, The Hon. James:  SecNav, p. 273-4.

FOSTER, Vice Admiral Paul:  visit to Alaska - mission for President Roosevelt, p. 107 ff; p. 155-8; p. 288.

USS FRANKLIN:  flagship of Adm. Davison for Task Group 58.2, p. 170; hit by kamikaze in Philippines, p. 189; p. 204; p. 214; p. 216; bombed off Okinawa, p. 216-9 ff; attitude of skipper towards crew members who had gone over the side at time of fire, p. 224-5.

FROMAN, Dr. Darol K.:  scientific director for the Einewetok Tests, p. 275-6; p. 283; p. 285.

FUCHS, Claus:  American scientist who turned over atomic secrets to the Soviets, p. 281-2; p. 291.

GALLERY, Rear Admiral Dan V.:  Division Commander, Mediterranean, 1951 - p. 292-6; flies Sky Raider from CORAL SEA, p. 297-8; p. 300; p. 307.

GARDNER, Admiral Matthias (Matt) B.:  p. 220; takes temporary control of Task Force after Kamikaze attack on the USS FRANKLIN, p. 222.

GATES, The Hon. Thomas S.:  p. 331 p. 336; p. 349-50.

USS GILLIS:  Seaplane tender - p. 88.

GRAVES, Dr. Al:  Los Alamos Lab, p. 275; p. 280; p. 283-5.

GURNEY, Marshall:  involved with Russell in OAKS and OCORNS program, p. 152-3.

HALSEY, Fleet Admiral Wm.:  p. 179-180.

USS HALSEY POWELL:  DD damaged in kamikaze attack on CV HANCOCK, p. 221.

USS HANCOCK:  p. 214; p. 216; Admiral Davison transfers flag from USS FRANKLIN to USS HANCOCK, p. 220-1.

HEBERT, The Hon. F. Edward:  Chairman, Armed Services Committee of the House of Representatives, p. 327-8.

HIROSHIMA:  Russell's visit in September, 1945, p. 236 ff.

HOFFMAN, Melvin (Boogie):  assigned task of flying captured ZERO and discovering strengths and weaknesses, p. 121; p. 123.

HOLLOWAY, Adm. James L. Jr.:  number 2 turret officer on BB WEST VIRGINIA, p. 32.

HOOD, Lt. Clark:  Operations Officer (VP-42), lost on first flight of B-24s against Japs in Kiska, p. 136-7.

HOOVER, Admiral John:  becomes deputy CincPac after Adm. Towers - remains only 20 days because of unpleasant mess that results from dinner for Gen. Adler of the N.Y. TIMES, p. 228 ff; p. 230-1.

HOSOGAYA, Vice Admiral B.:  in command of Japanese 5th fleet amphibious force that took Kiska and Attu - June 1942, p. 146-7; p. 245.

HOUSE, Wm. Charles:  2nd class aerographer's mate - captured on Kiska Island, p. 133 ff.

HULL, General John E.:  Commanding General, Army Forces, Middle Pacific, p. 271; p. 274-5.

HUNT, Wiley:  Navigator on the Catalina patrol plane shot down by Japs on June 3, 1942 - his story when captured and interrogated on the MAYA (Jap. Cruiser), p. 124 ff.

INONU, The Hon. Ismet:  Prime Minister of Turkey, p. 361-3;

IWO JIMA - CHI CHI JIMA:  operation against, p. 170 ff; p. 196; p. 203-4; p. 206.

JAPAN:  Russell's first trip to Japan (1920), p. 14-15.  U. S. raids on mainland (1945), p. 212-215; Russell in Japan - early Sept. 1945 - his impressions of effectiveness of U. S. raids, p. 231 ff; usuable planes Japanese had on hand against probable assault of the homeland, p. 234 ff.

JAPANESE NAVAL ACADEMY - At Eta Jima:  p. 197 ff.

JAPANESE WAR PLANS:  Russell's outline of Japanese strategy in the Pacific - as discovered in post war era, p. 144-5.

JUNYO - JAPANESE CV:  in raid on Dutch Harbor, June 3/42), p. 114; p. 125-6.

KAMIKAZE:  p. 188-192; Russell visits the kamikaze museum at the Japanese naval academy (1973), p. 196 ff; the kamikaze room, p. 199-200; the kaiten, p. 199 Russell discusses the Japanese concept of 'no surrender', p. 200-3.

KENNY, General George: p. 187-8.

KIMIKAWA MARU: p. 243-4.

KING, Samuel Wilder: p. 28; gives a luau, p. 29-30; recollections of the King family and the Paul Burns family, p. 29 ff.

KISKA: p. 89-90; p. 102; p. 108-9; p. 111; the Japanese landing on June 7, 1942, p. 133 ff; the loss of Clark Hood, flight officer in B-24 attack on Kiska, p. 136-7; p. 142; p. 147-8; p. 201; p. 250; evacuation of Kiska, p. 251 ff; p. 260.

KNISKERN, Rear Admiral Leslie A.: preliminary design officer in Bu Ships, p. 79.

KODIAC ISLAND: new N.A.S. (1941), p. 85; p. 87-9; p. 91; p. 102; p. 119.

KOMANDORSKI ACTION: Rear Admiral Sock McMorris and the Japanese force, p. 245 ff; reasons why the Japanese broke off the engagement, p. 248-9;

KURITA, Admiral T.: p. 178-9; p. 181; his post-war explanation for actions, p. 183-4.

USS LANGLEY: Russell makes his first carrier qualifying landings in 1929, p. 42-3; story of an irregular landing aboard the LANGLEY, p. 43-4; p. 65-6; a description of early attempts at arresting gear, p. 69-70; p. 72-3;

LEBANON: p. 342-3.

LEE, Vice Admiral Willis A. Jr.: p. 180; p. 182-3.

USS LEXINGTON: p. 72.

MAYA - Japanese CA: part of naval Task Force that attacked Dutch Harbor, June 3/4, 1942, p. 125-6.

McCAIN, Admiral John Sydney: p. 46; chief of Bureau of Aeronautics (1943), p. 153-4; p. 169; p. 172.

McCORMACK, General James Jr. (Jim): Director of Division of Military Application, AEC, p. 269; p. 273-4; p. 352.

McMORRIS, Vice Admiral Charles H. (Sock): p. 245; p. 247.

MIDWAY ISLAND: p. 145-7.

MILLIKAN, Dr. Robert A. - President of Cal. Tech (1932) p. 61.

MITSCHER, Adm. Marc: p. 172-3; p. 177; p. 180; p. 207-8; p. 221.

NACHI - Japanese CA: flagship of Adm. Hosogaya in Aleutians, p. 245-7.

NASH, Capt. A.R. (Daddy): C.O. of VP-42 (1941), p. 83-4; p. 86-7; Russell relieves him in command (Aug. 1941), p. 93.

U. S. NAVAL ACADEMY: Russell's appointment to the Academy, p. 20 ff; plebe summer, p. 22 ff; demerits and their consequences, p. 23 ff; cruises, p. 24-25; aviation summer, p. 25.

NAVAL AVIATION: Russell's introduction, p. 25; flight training, p. 26.

NELSON'S ISLAND: (Aleutians) p. 87.

USS NEW JERSEY: p. 192.

NEWPORT NEWS SHIPBUILDING CO.: p. 71; p. 75-6.

NEWTON, Rear Admiral John Henry Jr.: replaces Admiral John Hoover as Deputy CincPac, p. 229.

OAKS AND ACORNS: names given big and little bases which were planned for Pacific - Russell involved in this program (1942-3) - takes over maritime school at Port Hueneme - a training spot for Seabees, p. 152.

OFSTIE, Vice Admiral Ralph: p. 238-9; p. 257; p. 269.

OKINAWA: p. 206.

OLDENDORF, Admiral Jesse Barrett: p. 180.

OP-05 - AIR WARFARE DIVISION: Russell takes over Division (1952), p. 310; new airplanes and other developments, p. 312-3; angle deck, p. 314; steam catapult, p. 314-15; air refueling, p. 317-8; concepts for new planes that came later, p. 320-1 the SEAMASTER, p. 321.

ORANGE WAR PLAN: p. 98-99.

SS OSSINING: Grain bearing steamer on which Russell served at end of WW I, p. 8.

OZAWA, Vice Admiral J.: p. 178; p. 182; p. 186.

PALAU ISLANDS: assault on, p. 169 ff.

PARSON, Rear Admiral Wm. S.: (Deke): p. 269; p. 276; p. 282.

HM PAUL, King of the Hellenes: p. 359-60.

PENSACOLA: In 1928, p. 35 ff; comments on senior naval officers who took the course in that year, p. 36.

PERT: idea developed for POLARIS program by Gordon Pehrson, p. 332.

PG SCHOOL (1932): a course in aeronautical engineering, p. 58; Cal Tech, p. 58.

HRH PHILIPP, Duke of Edinburgh: skipper of HMS MAGPIE - at party in Bari, Italy, p. 295-6.

PHILIPPINES CAMPAIGN: p. 173 ff; Leyte Gulf, p. 177 ff.

PIRIE, VADM Robert Burns: p. 40-41.

PLANE TYPES: Russell's comments on :BF2C-1 (Curtis-Hawk biplane), p. 62-5; F2F, p. 63.

POLARIS: Russell's story on the role of BuAir in pushing the idea of ballistic missiles in submarines, p. 330.

RABORN, Vice Admiral Wm. F. Jr.: p. 331-2.

USS RANGER: p. 65; p. 72-3.

RENFRO, Rear Admiral Edward C.: Chief of Staff to RADM Gallery in Mediterranean (1951), p. 298-9.

USS RICHMOND: in Komondorski action, p. 245; p. 249.

RICKOVER, Admiral Hyman: Russell's first encounter with him, p. 75; p. 349-351; comments on his accomplishments, p. 352-4.

SS ROBIN GRAY: p. 13 ff; coaling ship - in Japan (1920), p. 15-18.

RUSSELL, Admiral James S.: personal data, p. 1-5; he goes to sea as deck hand in merchant ship, p. 6 ff; other adventures at sea, p. 7-19; how he came to the Naval Academy, p. 19 ff; his courtship and marriage, p. 39; becomes a Commander and recalled to Washington (Oct. 1942), p. 143; becomes Vice Admiral as he leaves BuPers to become Deputy CincLant, p. 338; retirement, April 1, 1965, p. 366; post retirement assignments for Navy and Department of Defense, p. 366-9.

RYUJO - Japanese CV: in raid on Dutch Harbor(June 3/42) p. 114; p. 120; p. 128. her records of Aleutian actions - as obtained in post-war era, p. 243 ff.

USS SALT LAKE CITY: in Komondorski Operation, p. 248-9.

SAN BERNARDINO STRAIT: See entry under LEYTE GULF; Admiral KURITA.

USS SANTA FE: p. 214; her rescue operations of crew members from the USS FRANKLIN, p. 219.

SANTIAGO, Cuba: picture of city in 1920, p. 16-17.

USS SARATOGA: p. 72.

SEABEES: p. 152.

SEAMASTER: p. 321; p. 333-4; Adm. Mountbatten inspects the design at Martin plant, p. 334.

SEA OF MARMARA: see entry under USS CORAL SEA.

SHERMAN, Adm. F.C. p. 34.

SHUMAGIN ISLANDS (Dolgoi Harbor): p. 90-1; p. 105; p. 117.

SITKA: p. 96; p. 102.

SLOTIN INCIDENT: see entry under Dr. Al Graves.

SMEETON, Vice Admiral Sir Richard: p. 205.

SPRAGUE, RADM Clifton A.F. (Ziggy): flight officer on new YORKTOWN, p. 72; p. 82.

STARBIRD, Col. Dodd: p. 271

U. S. STRATEGIC BOMBING SURVEY: Russell joins team of Admiral Ofstie in fall of 1945, p. 238 ff; General Orville Anderson's subsequent report dealing with Air Force claims, p. 255-6; p. 258.

SYMINGTON, Senator Stuart: investigates a so-called airplane lag - President Eisenhower insists that Navy be included, p. 326.

TAI SHAN ISLANDS: evacuation, p. 311.

TASK GROUP 58.2: under command of Adm. Ralph Davison with flag in CV13 - USS FRANKLIN - operations in central pacific, p. 169 ff; the Palaus, p. 173 ff; the Philippines, p. 173 ff; night fighters, p. 175-6.

THACH, Admiral John: (Jimmy) flies against the captured Jap zero in developing counter techniques, p. 121.

THEOBALD, RADM ROBERT A.: p. 122-3; p. 158.

TONGUE POINT - mouth of COLUMBIA RIVER: UP-42 partially deployed there at outbreak of WWII, p. 98; difficulties in operating, p. 101-2.

TOWERS, Admiral John: Russell goes to Pearl Harbor with Adm. Davison (1945) and takes a staff job with Towers, p. 225; Towers reports on an earlier quarrel with Adm. King, p. 225-6; his retirement, p. 263.

TRUMAN, President Harry S.:  makes decision to use Eniwetok Atoll for atomic tests, p. 272-3.

UCLUELET ARM - Vancouver Island:  site of RCAF base - used by U.S. VP-42 at outbreak of war, p. 98; VP-42 operations from this base, p. 99 ff.

UJELAND:  p. 271-2; p. 277.

UMNAK:  p. 136-7; p. 143; p. 261.

UPDEGRAFF, RADM WM. N.:  (Billy) Station Commander, Dutch Harbor, p. 104.

U-2:  the Power's flight and his capture, p. 347-8.

VB-5:  Russell becomes engineer officer, p. 62 ff; attached to USS RANGER, p. 65; p. 67; p. 71.

VCNO:  Russell comes back to Washington as Vice Chief to Admiral Burke (CNO), p. 340 ff; his work with the Franke Board on reorganization of the Navy, p. 340-1; his recollections of Arleigh Burke as CNO, p. 342-5; Bay of Pigs, p. 345-7; development of the USS NAUTILUS - North Pole Project as means of offsetting impact of SPUTNIK, p. 348-50.

von KARMAN, Prof. Theodore:  Head of Department of Aeronautics, Cal Tech. (1932), p. 59-60.

VP-1:  (Flying Boat Squadron); p. 54-7; merits of the flying boat, p. 57-8.

VP-42:  (Seattle):  Russell joins squadron July 1941, p. 83; mission to Alaska, p. 85 ff; visit of Russian PBY's at Kodiac Island, p. 92-97; rotated out of Alaska (Oct. 1941), p. 98; December 7, 1941 and Orange Plan deployment, p. 98 ff; return to duty in Alaska (Jan. 1942), p. 102 ff; the Catalina accident at Dutch Harbor, p. 103-7; story of former Chief Aviation Pilot Campbell and his sighting of the Jap fleet, p. 144-17; pilot losses, p. 118-119; p. 128-30; loss of Catalina on mission of mercy, p. 129 ff.

WARDER, Rear Admiral Frederick B. (Freddie):  p. 302-2.

USS WEST VIRGINIA - BB:  Russell's first tour of duty after graduation, p. 25 ff; p. 34; with a float plane squadron, p. 41-2; catapults on the West Virginia, p. 46-7; p. 49.

USS WILLIAMSON:  Seaplane tender - Knappy Kivette, skipper - takes Gen. Buckner from Kiska Harbor, p. 109; p. 157.

WILSON, The Hon. Charles - SecDef:  his idea for a ballistic missile in submarines, p. 330; p. 332.

SS WISHKAH: WWI ship in which Russell had his first duty at sea, p. 7.

WITHINGTON, RADM Freddie: p. 27; p. 32.

YAMAMOTO, Fleet Admiral I. (Japanese), p. 146-7. His shrine at Eta Jima, the Japanese Naval Academy, p. 198.

USS YORKTOWN: Russell ordered to fitting out, p. 71; his previous experience in carriers translated, p. 72-5; p. 77.

ZERO - Japanese plane: Russell's story of the downing of a Japanese ZERO - on Akutan Island - cuts its use by U. S. in developing counter tactics, p. 118 ff.

www.ingramcontent.com/pod-product-compliance
Lightning Source LLC
Chambersburg PA
CBHW082149070526
44585CB00020B/2142